CHILDREN AND YOUTH
Social Problems and Social Policy

CHILDREN AND YOUTH
Social Problems and Social Policy

Advisory Editor

ROBERT H. BREMNER

Editorial Board
**Sanford N. Katz
Rachel B. Marks
William M. Schmidt**

L. EMMETT HOLT
Pioneer of a Children's Century

R[obert] L[uther] Duffus

and

L. Emmett Holt, Jr.

ARNO PRESS
A New York Times Company
New York — 1974

Reprint Edition 1974 by Arno Press Inc.

Copyright © 1940, by D. Appleton-Century Company, Inc.
Reprinted by permission of Hawthorn Books, Inc.

Reprinted from a copy in
   The Columbia University Library

CHILDREN AND YOUTH
Social Problems and Social Policy
ISBN for complete set: 0-405-05940-X
See last pages of this volume for titles.

Manufactured in the United States of America

Library of Congress Cataloging in Publication Data

Duffus, Robert Luther, 1888-
   L. Emmett Holt; pioneer of a children's century.

   (Children and youth: social problems and social
policy)
   Reprint of the ed. published by Appleton-Century,
New York.
   1. Holt, Luther Emmett, 1855-1924. I. Holt, Luther
Emmett, 1895-   joint author. II. Series.
RJ43.H6D8   1974   618.9'2'000924 [B]   74-1683
ISBN 0-405-05960-4

L. EMMETT HOLT
Pioneer of a Children's Century

L. EMMETT HOLT
1900

L. EMMETT HOLT

Pioneer of a Children's Century

By

R. L. DUFFUS

and

L. EMMETT HOLT, Jr.

Foreword by

EDWARDS A. PARK, M.D.

Professor of Pediatrics
Johns Hopkins University

D. APPLETON-CENTURY COMPANY
INCORPORATED
New York   London
1940

Copyright, 1940, by
D. APPLETON-CENTURY COMPANY, INC.

All rights reserved. This book, or parts thereof, must not be reproduced in any form without permission of the publisher.

PRINTED IN THE UNITED STATES OF AMERICA

PREFATORY NOTE

THE earlier chapters of this volume are largely from the pen of one of us (R.L.D.); the later ones were largely written by the other. But there is hardly a chapter in which both of us have not had some part. It has been an enterprise in which it has been a joy to cooperate. Needless to say, without the help of various members of Dr. Holt's family, his friends and associates, the task would have been quite impossible. Particular acknowledgment is due to Olivia Holt who collected much of the material for Chapter III and wrote parts of that chapter.

R. L. D.
L. E. H., JR.

FOREWORD

IN the years 1903, 1904, and 1905 I was a student under Dr. Holt at the College of Physicians and Surgeons, New York City. Dr. Holt had been appointed to the professorship of Diseases of Children in 1901. His name was known from one end of the country to the other and his word was law, not only to physicians, but to countless parents faced with the responsibility of bringing up children. He dominated pediatrics, that branch of medicine which has to do with the diseases of children, as no one has done since. He was the authority; there was no second. We students regarded him as one of the great men of the medical school and watched him and listened to him with awe.

I remember him vividly. He was then fifty years old, at the very height of his influence and fame, a small, slender man, immaculately dressed, with an abundance of hair, half gray, half dark, parted exactly in the middle. Not one hair was out of place. He spoke in short, crisp sentences, in a voice low and clear. His manner was deadly earnest. In intense moments, as he looked up at us in the benches of the amphitheater, he would wrinkle his forehead. Except for an occasional illustration taken from his private practice, there was never any digression from the steady progression of facts. His lectures were formal, and events. The assistants who worked at the neighboring Vanderbilt

Clinic used to follow behind him into the amphitheater and take their seats in the front row. Private practitioners, who often attended, usually sat with us in the upper benches. The lecture ended, as it had begun, precisely on time with the topic completely presented.

The informal clinics, conducted at The Babies Hospital, however, were more interesting to us and were the best of their kind I have ever known. They were informal, almost conversational, and showed Dr. Holt's powers to yet greater advantage. Each student was in turn assigned a patient and required to present the case. When he had finished, Dr. Holt began a catechization, bringing out new ideas and testing knowledge and convictions by leading toward pitfalls with an artfulness which would have made Socrates proud. The teaching was directed at the individual student; the rest of us were brought in as the court of appeal.

In his teaching Dr. Holt chose the common conditions and diseases, those which he knew would confront us as practicing physicians. I recall interesting hours devoted to the small humdrums of pediatric practice—thumb-sucking, habit spasms, bed wetting, diaper eruptions, and so on. Afterwards, as an intern at the New York Foundling Hospital, I learned that he actually had little real interest in the rarities. Disease made its appeal to his conscientious mind exactly in proportion to its magnitude as a practical problem.

In his teaching he always laid great emphasis on treatment and showed a predilection for disease for which there was effective treatment. "Well, doctor," he would finally ask, "what are you going to do for this patient?" He was also greatly interested in prognosis.

FOREWORD

At one time, as a part of the routine of ward rounds at The Babies Hospital, he required of himself and members of the house staff that predictions be made in writing as to the future course of the disease. These were placed in sealed envelopes on the patients' charts to be opened after all was over. He loved games which involved memory and shrewdness of judgment and this was a game.

The statistical aspects of disease made a particular appeal to Dr. Holt. He taught from tables and charts whenever possible. Clinical medicine was then in the descriptive stage. The frequency with which pneumonic consolidation occurred on the left side of the chest as compared to the right or the number of paroxysms per diem in whooping-cough were to him questions of absorbing interest. His assistants worked furiously over case records in order to assemble the statistics of disease. He ruled his assistants completely and infected them with his feeling of obligation to work incessantly in order to increase medical knowledge. Once, I recall, he asked a fellow intern of mine at the New York Foundling Hospital, Dr. George Smith, to ascertain from the autopsy records the frequency of death from acute general miliary tuberculosis. Smith worked the entire night and all the following morning. When Dr. Holt arrived for two o'clock rounds, Smith placed in his hands the completed data. But he was completely crestfallen, for Dr. Holt accepted them and put them in his pocket without any sign of surprise, remarking merely, "Thank you, doctor." As President Eliot of Harvard might have said, he was "economical" of praise. His distinguished assistant, the late Dr. John

Howland, once described to me the nearest approach to praise which he ever received from Dr. Holt. It was on an occasion when he had discovered unsuspected appendicitis in one of Dr. Holt's patients. Dr. Holt hurried to the scene and concurred in Dr. Howland's diagnosis. As they left the house together, Dr. Holt remarked, "Well, doctor, it pays to keep your eyes open." It was painful sometimes to observe how his assistants jostled and vied with each other to win his favor. Appreciation was there in full measure but remained inarticulate.

Dr. Holt devoted much time to teaching us the art of medical practice, how to enter the sick room, what to say, how to break the news that a child was mentally defective, and so on. When confronted with the latter problem, he used to emphasize the importance of erring on the side of optimism. The physician would not be forgiven if the predicted fell short of the actual outcome. Never remove all hope; always point out that some improvement will occur with increase in age. These two dicta were founded on sound psychology. He had a great natural interest in behavior problems and remarkable intuition in sensing their true nature. His handling of mentally defective children, who were sent to him from all parts of the country, was masterly. He was a pioneer in what has since become child psychiatry. If Lee was every inch a soldier, Dr. Holt was every inch a physician.

As in the case of many eminent teachers, Dr. Holt's greatest power lay in unconscious example. To take care of a patient perfectly, it was necessary to know all the details of his life, even the most insignificant ones.

His systematic interrogation of the mother and his painstaking examination of the child left unforgettable impressions. In all cases he would inquire into the diet in minute detail; for example, not only how much bread the child ate but when, what kind, fresh or stale, if with butter and how much. He would also learn the child's habits of life and occupation every minute of the twenty-four hours. No matter what the difficulty, he would have the diet and daily routine perfect. He invariably measured his patients to see if they came up to standard, even if the complaint was "warts." He put all information in writing. He always saw the child as a whole, that is, as a young, growing developing human being placed and required to move in the complex environment of society; a viewpoint in advance of his time. The greatest personal debts which I owe Dr. Holt lie in the early inculcation of the importance of exact, systematic, comprehensive study, and of an outlook upon the child of large perspective quite apart from local needs.

Dr. Holt's great interest in teaching was in part a natural outcome of his ability as a teacher, but it was in greater part due to his feeling of responsibility that each one of his students should leave his tutelage a fully trained physician. An overwhelming sense of duty ceaselessly drove him forward. Was not perhaps keeping the child well the greatest service? Accordingly, early in his career he threw the full force of his energy in the direction of preventive medicine. His little book for the guidance of mothers, *The Care and Feeding of Children* was written with the idea of prevention of disease. His efforts to improve the milk supply of New

York City represent another example. The formation of the American Child Health Association was the culmination of these activities. Of all the groups of practicing physicians to-day, the pediatricians are the most liberal toward the development of preventive medicine. When Dr. Holt fashioned pediatric attitude in this country, he made them so, for prevention was made a full half of the pediatrician's responsibility.

In his clinics and lectures Dr. Holt often praised private practice and was fond of pointing out that it was in private practice alone that one could learn to judge the outcome of disease. Later on he recognized the importance of scientific investigation and once asked Dr. Howland if he thought he had become too old to enter the laboratory. In his later active years, Dr. Holt did organize and conduct an important series of investigations in the field of chemistry at The Babies Hospital, but did not directly participate in them himself. In the beginning Dr. Holt looked askance at the development at Johns Hopkins of a "full time" clinic in which the physicians did not do private practice. Later he became convinced of its value. Dr. Howland used often to remark to me that Dr. Holt preserved an open mind and, though seeming entrenched, could always be convinced. He usually added, "His mind's as quick as a steel trap" or "His deed is always better than his word."

Dr. Holt could not tolerate dishonesty; it made every fiber of his being bristle. When an eminent pediatrician helped himself to passages from an article written by Dr. Howland and Dr. Marriott and published them as from his own mind, Dr. Holt was filled with righteous anger. He had the two articles typewritten in parallel columns and sent them to the author with the message, "What is your explanation of this?" Dr. Holt was extremely matter-of-fact and direct. Once when he was visiting the Harriet Lane Home in Baltimore, Dr. Howland surprised me by asking me to show him over the wards. Dr. Holt asked two questions: "Doctor, what is the number of cubic feet of air per patient," and, "What is the percentage of horse-hair in the mattresses?" Dr. Howland must have known what was impending! One finds in Dr. Holt's letters to his family advice in the form of aphorisms and in his discussions with us he frequently resorted to aphorisms which evidently were the product of his experience. I was always interested in this trait. It threw light on his mental processes. As experience accumulated, his mind kept formulating it into rules of thought or procedure. These came automatically to guide subsequent action. But with his matter-of-factness went a dry humor which emerges pleasingly from time to time in his letters.

A biography of Dr. Holt has long been awaited. For the first quarter of the present century his name was on the lips of all physicians and great numbers of lay persons on all matters pertaining to the health of the child. He was generally acknowledged to be a master in the art and science of medicine and a brilliant teacher, but the part he played in this country in the birth of pediatrics and in the development of public health, particularly as applied to children, and in the fostering of scientific medicine is not generally known. Dr. Holt's letters, particularly, give an insight into the character of the man whose reticence was such that few even among his colleagues knew him intimately. But the story of his life is a document of no little interest quite apart from its human appeal. It was an inspiring life, not the life of a romantic figure, but of a man of deeds. Few physicians in this country have left behind them accomplishments of so much importance and to very few do the medical profession and laity owe so much. Dr. Holt was the outstanding figure in American pediatrics of his time, was one of the great physicians and educators which this country has produced and will abide as one of the great figures of American medicine.

E. A. PARK

CONTENTS

	PAGE
PREFATORY NOTE	v
FOREWORD, BY E. A. PARK, M.D.	vii

CHAPTER		
I.	INTRODUCTION	1
II.	SABRAH CURTICE AND THE HOLTS	7
III.	THE HOLT BOYS	20
IV.	MEDICINE	36
V.	THE DAWN OF A NEW ERA	49
VI.	BACHELOR DAYS IN "THE FLAT"	55
VII.	AN INNOCENT ABROAD	69
VIII.	AMERICAN PEDIATRICS	87
IX.	CRUCIAL YEARS	102
X.	TWO BEST SELLERS	115
XI.	L.E.H. TO L.M.H., 1866-1902	122
XII.	MEDICAL RESEARCH, INCORPORATED	136
XIII.	INTERLUDES	146
XIV.	INFANT MORTALITY	161
XV.	VIRGINIBUS PUERISQUE	179
XVI.	NEW VISTAS	200
XVII.	CHILDREN OF TO-MORROW	214
XVIII.	CANNES, 1919	232
XIX.	REWARDS	257
XX.	FAR HORIZONS	267
INDEX		287

ILLUSTRATIONS

L. Emmett Holt	*frontispiece*
Sabrah and Eliza Holt	*at page* 16
Horace Holt	17
The Holt house at Webster, New York	24
The Holt children	25
The Rochester faculty in 1877	32
Emmett Holt in college	33
L. Emmett Holt	64
John B. Calvert	64
James Duane Squires	64
Diphtheria mortality in New York City	101
The American Pediatric Society	110
The Babies' Hospital	111
The Rockefeller Institute Board of Scientific Directors	166
Antivisection propaganda	167
Infant mortality in New York City	176, 177
Cannes Conference	260
Dr. Holt in China	261

I

INTRODUCTION

WHEN Luther Emmett Holt took his degree in medicine in 1880, one out of every four babies born in New York City died before the end of its first year. Some cities were worse off than New York, some country districts and small towns better off, but the ratio was representative. The babies of the poor and ignorant in overcrowded tenement districts, and those unfortunate enough to be in institutions had far less chance of survival. Poorly fed and poorly nourished, they fell an easy prey to infections of all kinds, and every summer with as much certainty as the upward curve in the thermometer came the sharp increase in the death rate caused by diarrheal disorders.

There had been, it is true, some improvement over conditions in the eighteenth century, when from 90 to 99 per cent of infants admitted to foundling institutions died, and when Malthus could truthfully say that the surest way of checking the growth of the population was to multiply infant hospitals and asylums. But the improvement had not gone far.

Pediatrics, that branch of medicine dealing with the care and diseases of children, did not exist as a recognized field of endeavor in the United States. The care of the sick child was in the hands of the obstetrician or the practitioner of internal medicine whose interest was chiefly in adults. The training of the doctor in this field consisted of a few casual lectures on children sandwiched into the course on obstetrics. One or two physicians had interested themselves in children and had written treatises on the subject, but they had not penetrated far, nor had their influence been widespread. Medicine as a whole was static. It embraced a body of knowledge handed down from generation to generation which few sought to challenge or to enlarge. The care of the child was not regarded as the province of the physician. It was the undisputed domain of the mother and grandmother, and here again the traditions were passed along from one generation to the next.

In 1924 at the time of Dr. Holt's death a vastly different picture presented itself. Information on infant care and hygiene—based on the best medical knowledge—was the property of practically every educated mother, and much had been done to educate children themselves in matters of health. Medicine had become a dynamic science. Disease was being studied by doctors everywhere—at the bedside, in clinics, in laboratories. Medical knowledge was expanding with unbelievable rapidity. And the diseases of children had assumed a place of major importance. Practitioners engaging in this specialty were to be found in every corner of the country. Full professors of pediatrics giving extensive courses were to be found in practically all medical schools. University departments of pediatrics and research institutes were springing up in the leading medical centers with staffs of workers devoting

INTRODUCTION

themselves to the study of disease in childhood, and numerous scientific societies and several special journals had been created to diffuse the new knowledge in this branch of medicine. The results were depicted by that infallible score-board, the infant mortality rate. Down it had come steadily, year by year, to less than one third of the previous figure.

The period between 1880 and 1924 saw the awakening of the science of medicine. It was a period of increasing social consciousness which permitted great advances in public health. In this renaissance it is hardly thinkable that the infant and child could have escaped. Such a development can not, however, be considered apart from the individuals who brought it to pass. Certainly no one person could take the credit for such an achievement. It was the product of many workers on many different fronts, of many leaders and a large army of followers. Yet if one individual were to be singled out as typifying America's accomplishment in those years in saving the lives of her children, that individual would be Emmett Holt. His contribution was not that of the great investigator whose discoveries are epoch-making. He was not of the mighty tribe of Lister, Pasteur, or Koch. Nor was he unique in possessing those traits of character and intellect which make for the highest skill in the practice of medicine. His outstanding contribution was, as he once expressed it, to be a "middleman" of science—one who formed a link between the producer, the research worker in the laboratory, and the ultimate consumer, who might be the practising physician, the health worker, or the public. His function was to translate the new knowledge into practical results and to diffuse those results far and wide. He was above all an educator.

Thrown by a fortunate chance, at the beginning of his career, into intimate contact with one or two spirits who were sowing the first seeds of the newer medical science in this country, Holt followed its growth eagerly and grew with it, and saw to it that it spread to his chosen field. In the combined effort to cultivate that field, an effort which succeeded within one brief generation in converting the field from a barren pasture with only a few blades of grass to a fertile domain producing bumper crops, he was a leading spirit—in time the outstanding leader. He obtained for his specialty a secure place in the sun, and through his own efforts the crops from that field were distributed to all in the land.

What was the background of such a singularly effective life? He was the product of a soil and of a tradition that are rapidly passing—a pure New England ancestry, a boyhood spent on a farm in upstate New York, a family with Puritan traditions which were instilled into him from the cradle.

In twentieth-century America the word Puritan has notoriously become a term of reproach, employed to describe a certain sourness, narrowness, and intolerance which did indeed exist among the early settlers of New England, as among all peoples, in all ages and under almost all religions. That this temperament was more common in New England than elsewhere is matter for debate. Certainly there are abundant traces of it in ancient Sparta, in Republican Rome, in the Italy of Savonarola, and in the modern as well as the medieval life of Spain and Northern Europe. But the Puritan movement developed also a quality of conscience and self-reliance which has been one of the driving forces of humanitarian progress for at least three centuries.

The Puritan stock is still to be found in the old New England communities and in other regions which have felt the effect of the great New England migration to the West. If these Puritan descendants are farmers their farms are prosperous and well-kept. If they are storekeepers they count their pennies but their weights are honest. If they are carpenters their houses stand, or are worthy of standing, for generations. If they are physicians they render themselves indispensable to a whole countryside. They are a sober race, yet if they lack gaiety they commonly have humor. Artists have been rare among them, yet loveliness was not absent from the churches and homes they built, and they have had a shy instinct for beauty in nature. They are not given to emotional demonstrations, yet it would be untrue to say that a New England pulse beats more slowly than one in Virginia or in Naples. But their nature finds highest expression in their well-developed sense of responsibility. They regard life as purposeful and think of themselves as failures unless they have been in some degree useful to their fellows. They measure usefulness in tangible terms—in schools, roads, churches, charities, hospitals. Their dreams are solid, and though their heads occasionally penetrate the clouds their feet are on the earth.

Of this tribe Emmett Holt was a true child, though he was born a few miles outside the frontiers of New

England proper. But he was able, as not all of that doughty stock have been, to translate Puritanism into nineteenth- and twentieth-century terms. His horizons widened with every year of his life. He used the tools of modern thought and science as effectively as his forefathers had swung the ax and held the plow, and as simply. He extracted from the religion which his mother impressed upon him, not its rigidity and formalism, but its overpowering urge to action. He did what lay nearest to his heart, in an eminently practical manner, without noise or ostentation. He was rightly proud of his ancestry but he instinctively improved upon it. He showed that though Puritanism had altered, its virtues and its vigor were not extinct, for in him it achieved as much effectiveness as it had done in other scenes and other ways three centuries earlier.

Emmett Holt will be long remembered for his tangible gifts to his generation. He attained in his field a position comparable with that of Osler in general medicine. But he is also a symbol of importance in American life. He represents the transmutation of an old and perhaps outworn tradition into the gold of a new era.

II

SABRAH CURTICE AND THE HOLTS

LUTHER EMMETT HOLT was born in Webster, New York, a few miles from Rochester, but his background on both sides of the family was straight New England. Nicholas, the first of the American Holts, came to this country, not indeed in the *Mayflower,* but fifteen years after the arrival of that deeply laden vessel. He settled in Andover, Massachusetts, where his sixth son, also called Nicholas, lived and died. Ultimately a large tribe of Holts accumulated about Andover; twenty-four of that name are said to have marched to the Concord and Lexington fight in 1775. But the Holts of the direct line had moved West before the Revolution. Abiel, son of the second Nicholas, moved to Windham, Connecticut, where he died, and Abiel's son, Nathan, following the slow drift of the westward movement, went a little farther and died at Willington. There the Holts rested a long generation, while a second Nathan was born, grew up and died. His son, Constant, Emmett Holt's grandfather, was born in Willington in 1787.

Constant was twenty-five when, in 1812, he decided to leave the land of his fathers and strike into the Far West—for so it must have seemed, and so it was, according to the speed of travel in those days—where land was at once cheaper and more fertile. He was one of the many who were leaving the rocky farms about the old settlements and sowing the seed of New England far and wide. He did well to leave. A hundred years later his grandson, Emmett, found Willington "half a dozen white houses," sleeping peacefully if not prosperously in the sun, with the last Holt of the name, a man nearly eighty, reflecting in his contentment and serene indifference the mood of the little town.

The expedition consisted of two ox-carts—one containing Constant and his bride, Sally Dart, and the other his cousin William, his wife and worldly possessions. It took them three weeks to reach Western New York, following roads and Indian trails; at the site of the village of Webster they halted and decided to settle. A few settlers had preceded them, but it was mostly virgin forest which had to be cleared; logs had to be hewed for the settlers' cabins. Constant's young bride survived the rigors of frontier life for one year only and the widower continued the task of clearing his acres and building his home alone.

Sixteen months later a new bride, Sally's sister, Sibyl Dart, was brought from Willington. She became the mother of four boys, one following the other in quick succession. This marriage, too, ended in tragedy, for Sibyl died when the eldest was but six years old. The task of making a home for the motherless boys proved more than difficult, and after a few months Constant, taking the youngest child with him, again drove back to Willington, returning with a third wife, Polly Sibley. The new wife was desperately lonely and homesick in the wilderness. She would go to the creek in the middle of winter and stand with her feet in the icy water, hoping to catch a cold that would kill her. For her benefit a return visit to Willington was made, and seems to have had the desired effect. After a few weeks she told her husband that she felt that she must get back to the little boys who needed mittens, stockings, and warm clothing for the winter. She proved a most successful stepmother, and from then on there is no mention of homesickness.

The land was well chosen, though it never brought wealth to either Constant or Horace (the only one of Constant's four sons who took up farming). For a time the Holt apple, which Constant developed and Horace perfected, enjoyed a considerable reputation. Silkworms furnished a nice profit and kept the spinning-wheels ahum during many months of the year. For two generations there was no more wandering. If Horace, in his mature manhood, felt the pull of the California gold fields or of the fabulous prairies of Kansas and Nebraska he resisted it. Webster's primitive log huts were succeeded by houses of sawn boards. The forests shrank, and orchards and fields of grain replaced them. White churches lifted their steeples, and roads sprawled about the countryside where only blazed trails had run before. A community was formed, with sober, steady-going traditions; and in all this the Holts had a worthy share.

The Curtices, too, were early settlers in Webster. They were descended from Henry Curtice, who came from England in the *Elizabeth and Ann* in 1635— perhaps on the same voyage as the first of the Holts.

Henry Curtice was a "gentleman" and a "proprietor" in Sudbury, Massachusetts. One of his descendants, Emmett Holt's great-grandfather, was living near Andover, Massachusetts, when he heard the signal gun fired in April, 1775. He left his plow in the furrow, summoned his five sons, and with them marched to Lexington, not to be mustered out until 1781. Ebenezer Curtice, one of the five sons, lived for a while in Amherst, New Hampshire, and in 1817, on the threshold of a hale old age, went with two of his sons into the wilderness where the town of Webster now stands. One of these sons was Ziba Curtice, who, like his neighbors, the Holts, carved a farm out of the forest by main strength. They were a doughty, as well as a religious race; on Sunday Ziba and his wife Mary would walk four miles to church, usually carrying a baby. One of their six children, Sabrah, a spirited girl with auburn hair, married Horace Holt. Emmett Holt was the third child of that marriage.

Horace Holt managed his farm well, and his land yielded apples, cherries, pears, grapes, and peaches in abundance. He was industrious and resourceful, and when he felt the need of more money with which to provide for the education of his children he spent his winters—for most farmers a period of comparative leisure—in selling nursery products. His formal education had been limited, yet he appreciated books and made the most of his cultural opportunities. He was a shy man, but in his quiet way was always influential in the affairs of the community, and especially of the church, which was, first and last, with the Holts, the Baptist church. But the central figure in the Holt household was the former Sabrah Curtice. Once Horace found it hard to punish his children for some small misdemeanor and asked their mother to do it, because, he said, she didn't hate to do it half as much as he. Her answer, a characteristic one, was that as he had promised the punishment he must be the one to go through with it.

Sabrah was a woman of deep convictions, of unswerving purpose, and of quiet energy. She accomplished a good deal without fussing or worrying. She read everything available, talked well, loved the society of her kind, and was able to give sound advice with sympathy and tact. She could gossip, but never maliciously, and when people were in trouble they sent for her. Her opinions, especially on the subject of religion, might seem narrow to people of this age. When her daughter married a Presbyterian clergyman she accepted him unreservedly, but it was plain that she grieved because he was not a Baptist. How could Eliza (her daughter) "fellowship" a baptism that was not according to inherited tradition? At a later date she took a secret delight in indulging her "depraved nature" by seeing that her granddaughter witnessed at least one Scriptural baptism, even if she never saw another. But firm as were her convictions, she had a sense of humor that made bigotry impossible.

She had a knack of observing and of writing down what she observed that makes her letters most interesting reading. In fact, as a picture of the life and manners of her time, in the small village she knew best, they are historical documents of no little value. She knew the art of small things—of preserving, by a trivial stroke or two, the color of a moment. "It is now half-past five A.M.," she would write; "the train has just gone up. Pa is milking. Caroline building fire." For a boy away from home that picture was as good as a yard of news. He could see and hear and smell it all—the table in the dim lamplight, the crackle of the fire, the dry-wood smoke. Again: "I went to church Sunday evening a week ago, and to prayer meeting Wednesday night, and to sociable Thursday, and put up six qts. ripe cucumber pickles and four qts. pickled pears, and canned five qts. of pears Friday, and since then have done as little as I could get along with." She could convey a mood, too: "Well, they are all through packing, and all is quiet, and a sad sense of loneliness already begins to creep over me, as the wind howls and the cold creeps in at every crack, and I think of all my dear ones scattered in every direction."

One sees, in almost every letter, the reflection of the life of the staid little town, a kind of existence now almost legendary. Webster, ten miles from Rochester, was as isolated as it would now be sixty miles away. In Emmett's boyhood there was no railroad. On occasion people drove in to the city, but such jaunts had to be planned: one did not undertake them on the spur of the moment. But it must not be supposed that life in Webster was as benighted as the mere absence of motion picture theaters, automobiles, radio sets, and similar means of enlightenment might imply to a citizen of our own generation. The village had an indigenous culture. Practically all the social activities were concentrated in the churches. There was a constant migration westward and cityward, but the country town had not yet started to decay. It was still an excellent environment—perhaps the best environment —in which to lay the physical and cultural foundations of a career. There was something of Main Street in it, but there was also a broad humanity, a ready charity, and a local pride and self-reliance not easily understood in these migratory days.

The general run of its diversions the village had to provide for itself. Sabrah wrote:

Our donation finally went off Tuesday night. But it was a terrible night, for it commenced snowing Monday night, and the going was awful. There was too much snow to go with wagons, and sleighs cut right down through into the mud, which was six inches deep and all soft. As a result there were only about fifty there, and two thirds of them were boys from eight to eighteen. We took in $87.50. Wasn't that doing well?... Friday night we had a little surprise party (nine in all). They came in one load in a big sleigh, and sat on straw in the bottom of the sleigh, and they were in high glee when they came in, and kept it up all the evening. Stayed until eleven. We treated them to apples and popcorn, and they ate two pans full of the latter.... I only wished, as I always do when I have young company, that the boys were home.

Or:

The Spell last Friday went off nicely, they said. Not a big turn out but a fair house. At first they had an old folks' spell down, and Mr. Lyman Wall bore off the palm. But at the next trial Belle came off victorious over all, Mr. W. included, and took the prize, which was Whittier's Poems.

Again:

Mr. Seeley's donation passed off pleasantly. His net proceeds were $75; they had oysters, so that took some off.

In another letter:

Em Potter is doing nicely. She took three of her paintings to the fair at Dover and got a prize on each one.... The school board in Webster had a terrible time, as they were about equally divided and Dr. Maine wanted to be on both sides.

And how well the genial side of life in the little town is reflected in such incidents as this:

Curt [Emmett's brother] went up and mowed the lawn in front of the church. After he got through he put the lawn mower in the Democrat under the shed. The Copelands and Em Potter, seeing Curt's coat and cuffs lying on the grass, took them home, and said nothing. This morning Curt went up to Hendee, the Justice of the Peace, took out a search warrant, and then, armed with a shot gun, pistol and revolver, marched up to the Potters' door in his shirt sleeves and rang the bell. Em came to the door. Curt in a very solemn manner, in the name of the Commonwealth of the State of New York and town of Webster and "Bob" Hendee, demands property which he intends to take peaceably if he can, forcibly if he must. Em pretended to be terribly frightened, and began shaking fearfully, but ended with a hearty laugh. Having summoned the whole family, who were at breakfast, he read the warrant and they all appreciated the joke. Em brought the stolen property from its place of concealment, and Curt put them on and came home.

. . . .

The human drama passed across the stage, and Sabrah Curtice felt the humor and pity of it. There is Uncle Luther, who, dying, is chiefly concerned because he has "gone into buying apples with Jim Thompson and vats with L. Billings, and then potatoes and produce on commission, and all this is unsettled." There is Uncle Nelt, who can rise at a revival meeting to be prayed for, "with true tears and penitence," but is capable later of stirring up a row with the other leading members of the church over the remodeling of the house of worship. There is "Miss Stephens of Rochester (sister of Othello Hamlet Stephens)" who comes to display the talents of an obviously histrionic family in the Webster school. There is Dr. H., once "one of the very best of physicians," but now "a perfect wreck" from liquor and opium. "How old and shattered and gloomy he seemed!" cried Sabrah, thinking, no doubt, of her own boys, adrift in a world of temptations. "It did seem dreadful—as smart a young man as he used to be, and temperate and a member of the Presbyterian church." There is Mr. Emmett, the Sandy Creek revivalist, whose father "is an Indian chief and his mother an educated English lady." Mr. Seeley, the Baptist minister, preaches a bitter farewell sermon, blaming the dashing young intruder for his estrangement from the congregation.

There is a friend whom one can not help feeling sorry for, "he has so little sprawl." Horace Holt's three brothers come to dinner and "Mr. Lovell said he didn't remember of ever seeing four nicer-looking old men in one family in his life." There are church sociables, Sunday school picnics, excursions to Niagara

Falls. A new minister is found after much "candidating"; the fruit trees blossom and bend with their burdens; there are summers and winters, births, weddings and funerals. And so the little, old-fashioned town presents itself, with its quaintness and sturdiness and sympathy and not much of its reputed meanness.

The picture of Emmett Holt's mother comes out clearly, too—her cheerfulness in spite of poor health, her vivid, almost uncanny, insight into human motives, her quick, sensitive nature held in leash by a will so strong that it gave her the semblance of serenity. Horace Holt, walking through his orchards to see if the pears are ready to pick, reasoning with Uncle Nelt about that impulsive old gentleman's domineering attitude in church affairs, getting patiently out into the mud to lead the mare home on a dark night, helping Charlie, the hired man, with his lessons in the evening, writing to his son what the guests had to eat at the wedding, instead of telling what the bride wore—he is a more shadowy figure, yet with a kindliness, almost a sweetness, about him. Horace might have been a bookish man had he had time and opportunity. He transferred his ambitions, as such men usually do, to his sons. He must have longed for their success because he sacrificed for it.

Sabrah, too, looked far ahead. She had both an otherworldly vision and the wisdom of this earth. She strove persistently to teach her sons self-confidence. "I don't see why my boys can't do big things as well as others," she wrote to them while they were in college, "and I know they can, if they will only think so." Such phrases occur again and again. "I should very much

SABRAH AND ELIZA HOLT
1851

HORACE HOLT

dislike to have either of my boys attempt anything and fail." ... "I never want my children to do anything that is right and for their improvement at the halves."

"Now, Emmett, live within your means, and on no account run in debt for anything, as you value your peace of mind, or the respect and esteem of your friends. There is no one whose opinion is worth anything but will commend you for your economy, though you don't live in the style they do." "I would like very much to see you Saturday, but if you feel that you will have to neglect anything which you ought to do to come, Ma would not wish you to." These injunctions Emmett obeyed literally. He never tolerated failure. He never went into debt or allowed an organization with which he was connected to go into debt or live beyond its means. The qualities of concentration and perseverance which his mother embodied and impressed upon him were to bear ample fruit in his career.

Sabrah's God was an intimate and personal one, whose approval she earnestly sought. Preferably He was a Baptist God. "Emmett," she once wrote, "when you choose a wife, I do hope you will get a Baptist. As you prize your everyday Christian life and Christian usefulness, pray much over this subject now before your affections are so enlisted as to blind your better judgment." But she would also say, "Let it not be enough that you observe the outward forms of religion, but remember God looks into the heart, and He has given you powers to be employed for Him." And: "My earnest and daily prayer for you is that you may be an instrument in the hands of God of doing much good in the world."

She longed, as other mothers have done, to visualize her son's life away from home, and to enter into it. She made his friends her own, though she might never see them in the flesh. She was concerned about his clothes, his social life, his daily routine. She worried about his colds. She even read his technical papers when he began to publish them. And he was twenty-eight and a successful physician when she wrote to him:

Emmett, we have all been talking it over since you left, and have decided that you were getting round-shouldered, and Pa says it is because the pillows sent you were so large and full, and I do not know but he is about half right. When I realize that one-third of our time is spent in bed, I do think much depends upon our position there, and now if you will take those pillows for your spare bed I will send you some small ones for your bed, if you will sleep on them. I presume at first it will not be as pleasant, but you will get used to it after a little while.

She even had good advice for him in his love affairs, which he seems to have confided to her without reserve—a fact which tells much about the relations between Sabrah Holt and her son, for few men have been more reticent about themselves than Emmett Holt. "Don't look for a mature woman of forty in a girl of twenty," she wrote, "and remember that we can't find perfection in this world, and if it was possible we are so imperfect ourselves that we could not harmonize the two." She also warned him against the reprehensible practice of paying attention to more than one young lady at a time.

These letters, many of them written before daylight on winter mornings, or late at night, after the household work had been done and every one else had gone to bed, throw more than a little light on the career of Emmett Holt. In later life, it probably never occurred to him to worry about creeds, though he remained to the last a member of his mother's denomination. If the choice had had to be made he would never have allowed his religion to interfere with his science, but for him there was no clash. The precepts of conduct—the militant view of life—which Sabrah impressed upon him, day after day, made up the practical part of his religion. He would have been, in any case, a man of mark, for he had native intelligence, physical energy, and will power. He was ambitious. But Sabrah Curtice made it inevitable that he should care more for skill and knowledge than for wealth, and count usefulness an essential ingredient of success. A man with such a mother could not view his life as a scramble for power and position. He had to regard it as a moral issue.

III

THE HOLT BOYS

EMMETT, born on March 4, 1855, was the youngest of Horace and Sabrah Holt's three children. The first was Eliza; then, after a considerable interval, came Curtice; then, after two years, Emmett. Eliza, as seen in an old family photograph, was a demure and grown-up young lady when her two brothers were still in knee-pants. When she was not having her picture taken she seems to have been less demure. She married Eugene Cheeseman, then principal of the Webster Academy, where the young Holts went to school; later Mr. Cheeseman became a Presbyterian minister, and Eliza, both as an elder sister and a minister's wife, wrote them letters full of excellent advice, letters which contain much engaging information as to the life of a country clergyman and his family in the seventies and eighties. It was Eliza's little daughter, Belle, who "washed and brushed her cat's hair and said, 'He looks just like Uncle Emmett when his hair is brushed so.'"

Emmett is remembered as an active boy, well developed mentally and with a streak of fun in his make-up. "I was there at the old Holt home all the summer of 1863," writes his cousin, Emma Holt Cox. "The boys were attending the 'little red school-house

THE HOLT BOYS

down North' that spring. Emmett was called upon for a composition—his first attempt in that line. It was headed 'C.M.T.' which, he went on to explain, meant 'Curt's Mud Turtle.' ... When I was there again, in 1867, if there was an Irish song to be sung, or a Dutch dialect recitation wanted, Emmett, who was brimming over with mischief, was always in demand."

Eliza Cheeseman, in a letter written to her brother in 1906, also gives a glimpse into the life of those far-away days. Dr. Holt had been relating some of his boyhood experiences to his own children, and had asked her to refresh his memory.

Indeed, I do remember the Sunday school picnics [she wrote], but hadn't recalled them for years till your letter gave me food for thought for a whole afternoon.... I wonder if you were too little to remember a big union one held down Lakeside way—it seems to me the woods were Boynton's—and just as the long tables were all set, loaded with food, a shower came up and in spite of the rush to hold umbrellas over the tables and themselves, too, some frosted cakes and chicken pies got a soaking, as well as some white muslin dresses, but the sun came out in a few minutes and dried the dresses, and there was always plenty of provisions.

I suppose you didn't tell them what you ate. For breakfast crackers and coffee, then, after the long ride, boys could eat everything, and you had chicken pie, pressed chicken, cold baked chicken, and sometimes other kinds of meat; with these went two or three "raised biscuit," pickles, jelly or jam and cheese, then wild blackberry pie (wasn't it good?) and all the other kinds known to that generation; lemonade to drink all through dinner by the children, and coffee for the old folks, made at an outdoor fire, or brought cold from home; after pie came cake—as many pieces as your teacher would pass you—nice, rich cake it was, too; then came the watermelon, furnished by Billings always, and if the season had been a prosperous one you had candy. And you ate all these things—and still live. Oh, well, they didn't know any better, and had no books on "Care and Feeding"; so they didn't get sick.

Weren't you old enough to remember some of the war meetings in the latter part of the war? Those weren't so interesting as in the early part, for war was a serious thing later, but you must know of some, for you sang in the days when "little Emmett Holt" was a star attraction at any entertainment. When you came on the stage you were always greeted with applause and audible whispers of "Ain't he cute?" Don't you remember "The Pickets" that Curt and Zibe sang the night you sang "Little Sam" or "Good-Bye, Jeff," and how proud father and mother were of their little boys, and how they told them so, too?....

. . . .

"Little Emmett Holt," as one sees him in these daguerreotypes, was being pushed forward by parents who believed that every member of the family, young or old, should do his duty. With the Civil War the curtain falls on the stage career of this popular artist, and when he reappears on the platform, years later, as teacher and lecturer, it is with a reluctance and a shyness undetected in the days of "Good-Bye, Jeff."

Dr. Holt himself touched upon this halcyon period in a letter written to his sister in 1900:

I have just come from telling Calvert and Emmett stories before their bed-time. The most popular ones always are those rehearsing what I did when I was a little boy. To-night the subject was the trip to Springwater made at the time I fell in the mill race, wore Nate Kellogg's trousers, etc. It was immensely popular with my audience and parts of it were encored with much enthusiasm. Then I gave them a verse of "Old Shady" and selections from "Johnny Smoker" which pleased them very much. How many memories those old songs bring back, and how long ago it seems since I was a little boy like Calvert, singing those songs and cutting up generally as we boys did at that age. I have lived those times over more of late than in many years, as the children are always wanting more details and my memory and my imagination are both severely taxed to meet the demand.

. . . . .

Both the Holt boys worked about the farm as they grew old enough to do so. More than half a century later Dr. Holt still remembered the ominous rattle of his mother's broom against the downstairs stovepipe, a rising signal not to be ignored by the sleepers above. It took will power to get up before daylight on a cold winter's morning, go out in the cold barn, feed the sheep, milk three cows, and clean out the stalls—all before breakfast. And there were the same chores in the evening.

When the Holt boys left the "little red schoolhouse down North," they went to Webster Academy. The curriculum here was limited, but there was nothing to prevent its being thorough. Emmett learned Brown's Grammar by heart, and it was probably from Brown that he derived his disconcerting habit of quoting paragraph and clause, with invariable correctness, when a difference of opinion arose over grammatical usage.

Rochester University, to which the Holt boys went in 1871, after their four year course in the Webster Academy, was a Baptist denominational school, presided over by a faculty of less than a dozen men, headed by Martin B. Anderson. Perhaps it was more liberal than some institutions of the day, for the faculty contained at least one Methodist, Professor Samuel Lattimore. He had hesitated on account of his denomination to accept a call there, but had been assured by the President that this fact would never prove a source of embarrassment to him, and it never did. The course of study offered by the University in 1871—all of it required—was, after the manner of the day, heavily loaded on the classical and ethical side. The subjects taught were Philosophy (Mental and Moral), Political Economy, Art, Greek, Latin, Modern Languages, History, Logic, Rhetoric, English Literature and Composition, Mathematics, "Natural Sciences," "The Principles of Chemical Philosophy," and a surprising course on the 241 bones in the human body. Most of the students came from the vicinity of Rochester; there were about 150 in all, twenty-five in the graduating class.

Under such circumstances the contact between faculty and students was a close one, and men of strong personality left their mark upon the boys as few professors in large modern institutions have a chance to do. If there was one personality that was stamped upon the Rochester boys it was that of President

THE HOLT HOUSE AT WEBSTER, NEW YORK

THE HOLT CHILDREN
N. Curtice Holt——Eliza Holt——L. Emmett Holt
1859

Anderson. He was the grand old man who had steered the University's bark from its first humble beginnings twenty years before, when it started in a defunct downtown hotel. Anderson was the leading citizen of Rochester, an imposing, magnetic person, with a Jovian head, a considerable degree of eloquence, and he was, after the fashion of the time, a great educator. When he made a trip to Europe he had the pleasure of being mistaken for Garibaldi. A self-made man who started life working in a Maine shipyard, he had worked his way through college, had been successively a professor of Latin, Greek and mathematics, a preacher, and a religious journalist; he had had a well-rounded experience, and knew how to draw on it effectively when he talked or lectured. His chapel talks were almost as good as Sabrah Holt's letters—which is saying a good deal. He had a way of stimulating ambition, of an idealistic sort, just as she did. "Nineteen men out of every twenty are waiting to be led... waiting to have some one tell them what to do. It is a moral duty for a man to be strong; to go up to that height where men are scarce." He said, perhaps as early as any college president, "A college can do a great deal for a man, but it cannot furnish him brains." In an age when the great fortunes of the country were being made and applauded, he punctured the glamour of the successful business career, discouraged his graduates from following it, yet was succeesful in persuading men with money to give it to the University. Obviously Rochester under his administration was an institution to which Sabrah and Horace Holt could safely entrust their boys. Dr. Anderson might not make original thinkers, but he could instil a profound respect for learning; he could mold character.

Like all strong personalities Anderson had his cherished prejudices. He could say in chapel: "I shall never feel right until I have thrashed a plumber." He could make disparaging remarks about Darwin and Huxley to his class in philosophy, viewing them as annoying and inconsequential worms in the pathway of true religion. But the balance is heavily weighted on the positive side. In his course on Art he imparted more than a superficial esthetic appreciation to many an upstate New Yorker. And surely he was prophetic in glimpsing many of the economic changes that have since come about—the reaction against the exploitation of the country's natural resources, against unfair competition and the privileges of hereditary wealth. As an educator his vision for the college was one of quality rather than size, a policy which he carried to the point of refusing state funds which might lead to expansion. He was admired outside of Rochester and was obliged to decline several flattering offers, among them the presidency of Brown University and of the University of Chicago.

He had an austerity that made the student summoned to his office quake with apprehension, but more often than not the summons would be merely for a friendly chat: "I have been wanting to talk to you about your work in college; how are you getting on and what are your plans for your life work?" On hearing that a certain very conscientious student, John B. Calvert, took little or no exercise, he sent for him and prescribed thus: "You are looking pale. Walking is the best exercise. You must keep in the open; walk more; walk more!" For although he discouraged athletics, feeling that they diverted valuable energy from the brain, he did not cultivate the lowly grind in his garden of learning. He had a real personal interest in all his boys. There is pleasant mention in one of Sabrah Holt's letters of his visiting Webster and driving up to the Holt farm just to see "where those boys were raised." One may imagine the mixed feelings of apprehension and pride with which "those boys" read the account of "Prex's" call.

The Rochester faculty, nine in number (including Elijah Withal, janitor), make a most august showing as photographed at that time, but there were many rich personalities obscured behind the forest of whiskers: Kendrick, the scholar who recited Homer for sheer love of it; Morey, who could make Roman history seem pertinent even in upstate New York in the seventies; Lattimore, keen and kindly, as quick to detect the hidden personal troubles of the students as their mistakes in chemistry, and as anxious to rectify both. Chance had led Lattimore into a career of science: it was the only vacant chair in the small upstate college to which he first applied for a job, and "he would as soon teach that as anything else." Luckily it was a perfect fit. Lattimore not only taught all the science courses at the University but acted as toxicologist for the city of Rochester as well. He instilled into his pupils lessons in accurate observation and a love of scientific truth that were not easily forgotten. To-day on the campus a glacial scarred rock marks his grave, and on it (as he directed) are inscribed the words: "He found God in the laboratory."

And there was Gilmore, who held down the several chairs of literature, logic, and rhetoric (invective, esthetic and ethical rhetoric, be it noted)—a disciplinarian, a pedagogue of the old school. He had no doubts on any subject, and any which survived in his students must have been hardy doubts indeed. "Of two contradictions," he admonishes his class in logic, and one can almost hear the impact of fist on table, "one or the other must be true; there is no middle course." Like his colleagues he used few textbooks; he would simply give out a question and dictate the answer for the students to memorize. Question: "How can a poor literary style be rendered more smooth and flowing?" Answer: "By reading Addison and Irving." Or: "What is the primary requisite in Esthetic Rhetoric?" Answer: "Elegance." A mistake in spelling affected him like a knife stab, and he was inexorable in his standards of penmanship and of graceful sentences thickly seeded with commas. "Miserable epistolary specimen," he wrote on the margin of Emmett's first literary effort—a letter to an imaginary friend Charlie on "How I Spent My Vacation," and though the ink is faded the sting is still there:

FRIEND CHARLIE:
On looking over my unanswered letters the other day, I found one of yours among them and hoping that you will pardon me for neglecting it so long, "I take my pen in hand" to inform you how I have spent my time since last July.

After leaving your place, I went to Pittsburgh to see

my aunt, and spent about a week sight-seeing; from there I came directly home—I don't think Hemlock Lake and the surrounding country ever looked so beautiful as on the morning I reached home.

Charlie, if you want to be appreciated, go away and stay a couple of months. I don't think I was ever made so much of, as during the first week after I came home. Father never seemed so glad to see me and Mother met me with tears in her eyes. I begin to think that "there is no place like home...."

Give my best regards to your parents, your sister, and that Miss —— of whom you wrote so much in your last.

Answer as soon as possible, and be sure to come down next summer. Ever your friend,

L. E. HOLT

Under Gilmore's firm guidance, Emmett traveled far. Four years later "Friend Charlie" would hardly have recognized his humble correspondent in the impassioned author of "Amid the tottering of thrones and the crash of falling empires, he alone seems to have maintained his equilibrium"—this of Edmund Burke. Fortunately for posterity, the Gilmore touch does not survive in postgraduate writings. Gilmore might mold the written word, born in deliberation, but there was a far more difficult hurdle for boys raised on a farm—to overcome the various ungrammatical expressions of rustic speech which were second nature to them. The college pedagogues seem to have despaired of this task, but the Holt boys were fortunate in having drawn as a room-mate an urban Massachusetts boy, Benjamin Bulkley. He felt very keenly the handicap rustic speech would prove to them in later life and spent no end of effort over them. The efforts were greatly appreciated at a later date; they were apparently more successful than those with a less apt classmate who, when shown a sentence containing the expression "hadn't ought," remarked: "Why I see what's wrong with that; the 'had' hadn't ought to be there."

Emmett was but sixteen years old when he went to college, and unlike his brother Curt was not prominent in college politics. Curt had always been a better mixer, and there is no doubt that his popularity aroused in his younger brother a resolve to square himself through some special achievement since he could not do so by personality alone. So when Curt rose to be president of '75, Emmett looked on admiringly, perhaps a little enviously, and bided his time. For he was not one to take a resolve lightly.

He was not a spectacular contender for scholastic honors. He was seventh from the top of his class in the senior year, but the prizes seem always to have been carried off by some one else. He and his brother sang in the glee club and were members of the chess club, and Emmett probably played baseball, too, though his name does not appear on the lists of those marvelous nines which won or lost hotly contested games by such scores as 37 to 24. As the lightweight in '75 he wrestled against the lightest man in '76 and won. Indeed, he is remembered as a boy with an almost uncanny habit of victory. He was apt at croquet, as he was later at billiards, tennis, and golf—never, indeed, of championship material, but always an accurate, determined player. He was compact, lithe, and full of a superb vitality which lasted him almost to his dying day.

The Holt boys were both members of Delta Kappa Epsilon, which was then, like the other fraternities, essentially a literary society. The members met in secret once a week (usually in a hired room over a store), read their own compositions, criticized, coached each other for competitive orations, and were mutually uplifting.

As "Prex" frowned on dormitories, preferring the influence of a "good Christian home," the boys lived in plain quarters at 28 Pearl Street. In their room was a stove for which they had to carry up the fuel. One day in their Freshman year a debate arose as to which of two ways of getting from 28 Pearl Street to the campus was shorter, and Emmett persuaded his brother to make a bet, by the terms of which the loser would be compelled to carry up wood for the remainder of the month. Emmett won by a few feet. Next month there was a similar bet on some other subject, and the tradition in the Holt family was that Curtice carried up the wood during the entire four years of his stay at Rochester.

Almost every week the boys went home to Webster, their father usually driving up to meet them. Between times Sabrah wrote them letters full of encouragement and sage counsel:

You know I would be very glad to have you home this week but I would not wish you to neglect any of your studies, and especially your orations. I want you to spare no time or labor to make them what you and your friends would be proud of.... It may not be as easy for you as for the others but you know the Bible says: "Where the steel is dull you must put forth the more strength." ... One thing more, Curt. I don't want you to go around with that Mrs. Nichols. She has a husband and let him wait on her, or if Clark being her cousin sees fit to take her, it is well enough. I don't want my boys to have the name, much less the shame, of going with married women, be they ever so pleasant, highly educated or accomplished.... What would you think if Eliza should be going off to lectures with young men when Eugene is gone? I should tell her very soon what I thought about it.

Eliza, too, has her innings. She writes to her brothers:

I've heard *so many things* lately about *Rochester girls, and girls of good respectable families too*—deacon's daughters some of them—that I am *perfectly disgusted with the whole of them* and feel almost as if I didn't want you to get acquainted with *any* girls. Association with any ladies that are not perfectly pure and upright in their character will certainly exert a debasing influence upon any young man, and any lady's society that doesn't make a man nobler, purer and more true to his manhood is not such as I wish my brothers to be in.

In spite of these constant admonitions from home and notwithstanding the influence of daily chapel and weekly prayer-meeting and church sociable, the Holt boys were not altogether models of virtue. They bet heavily at croquet and were in the thick of the inter-class gum-shoe fights—historic moments of stealthy

THE ROCHESTER FACULTY IN 1877
Morey   Filmore   Robinson
Mixer   Kendrick   Anderson   Quinby   Lattimore

EMMETT HOLT IN COLLEGE

ambush followed by sudden and terrible chastisement. The faculty itself was not exempt from attack. When the unpopular Professor of Mathematics was engaged at the blackboard a hail of chalk was likely to descend suddenly on his head, or failing that, some one would hurl the coal shovel thunderously across the room.... And the Holt boys were regrettably among those present. Mathematics was required for all—through calculus—but the resentment against this unpopular subject found expression in a ceremony, "the interment of calculus," which took place at the end of the course. Once a copy of the hated volume was under the sod there was great jubilation.

The evening serenade was a cherished diversion of this period. Sometimes it was abused, as on the night when a popular professor appearing wrathfully at his window in a nightshirt shouted to his adorers, "What! Seventy-six again! and for the second time to-night!" Seventy-six, unjustly accused and immediately suspicious, began to search the adjacent shrubbery and on discovering their impersonators administered fitting punishment.

The "Bone Man" was such a college tradition that he deserves special mention. Perhaps he was originally acquired for the osteology course, but whatever his past history he became in time a beloved fraternity mascot. He resided, apparently, with that fraternity making the best record in competitive orations, and whenever he changed his habitat, he was driven all around town on the front seat of a cart and thus joyfully welcomed:

Come, brothers, let's chant to the Bone Man a chorus,
Let's raise a glad anthem of welcome on high,
We honor his coming, as those gone before us,
And those coming after will do by and by,
But never! no, never! did sachems or sages,
Whose memory poets delight to revive,
E'er revel in honors more bright through the ages,
Than those that are lavished by Seventy-five.

There appear to have been thoughts of a medical career in the mind of the younger Holt boy even in college, if one may judge by the prediction of the class historian: "Emmett Holt," he said, "believes in hydropathy and little pills. Holt showed this water-cure tendency in college by keeping his face clean and by helping to put a member of the class of '76 under the pump. Holt, who is a high dilutionist, will present the following for feeding up a patient: 'Hang a small chicken so that its shadow will fall on a hogshead of water; for an adult three teaspoons daily; for a child apply infinitesimal calculus to find the proper dilution." Perhaps it was the influence of Lattimore that had steered Emmett's thoughts in the direction of medicine, but it was not until almost a year after he left Rochester that he announced his decision.

Four years pass quickly, and suddenly it is graduation day. The same old chapel, but to-day alive with friends, relatives and palms.... The proud parents from Webster.... Music by the Glee Club.... "Prex" in his most ennobling vein followed by twenty-one orations from the members of '75, all twenty-one characterized by the Rochester *Democrat and Chronicle* as "very fine indeed"... more music... prizes...

diplomas... the alumni banquet with its toasts and prophecies and its inevitable appeal for funds... and finally the formal reception by Dr. Anderson's "estimable lady."

Emmett was a few months past twenty when he graduated. He was charged with high ideals, but he was not trained to do anything but teach school.

IV

MEDICINE

PRESIDENT ANDERSON gave Emmett a letter of introduction in which he spoke of him as "a man of excellent moral character and scholarship, as well as of more than common ability." Thus armed he secured a position in the Riverside Academy at Wellsville, New York, to which he went in August.

"Everyone seemed very much surprised that you had gone," Sabrah wrote, "and the universal exclamation was, 'Wasn't it a sudden start?'" A few days later she added, "Emmett, we do miss you so much. Curt looks like half a pair of shears, for you have always been together, and I feel as though I could not have you separated." And again, a month later: "Well, I suppose you think you have earned $50, and have the satisfaction of knowing that it is your own, and you can do with it just as you please. I dare say you never felt so independent in your life before, and I doubt if you ever do again.... I don't know how much I would give to have one of our old-fashioned visits to-night. I would be willing to sit up till midnight, as tired as I am. Have you got over your cold entirely?... When I mend Curt's gloves or fix anything for him I always think of my other boy and wish I could do for him."

Emmett kept a cash account, in a little brown leather-covered book which is still in existence. Here, among entries for "letter paper," "stamps," "gloves," "hair cut," "horse fare," and so on, there appear two significant items. In September, 1875, he bought a physiology for one dollar, in December an anatomy for $7.30. He also bought baseballs and croquet balls, and spent small sums on "festivals" and "music." He could not altogether have neglected the lighter side of life. "We were very much amused at your account of your visit to the Rocks," says one of his mother's letters, "especially the circus part, and yet half frightened to read it. Did you get hurt much? Do be careful how you have much to do with strange horses, especially ugly ones."

March 4, 1876, was Emmett's twenty-first birthday. He wrote:

To-day, the solemn fact forces itself upon my mind, it matters not how much I may try to avoid or escape it, that henceforth I bear the burdens, assume the responsibilities and meet the trials and temptations of manhood. That to-day I cross the boundary line once and forever, with no possibility of ever retracing my steps.... For me the possibilities of youth have been decided. What has been realized, I asked myself. I look over my life and see its path marked with privileges not appreciated, opportunities, many wasted, others not half improved, duties to God and man not recognized, or worse, when seen, ignored. But, thank God, all my reflection upon the first twenty-one years of my life does not confront me with such solemnly-sad results, for with these there comes back the memory of Christian parents, a Christian home, and Christian teaching from my earliest infancy, and for these, if never before, I believe I am to-day truly thankful.

. . . .

This youthful solemnity was in part, of course, a reflection of Sabrah; he was speaking her language, as he spoke it to few but her. It also reflected Dr. Anderson and that excellent teacher of rhetoric, Professor Joseph H. Gilmore, and it reflected the epistolary style of 1876. Emmett Holt was taking life seriously and purposefully.

All that winter, no doubt, he was studying the bulky book on anatomy. In May he wrote: "I can hardly realize that five weeks in Wellsville are all that remain. I never saw a year go quicker than this one, but still it seems some time since I was home, and I think I shall enjoy getting back there.... For myself, I have *about* decided to go to studying medicine next year, but you need not tell any one, for I may change my mind." This seems to have been written in response to one of his mother's letters, twelve days earlier, in which she said:

My principal reason in writing now is that we had a session on your case when Pa was home, and decided if you were going to study medicine it was not worth while for you to spend any more time in teaching, unless you particularly desire to do so, for Pa says he can help you through now, with what you have to help yourself. He thinks and we thought, you would rather have some of your "portion" now than to spend any more time in teaching. Now you have the matter before you, and can do just as you think best.

What Emmett thought best was to go ahead with medicine.

In August, 1876, after completing his teaching and

visiting Webster, he went to the Philadelphia Centennial Exposition, and spent a day or two also in Washington and New York City. This little fling was characteristic. He had little money and was careful of every penny of it, but he was always willing to invest in an educative experience. In his note-book he entered, with his customary zeal for tangible facts, a list of the exhibits at the Exposition which had interested him, and followed it up with a memorandum about the cost of the Baltimore City Hall and some statistics about the then uncompleted Washington Monument. One can visualize his keen delight in memorizing these data and bringing them forth to share with the folks at home—a habit in which, as long as he lived, he always took delight.

By October his mind was made up, without reservation, and he went to Buffalo to attend the Medical College of the University of that city.

American medicine in the seventies was a far different institution from what it is to-day. Incredible as it may seem, quacks and faddists were then even more numerous, and the number of "diploma mills" led a European observer to remark that American degrees in medicine were to be "placed in the same categories as those amiable but meaningless distinctions conferred upon people dancing the cotillion."

The University of Buffalo, however, was not in this class. It was considered one of the better schools of the day, and its faculty included the best medical talent of the city. But by present standards the curriculum was woefully inadequate. Laboratories there were none, anatomy was to be learned from textbooks only, and such essential medical sciences as physiology and pathology seem to have been left for students to master for themselves. The microscope was neither mentioned nor used. The teaching consisted of a four months' lecture course on clinical subjects. Year after year the students listened to the same course of lectures, until having heard it three times, they were duly graduated. Emmett stayed only one, but he took careful notes, notes which give a fair picture of the medical wisdom of that period.

There were courses in medicine, surgery, the diseases of women and children, and materia medica. But how different from these subjects as taught to-day! Not a word was said about asepsis or surgical technic. Abdominal surgery with its almost uniformly fatal results was considered beyond the pale; there was, however, a considerable body of knowledge about many of the surgical specialties, such as orthopedics and nose and throat, while the course on fractures and bandaging leaves little to be desired to-day. The notes on medicine are more comprehensive. The descriptions of disease—the technic of physical diagnosis—these were familiar enough, but the causes of disease remained obscure. Night moisture, winds, and fogs were supposed to be responsible for malaria; poisons attaching themselves to the leaves of trees and emanations from freshly turned soil or various putrefying substances were thought to cause other fevers. Tuberculosis was considered a disease of the blood—hereditary; in fact, the marriage of tubercular persons was never to be condoned.

The medical knowledge of the day was static.

MEDICINE

Everything was known that could be known: there was no suggestion that new things could be found out. But perhaps there was one member of the Buffalo faculty who had a somewhat broader vision than his colleagues. Dr. Stoddard, the professor of Materia Medica, seems to have had one eye turned on the other side of the Atlantic, for at the bottom of a long list of causes of disease we find "bacteria," and there is mention of the Pasteur-Liebig controversy on the cause of putrefaction. Stoddard, however, had not entirely emancipated himself from the Middle Ages. Among his remedies were to be found bull's blood for internal use, and there was no doubt in his mind about the efficacy of a piece of bacon or ham hung about the neck of a patient with a sore throat. And what a delightful prescription was this: "One drop of capsicum in a teaspoonful of champagne." There were few diseases which could not be benefited by alcohol in some form, but many of the effective drugs of to-day were there, too, their doses determined, their action fairly well understood.

The medical student's real education was obtained outside the regular term of the school, when the student could either "walk the hospitals" or "read medicine" in the office of some practitioner. This survival of the old apprentice system had much to recommend it. A physician of character and knowledge could impart a great deal to his student assistant, not only in clinical experience, but in worth-while medical reading and in the less tangible traditions of the profession. Much, of course, depended upon the character of the preceptor; a charlatan produced charlatans, and a physician with ideals could inspire a younger man with the best ideals of the profession. The difficulty with the system was the limited number of physicians of quality who would accept student apprentices.

After attending one course of lectures at Buffalo in the spring of 1877, Emmett entered the office of Dr. J. W. Whitbeck of Rochester to read medicine, and remained for eight months. Whitbeck appears to have been a skilled surgeon and was undoubtedly a man of integrity. The association was probably a good one for the younger man, though it does not appear that it had a profound influence on his life.

Sabrah Holt, working and planning for the future, dreamed of seeing her son established as a physician in Rochester, where he might prosper and yet not be wholly lost to her. Indeed, it was some years later, after he had gone to New York City, that she wrote him: "The other night I woke up, and as usual when I can't sleep the future of each of my children comes up before me. I make out their courses as I would have them, and for you I thought how I would like to have you go in with Dr. Whitbeck in Rochester." But Emmett was to take root too deeply in the greater city. He did not forget the advice of President Anderson: "Young man, if you have got anything in you, go to a big place to fly your kite. When you get your kite up in a great center it amounts to something." And presently the chance did come for him to put up his kite in New York. The Hospital for the Ruptured and Crippled in that city had a vacancy for a student-interne at a small salary. It was first offered to a Rochester youth who had New York connections. This individual was, however, faced with the difficulty of deciding between the pursuit of ambition in the metropolis and the hand of an heiress who wished to remain in Rochester. The heiress won the day, and the position was left vacant. Through his college friend, John B. Calvert, then a divinity student, Emmett learned of the position and lost no time in applying for it. His application was successful, and he came to New York to take up his new duties in February, 1878, bearing a letter from Dr. Whitbeck saying that such "advice and assistance" as might be rendered him would be "worthily bestowed."

The Hospital for the Ruptured and Crippled had been established by Dr. James Knight in 1863 for the treatment of children between four and fourteen years of age. It was a pioneer effort, and had grown from a small beginning until at this time it occupied a spacious building at Forty-Second Street and Lexington Avenue large enough to care for two hundred children.

The new interne's duties permitted him enough time to continue his medical studies. The stipend was $400 a year. Emmett Holt arrived in New York with $27 in cash, as his account-book shows. It was a modest beginning, and there were years of struggle ahead.

After establishing himself at the Hospital, he registered at the "P. and S.," the College of Physicians and Surgeons, later affiliated with Columbia University. P. and S. probably furnished as good a medical education as was to be had in the United States. It was in many respects superior to that obtainable at Buffalo. Anatomy was still regarded as the most important subject of study, but it was learned by dissection rather than from books or lectures. The obtaining of cadavers for purposes of dissection was still beyond the pale of the law, and several of Emmett Holt's classmates, less fortunate than he in securing a hospital stipend, supported themselves and provided the medical school with cadavers by the practice of body-snatching. On dark and stormy nights there were expeditions to Woodlawn and other cemeteries with horse and buggy and a burlap sack, and there were narrow escapes from detection that must have made thrilling telling to their fellow medical students. The P. and S. had its outstanding personalities who lectured and gave clinics to the students; they were scholars and gentlemen of the old school. The teachers of that day were greatly revered and their words taken down as gospel. Nevertheless, the organized teaching of the medical school was quite inadequate for the graduation requirements, making it necessary for students to join "quiz" groups outside the curriculum conducted by some practising physician who needed to supplement his income.

Emmett Holt attended lectures, clinics, and quiz groups, but beyond a doubt he learned more within the confines of the Ruptured and Crippled Hospital from his immediate superior, Gibney, a warm-hearted Kentuckian who had taken the young assistant under his wing, and who remained his lifelong friend. In one of his last letters, written from Peiping in 1923, Dr. Holt wrote to Gibney:

Our friendship has now extended over a period of more than forty-five years, if my memory serves me right. Looking back over this long time I recall very vividly our first meeting in February, 1878, when I

MEDICINE

first came to the H. R. C., as we used to call it. You were very kind to the young medical student who had come to New York almost a total stranger, and he has never forgotten it. You taught me many things, more than you realized, I am sure—the value of keeping accurate clinical records, the importance of learning the *ultimate results* of pathological processes, the desirability of contributing to medical literature, even in a humble way; these are some of the things that stand out now in my memory.

I hope I have profited by your early words of advice and by your example. We have both of us done a good deal of hard work since those early days, which we can look back upon with some degree of satisfaction. As I write there comes back so vividly to mind the household of those early days. Averill in his office in the basement, whose book I used to sign every month on the receipt of $33.33—my munificent salary!— Egan walking up and down, wiping his perspiring forehead of a July day when the patients in Room IV would run up to numbers previously not recorded; and the house staff—H. the pockmarked from Minnesota, Joselyn the inimitable from New Hampshire, Swasey the man from Maine, last but not least Vance . . . with his endless discussion of the virtues and vices of the Yandells of Louisville. They were all good fellows.

The young student wrote to his parents with great regularity. Once he said: "I am getting sick of this writing-when-you-feel-like way of doing business, or rather not writing when you don't feel like it; so hereafter I am going to write twice a week, as formerly, and shall expect you to do the same." In an undated letter, written in 1878, he gives a sketch of his routine:

Pa, in his last letter, wanted me to be sure to answer his questions; so I will make that the first business, and I know no better way than to give you an outline of my day as it usually goes. The first bell rings at 6:45; at seven I get up and am ready for breakfast at 7:15. After breakfast I spend the time till 8:30, usually, in study. I then go down to the large office where I have my desk, and after looking over the morning paper, begin my writing. This office is a large one, and is the waiting room for the outdoor patients, of whom we have from 75 to a hundred a day. I spend the time here until noon, writing up the records of cases which have been discharged, getting the histories of the new ones admitted, seeing to braces left here for repairs, examining new cases in the small office adjoining, and when we have a larger number than the other doctors can manage easily I assist in examining, applying braces, prescribing, etc.

At twelve o'clock I lock up my desk and start down to the College to a lecture, or out for a walk or an errand, or perhaps go back to my room to read or study. At 1:15 we have dinner, and usually eat until two o'clock, when I go back downstairs, and repeat the morning's programme, except that the office is empty of patients, and the business clerks and myself are the only occupants. At four o'clock I close the books for the day, and my work is over, so far as my hospital duties are concerned. Only, when one of the other doctors is absent, I go up and help make the rounds through the wards upstairs, where we have about ninety boys and the same number of girls. We go up about five o'clock, and spend about an hour in bandaging, manipulating diseased joints, reapplying and adjusting braces. At other times I spend my time after four o'clock in taking a little exercise outdoors first,

MEDICINE

and then coming back and studying until supper comes at 6:15.

On three days in the week, Tuesday, Thursday, and Saturday, I go at four o'clock to my "quiz," which consists of a regular recitation at the private house of a doctor who makes a business of "coaching up" students, and prepares them for hospital examinations, etc. We have about eight in the class, and it makes an excellent drill, very much better than studying alone by myself. I get back from this at six o'clock, and spend my evenings in study, except Wednesday evenings, when we have office hours from seven to nine o'clock, in return for which I have Saturday afternoons off entirely, and my time all to myself from Saturday noon to Monday morning. Each day is the same and each week. I get from four to five hours a day to study, and take considerable time for exercise besides.

In another letter he writes: "Pa asks what the doctors get here. Dr. Knight gets $3000, Dr. Gibney $1500, and the other three $400, the same as I do. I do regular doctor's duty a good share of the time, and have much more time to myself, and many more privileges, than do the others." He had the impatience, even the unconscious cruelty of youth. He says:

You ask me if I don't like Dr. Knight and if so why not? I *don't* like him and for several reasons—none, however, concerning his relations to me, for I could not ask him to do better. In the first place he is an old man, and is completely under the thumb of the matron, who runs the whole institution, in one sense. As a physician he is a sort of granny, and treats all his cases in precisely the same way as twenty-five years ago, while the rest of the profession have been making rapid progress. In the third place his institution is a child of his own creation, and we are all inclined to be silly about our offspring, you know. He bores everyone with talking about it, about the perfect ventilation, the nice food, the dear children, etc., and soft-soaps the parents of patients, and also visitors, to an extent that goes quite contrary to my ideas of propriety and fitness.

In February, 1879, Emmett had this to report:

Examinations have been much more rigid this year than previously and 33 out of about 125 who came up for examination for their degree of M.D. were "plucked"—that is, they failed to pass. So you may imagine there were some sore heads among the boys. The spring term begins March 10, and I shall do about as much then as now in the way of lectures and dissection to get ready for next year's examinations.

But he himself had no reason to fear being plucked, for when he graduated, in the spring of 1880, he stood among the first ten in his class.

His graduation thesis was a paper on "Articular Osteitis of the Hip Joint," a subject of which Dr. Gibney had made a study. It was his first medical paper, a simple document, free from the rhetorical graces and falling cadences which had been encouraged at Rochester—a concise, straightforward presentation with a statistical analysis of the cases of the Ruptured and Crippled Hospital.

His high standing in the class enabled him to obtain a choice hospital internship. He chose the surgical service at Bellevue Hospital, for a surgeon he had made up his mind to be.

V

THE DAWN OF A NEW ERA

SURGERY in New York City in 1880 was barely emerging from the dark ages. Lister's first paper was published in 1867, but it had taken the better part of a decade for his views to obtain a foothold on the other side of the Atlantic. In Bellevue as late as 1871, 22 per cent of all open wounds developed erysipelas, and 40 to 60 per cent of all amputations terminated fatally, usually from pyemia. In the forties, Semmelweiss in Vienna and Oliver Wendell Holmes in Boston had first preached the doctrine of aseptic obstetrics, but as late as 1872 in Bellevue puerperal fever killed one in ten women who underwent childbirth. It was only in the later seventies that more than a handful of mothers were able to thank the author of "The Chambered Nautilus" for life and health. In 1879 had occurred that dramatic scene in the Paris Academy of Medicine when Pasteur had interrupted a discussion on the causes of puerperal fever by declaring that puerperal fever was of bacterial origin and was carried by doctors and nurses. To the speaker's retort that he feared the strange microbe would never be found Pasteur stepped to the blackboard and drawing what we now know as the streptococcus, said, *"Voici la figure."* During Emmett Holt's service at Bellevue only one case of appendicitis was diagnosed. The others were called colic, or otherwise described in general terms, and treated medically; and the patients, when soothing potions failed, were gathered to their fathers. Yet Bellevue was justly famous as a teaching hospital and was headed by men who had some claim to be considered farsighted and progressive. It was at Bellevue, in 1869, that the first regular ambulance service in the United States had been instituted. It was at Bellevue, in 1873, that the first training school for nurses in this country had been established. Prior to that time it was customary to employ "people from the penitentiary as attendants, nurses and general helpers." Such conditions were not abolished in a day. It is fair to suppose that they were exceedingly fresh, if not fragrant, in the memory in 1880 and 1881. But the wheels of progress had begun to turn. The influence of Virchow, the great German pathologist, was beginning to be felt. A pathological laboratory with Dr. Francis Delafield as director had been started in 1878 at Bellevue. The time was at hand when doctors were no longer to remain content with diagnoses made in the examining room or on the wards, but would insist on following the processes of disease to the autopsy room, where the microscope as well as the knife was now being used for the first time in this country.

The young surgical interne followed Gibney's advice to learn the ultimate results of disease. He was a frequent attendant at the autopsy room. But a recent arrival at Bellevue Hospital proved to be a more inspiring influence to him than Delafield, the pathologist.

THE DAWN OF A NEW ERA

A dynamic young physician from Connecticut named William H. Welch had just opened a bacteriology laboratory there. Welch had been lured abroad by the glamour of the new science. He had worked in the laboratories of the noted pathologists Von Recklinghausen and Cohnheim. He had learned the elements of microscopic pathology and something of the new science of bacteriology. A number of common microorganisms could be recognized by staining methods, although methods for the cultivation of bacteria outside the body had not yet been discovered. When Welch returned to New York hoping to teach and pursue his studies he had applied for a post at the P. and S. The authorities of this institution, however, failed to recognize the future "dean of American medicine." He had been coldly received and had then turned to Bellevue. In Bellevue Hospital he was given a small upstairs room for a laboratory, and soon he collected a group of fifteen or twenty enthusiastic young students. For seven years Welch continued to teach here until he was called to Baltimore to develop the Johns Hopkins Medical School. Many of his most distinguished pupils were those of the Bellevue group —E. L. Trudeau, William Stewart Halsted, and others. The enthusiasm of this little group and its significance were not lost upon the Bellevue house staff; in fact, most of Welch's students were hospital internes. Emmett Holt was one of them, and from the start caught the attention of his instructor as a particularly earnest young man who used to spend all his spare moments in the laboratory and the "dead house." There began an association and warm friendship that was to last throughout life. The seed of modern medicine had been carried over the Atlantic far more effectively by an outstanding personality than by any printed page. It took root and flowered in the minds and deeds of many. Holt was not to be one of those pupils who were to take up that particular torch and become primarily investigators of disease. Although he later pursued the problems of pediatrics into the laboratory, the needs of the sick patient always made a more urgent appeal than the satisfaction of solving a problem or answering a perplexing question. But the contacts at Bellevue had opened the young interne's eyes to the fact that medicine was advancing—was about to advance—by leaps and bounds, and that the leadership was in Europe. At the earliest opportunity he would go to Europe. But, at the moment, there was plenty to do with the task in hand.

His mother, as was her wont, followed his experiences closely and worried about him. "It seems to me," she said, "there is no man living who has greater opportunities for doing good than a physician, if he will but improve them." In April, 1881, she added this:

I should think you would feel like a man of forty with so much of care and responsibility upon you, and no one on whom you can shirk any of it. Doesn't it make you nervous, I'm glad it is not me, for it would soon make a finish of me. Though thirty years ago I was equal to most any emergency, and if you can only keep calm and cool yourself, you will, with God's help, be able to stand the strain. I am afraid you will have

THE DAWN OF A NEW ERA 53

to be too closely confined for your health.... You must certainly feel like a man, but don't let it make you conceited, just self-reliant. And never forget that you have the Great Physician of whom you can ask counsel, and who is always ready to give us just the help we need.

The new responsibility was perhaps that of house surgeon, with entire charge of the surgical wards at certain periods of the day or night.

Two months later:

Have you decided yet what you shall do, I have had a great deal of anxiety about you of late, feeling that you would very soon stand in the front rank, and in a hand-to-hand fight in the battle of life, and I often feel that I would so gladly stand in front and shield you, if I could but save you from the toils, cares, trials, anxieties, perplexities, and last, but by no means least, the many, many temptations.... In looking over your past I can see plainly how God has led you and cared for you.... I feel that he will hear and answer my prayer and keep you from all evil.

The choice of a career must have been much in the foreground of his thoughts as the end of the Bellevue interneship approached. The surgical training had been rigorous, and he had become no doubt a passable surgeon, but, as he himself realized, he lacked and probably would never acquire the exquisite manual dexterity required to reach the front rank in that field. The problems of internal medicine made an increasing appeal, but a further hospital training did not seem justified.

In the fall of 1881 his mind was made up, and he opened an office with Dr. Charles M. Cauldwell at 200 West 52nd Street. The building contained living quarters where Dr. Holt lived with two of his oldest college friends, John Calvert and James Duane Squires. Squires was a promising lawyer, and Calvert was studying for the ministry. On November 10th the following entry appears in Emmett's account book: "Sign ... $1.25." Was it on this day that he took the step of hanging out his shingle?

VI

BACHELOR DAYS IN "THE FLAT"

THE apartment at 200 West 52nd Street, affectionately known as "The Flat," served as bachelor quarters from the fall of 1882 until the winter of 1884. There could not have been in New York at that time a more exemplary group than Dr. Holt and the two friends, Squires and Calvert, who lived with him; certainly none ever sowed a milder crop of wild oats. They were all Baptists, all graduates of Rochester and members of the same fraternity. John B. Calvert, that same student whom Dr. Anderson had found "a little pale," was now assistant pastor of Calvary Baptist Church. His fine voice and the deep earnestness which underlay his sermons were a source of great pride to certain biased members of the congregation who, it is to be feared, actually welcomed absences of the pastor-in-chief. James Duane Squires, a budding lawyer, had been a boyhood crony of Calvert and was later his room-mate at college. His slight, if chesty, figure contrasted oddly with the impressive height and bulk of his friend Calvert and suggested the hen and chick relation which seems actually to have existed between them. The office at the flat was shared with another struggling doctor, Charles M. Cauldwell. Jovial and very fastidious, the son of a pillar of Calvary Church, he adopted the Flat as his second home.

Naturally the social life of the group centered in the Calvary Church. Sabrah Holt had urged her son to take a Sunday School class and had even offered to send him the *Sunday School Teacher* if he could not afford to subscribe himself. How surprised she must have been when she learned that he had become the spiritual leader of a class which, in Squires' opinion, gave early promise of becoming "a mutual admiration society." Squires also taught a class, though one less fraught with possibilities of romance, and such was the ability latent in this frail young man that he rose within a year to be superintendent of the whole Sunday School. He took his duties so to heart that on New Year's Day he felt it incumbent upon him to call upon every one of his Sunday School teachers—some sixty-five in all.

The church is thus the central theme in nearly all the letters to Webster.

New York, Oct. 19, 1884.

DEAR ONES ALL:

We have been quite gay this week. Tuesday night John entertained his Sunday School class here, consisting of about thirty old maids, and a few that were not so old, with a small sprinkling of stupid men. We had an awfully funny time entertaining them. I wish you might have seen them. They would insist upon sitting all around the room, as at a funeral. We showed off all our pictures and lectured at them, getting off all our old jokes, but I am sorry to say many were not appreciated. The few who could see the pictures while we were talking about them were, of course, much interested. But those who heard the speech and got the pictures about ten minutes afterwards, having meanwhile forgotten all that was said about it, got dreadfully bored and I finally desisted.

The absorbing topic now is the Cauldwell wedding. ... We shall combine on a wedding present as this is an "off year" financially. We shall buy something tomorrow, probably a cabinet. Charlie has told us of several things they *do not* want, e.g., already *ten lamps* have been sent and a dozen after dinner coffee sets. ...

I congratulate Curt on his easy nomination, and hope he will have as easy a walk-over at the election. Politics are getting very hot here. Mr. MacArthur has been offered $100 a night to speak for Blaine in New Jersey—of course he will not take the stump. How is Eugene and how is Pa's ear?   Love to all,

EMMETT

Usually the writer was too busy and absorbed to give more than the briefest mention of his social engagements, his jaunts to Staten Island and Asbury Park, the concerts, plays and operas he attended alone or in company. It is to Eliza's facile pen that one must turn for a real whiff of the social atmosphere of that day:

We had a splendid time at Dr. Johnson's Friday night. They just know how to entertain people and have everything to do it with. They have been abroad twice and have lots of nicknacks, costly ones, too; they have a large book of engravings by Doré, lots of stereopticon views, a portfolio four or five feet square on standards filled with *large* photographs of all the principal places of interest in Rome, Florence, and Sorrento and a large glass for viewing them, a splendid piano, etc. The house is just new, cost $13,000. and is furnished the handsomest of any house I was ever in, half the parlor was upholstered in blue silk rep and the other in crimson with puffings of velvet; the carpet was drab velvet... flowers in profusion as if it had been midsummer... and ice-cream two feet high with a whole basketful of cakes.

Dr. Holt's birthdays always made him solemn and retrospective.

New York, March 4, 1883

DEAR ONES ALL:

Twenty-eight years old today. I can scarcely realize it. In fact I forgot it entirely until the day was about half over. Well, it is a good thing to have a birthday occasionally to remind you that you are getting along in life. Five years ago last Wednesday since I came to this city! How little idea I had then that this would be my home now! I have worked hard and worked conscientiously, but have been rewarded beyond my brightest expectations.... I can never be too thankful that we three fellows have been thrown so intimately together and no one will ever know how much good their influence has done me. We have been mutually helpful in many ways. As our work has all been along different lines, no spirit of rivalry was possible, and we have, I think, all been successful.

So this birthday has set me thinking and running over the last few years, as I have sat here in my room alone by the fire, waiting for the others to come from church. John has just come in and sends regards to all

—especially congratulations to Curt on having a good Baptist wife.
With love to all,
. EMMETT

* * * *

His mother was still the dominant figure in his life, and the flying trips to Webster made him very homesick.

Here it is Sunday again [a letter runs], a damp, rainy morning and quite warm. Two weeks ago today Mother was sitting in the hammock and I lying on the grass beside her, visiting at the rate of ten knots an hour, and this morning I feel the same mood coming over me.

Or:

It seems a long time since I came from home and though I am contented here and enjoy the work, still I find nothing which can take the place of home; and I suppose I never shall....

* * * *

In the spring Curtice visited New York and brought back good reports:

Curt seemed to like your friends very much that he met; Dr. Gibney, he said, was such a free and easy sort of fellow, and not in the least what he had pictured him, and Dr. Cauldwell, he said, was a perfect gentleman, and so entertaining.

* * * *

Sometimes she became anxious, as when a dark rumor of card playing in the Flat reached her ears or when Will Holt reported "you were looking poor and thin. Don't be in such hot haste to make yourself known and felt in the world as to undermine your health and thereby cripple all your future." She sincerely hopes in another letter that he will not dine out more than twice a week, as otherwise he will overtax himself and not have enough time for letters home or "reflexion."

In July, 1883, Emmett sent his parents for a holiday trip. It is doubtful whether anything he ever did in his more prosperous years gave more happiness or brought him a richer reward. Sabrah confessed:

... I had to go to my room and give vent to my feelings in a good cry. Pa went up for the mail; and as the letter was one day later than usual he opened it before he got home, and when he came in threw it into my lap without saying one word. I took it up and read it; Lizzie, watching me and guessing at the contents, said, "Mother, what is the matter?" I handed her the letter and says she, "Mother, I knew what it was by your looks, and it is what we have been dying to tell you. ... " I have so long wished to go to the Thousand Islands that I had about given it up, but to go to Montreal I had never dared dream of, and now I can't realize that we are actually going."

The trip was made, and lived over again many times. Next December she insisted: "You are strictly forbidden to give Pa and me any Christmas gifts, for you know that we had ours last July, and it has lasted us and will, for years to come."

Practice came slowly to the young physician, and there was no such thing as limiting it to a specialty. It was general practice or none: obstetrics, minor surgery, tonsillectomies done in the office and sent home afterwards, were all a part of a day's work, and there were long gaps between them at first. He started a quiz class of his own—in anatomy—to fill in some of them.

The decision to aim toward specialization seems to have come early. Dr. George Fox, then beginning to achieve a reputation as a dermatologist, advised his ambitious younger colleague that the way to get ahead in medicine was to find some neglected field and study it thoroughly. The advice was taken to heart. Perhaps the two years' experience at the Ruptured and Crippled had impressed him with the fact that knowledge of medical disorders in children was well in arrears of surgical knowledge. The knowledge of children gained in that institution would be an asset. At any rate, the decision was made during his first year of practice to become a specialist in the medical disorders of childhood. It was made on practical rather than sentimental considerations, and from this time forward he followed that field without diverging.

Among private patients it was not possible to specialize, but there were dispensary and hospital opportunities in the chosen field to be found if one searched for them. A staff appointment in the Northwestern Dispensary, an active one to which many children came, was obtained without difficulty. A hospital service was not so easy to find, but here, too, the opportunity was not long in coming. The New York Infant Asylum, an institution harboring about 300 city foundlings, was located in Mt. Vernon. Its distance from the city—almost an hour by train—was such as to discourage the busy practitioners on its attending staff from visiting it frequently, and on the medical side it had been much neglected in consequence; in despair, the authorities were searching for a younger man with the time and the interest to devote to it. They found one in the person of Emmett Holt, and he in turn found in that institution an experience which was to give him a unique knowledge of disease in early life. There can be no question that the eight years at the New York Infant Asylum laid the foundation of his pediatric career. Winter and summer the trips to Mt. Vernon were made. He was met at the station in a horse and buggy by the institution's only interne, Dr. Charles G. Kerley, and driven up to the asylum where they made their rounds together. The infants were examined before they were sick and after they had recovered, as well as during all phases of illness. They were examined meticulously, and records were kept as they had never been kept before. Autopsies were performed on every fatal case, and the interesting material was taken down to Bellevue for microscopic examination and further study. There were other physicians at the time who were interesting themselves in children and were familiarizing themselves with children's diseases at the bedside, but not more than one or two who were in a position to interpret the clinical pictures by pathological observations. The opportunity which the Infant Asylum offered here was unsurpassed. For there was disease, unfortunately, and there were fatalities, too, in abundance: epidemics of contagious disease with pneumonia in their wake which would more than decimate its population within a few weeks, and, of course, every summer the enormous toll of deaths from vomiting and "summer diarrhea." Nothing was known at the time about replacing losses of fluid if it could not be retained by mouth. Treatment was by drugs alone, and they were singularly ineffectual. The day had not yet come when the successor of the New York Infant Asylum—the New York Nursery and Child's Hospital—put into practice a new method of caring for orphans: that of farming them out in individual homes rather than grouping them together in institutions where contagious diseases could do their worst and where, even with the best institutions, individual care was often defective. It was only with the end of the century and largely through the influence of Dr. Henry Dwight Chapin that the orphan asylum began to fade out of the American picture.

The observations made at the Northwestern Dispensary and the New York Infant Asylum were carefully recorded, tabulated, analyzed, and prepared for publication, and in 1883 there began a series of clinical publications on disease in childhood which made their author known to his colleagues as a shrewd observer and one who could express himself in an extraordinarily direct and simple style. There were no pediatric journals at that time; most of these articles appeared in the *New York Medical Record*. The first was a paper on malaria in children, based on more than two hundred cases collected from the Northwestern Dispensary. It would be difficult to find half a dozen in all the dispensaries of the metropolis to-day. Then followed others; perhaps it was the clinical picture of pneumonia in infants that was being described, or the difficulties in diagnosis between diphtheria and ordinary croup (it was before the days of specific bacteriological diagnosis), or the danger to infants, especially in summer, of improper food and improper feeding, etc.

The rewards of sound, honest work as always were in the doing, but the appreciation of others when it began to come must have been a source of satisfaction. His mother wrote:

Oh, I heard from you the other day, by way of a young doctor who was one of your quiz scholars and is now practicing medicine in Rochester. His name, if I remember right, is Buckner. The way it came to me was through Uncle George's folks. Abb Curtice's youngest girl, Florence, has been out of health for some time, and they have lately discovered that she has a curved spine. She has been doctoring with Watkins, but Sim insisted on their trying his doctor, who was said Buckner; and in talking over the treatment of such cases he spoke of Dr. Holt of New York, and his manner of treating them, and Sim began to make inquiries and found out it was you. B. said you were one of the best in New York and could get any position you had a mind to apply for.

The quiz class, too, appeared to be going well. Early in 1884 he wrote to his parents:

My men all got through their examinations very creditably. One of them was among the ten honor men of his class. He said he did not care about it on his own account, but was glad for my sake. I put one man through who had been a student of medicine over eight years, but had never had courage to come up to try examinations. He belongs to a very good family here,

JAMES DUANE SQUIRES

JOHN B. CALVERT
1883

L. EMMETT HOLT

BACHELOR DAYS IN "THE FLAT"

and they have been very kind to me. It is needless to say the family were delighted, and they give me all the credit.

I really feel a little guilty sometimes to think that I have coached some men so they have passed examinations, when they really knew so little, but it's my business to get them ready for the examinations, and it is that I am paid for. Good solid work tells, and the men themselves appreciate it when it is over, if they do not enjoy the process. Friday night I gave a little reception to my students of the winter past. They had just finished their examinations that afternoon. I had fifteen here—all nice fellows.... I had a good time, and they all seemed to do so. They made me a present of a very handsome framed etching, about two by three feet in size, and which must have cost at least $20. It was a very pleasant close to our winter's hard work.

Like all mothers, Sabrah both desired and dreaded her son's marriage. She felt marriage essential to a full and happy life; and she grieved to see about her in Webster young people who shied away from it:

What a change will come over them in the next five years! Those that don't marry will become staid old maids or bachelors, or frivolous and senseless in trying to make themselves or others believe they are still young.

Clearly her son was not to be numbered as one of these if she could help it:

Well, I am really glad to know that you at the "Flat" are waking up to the importance of something's being done to rescue you from that deplorable state of old bachelors, if 'tis nothing more than to pass resolutions, for that would seem to indicate that you are not quite easy, and therefore there is some hope.

She wanted full details about each young lady whom he met: What kind of mother has she? How old? How large? What color eyes has she? Good-looking? Good disposition? Is she neat and orderly? Is she a good Baptist? What are your prospects? Do you think she loves you? Would he send her the lady's picture if she returned it immediately without showing it even to Pa? To all of which her son replied dutifully, displaying some interest in the subject, and once even advising Charlie, the hired man, to marry and settle down.

She was almost as much interested in John Calvert's matrimonial prospects, for he had been a frequent and welcome visitor at Webster from college days on. She meets a certain Mrs. Wilkins, proud possessor of a Courtlandt quilt, and they indulge in a good gossip about "the boys":

Didn't your ears burn? Mrs. W. said many nice things about Mr. Calvert and Squires. Said she told John to pray for a wife and he (J.) said he didn't dare to for fear the Lord would send him some one he didn't want, and if he prayed for her he should feel he must take her whether he liked her or not. But you tell him from me that when the Lord sends the right one, he will send the love for her, too....

The Lord was evidently listening in, for not long afterward Sabrah asks: "Well, how is John getting on?

BACHELOR DAYS IN "THE FLAT"

Has not the disease reached the turning point? I believe fevers run from one to three weeks, do they not?"

In answer to his mother's query "What girl did you take to the Social Union?" Dr. Holt wrote a letter containing more than a hint of events to come:

DEAR ONES ALL: New York
 May 4/84

The Social Union was a great success—the attendance not as large as we had expected but we all had a good time—that is to say *I did*. I took one of my class, Miss Mairs, the one who took me to the concert. John said, "You had the best thing there unless perhaps I did." * She is certainly one of the sweetest girls I ever saw. The boys all think I am *going* fast. I am only sorry that she is not a little older—but if she were she would not be in my class—so that is some consolation.

Well, we have about decided to cross the "briney" this summer—John, Squires and Crandall, a friend of John's. I always thought it would be a great thing to go to Europe but now I am so near it, it seems like nothing at all. Not half so far as San Francisco from New York. We see people every day who are going and who have been—many of them several times.... When we get our plans more matured I will write more in detail. I shall run up home for a few days before I sail. Love to all.

EMMETT

Do not worry about the ocean passage. The Cunard Line is one of the oldest and is proud of its record of *never having lost a passenger.*

---

* Mr. Calvert escorted Miss Mairs' sister.

The bachelors started for Europe at different times, but with the aid of a Baedeker their plans had been meticulously worked out. At a certain day and hour all three were to converge and meet in a particular hotel in Visp and were to complete their trip together.

VII

AN INNOCENT ABROAD

JUNE 4, 1884, Wednesday. Off at 2:30 P.M. About 2000 down to see the steamer off. A body of Columbia students to see Professor Chandler. Very hot and oppressive. First sensations—on the whole I think I shall like it— Moon nearly full. Evening simply magnificent. Sea like glass. Spent the greater part of the evening talking French with Miss Marion Isaacs, a very bright school girl—old for her age—perfectly free and unaffected. She is not quite sixteen yet, speaks French beautifully, and has promised to give me instruction. Miss Jessie Merchant, also one of my S.S. class, a sweet, quiet, affectionate girl, engaged, Miss Marion's bosom friend, is the second of our party. Mr. Isaacs is about 50, a man who gave up business several years ago on account of his health, has traveled a great deal and always looks out to see that himself and his party are the best cared for and waited on party on the steamer or in the hotel; a man whom many dislike and many love. Mrs. Isaacs is small, quite pretty and seems to have taken a great fancy to me, so of course I shall like her.

Thursday, June 5. One of the days you read of— bright, clear, no fog. I hear there are some below sick. How can people be so foolish when there is really no occasion. It only shows how strong people's imaginations are.

Out of sight of land at last! How different the sensation is from what I always imagined. You seem to belong to a young world sailing through the water with no more thought of being lost or alone than when you compare the earth with the rest of the universe.

Commenced this morning to give the girls systematic lectures in physiology, and as they seem exceedingly interested and interesting, shall continue them we think through the trip—one hour each day. . . .

Friday, June 6. Another perfect day. Spent the morning as yesterday with my class in physiology. . . . Ship rolling a little in the P.M., and the berths are filling up. Racks on the table at dinner for the first time, but really no occasion for it. . . . Met the J's in the evening. Have not missed much in not meeting them before.

Saturday, June 7. Off the banks—foggy and cold. Ther. 46 degrees. Strange how one loses one's conception of time. It seems like a perpetual picnic, only one doesn't get anywhere. Have only seen one sail in three days. . . . In the afternoon a little excitement for the first time. The steamer began to lurch just as lunch was going on, and people tumbled about in a lively way. A lovely young lady showed the bottom of her shoes while making her way to the deck from the stairs. More room on deck than before. Have come to enjoy the roll, and no disposition to be seasick. Interesting young ladies are certainly scarce, have only seen one I would care to know and she is about twice my size and wears a maroon hat.

Sunday, June 8. Awoke early and sewed on buttons before I got out of bed. In the P.M. a strong head wind blowing. I got the girls all tucked up in their steamer chairs with myself between them, as for a sleigh ride in mid-winter, while I read "Evangeline" to them aloud. Among us all and the poem itself, we managed to get up a good deal of sentiment.... The evening the most beautiful yet. All grew sentimental. I don't wonder people fall in love on board the steamer and become engaged before the trip is over. If some people I knew were here, I might feel that way myself. The young ladies had almost to be driven to bed. It is dreadful to have the stern parent always at hand to send you in. Miss Marion is much humiliated to be sent to bed—before me....

Tuesday, June 10. Mrs. Isaacs came down to dinner with the delightful intelligence that she has spent the morning with the maroon hat's ma.... Spent a delightful afternoon with Miss Chatfield of Brooklyn—for such is the young lady's name and am making up for lost time very fast. She is a magnificent specimen of a girl, only too tall for me.

Wednesday, June 11.... The girls are doing splendidly in their physiology. Shall be sorry to quit myself. Can it be we have been on board a week?... A dense fog all the P.M. No whistle, as this is out of order. Everybody talking of landing and making their first preparations. About 7:30 was sitting in the music room when felt the ship's screw stop. "It is nothing—they are sounding," said some one. We soon started and then stopped again. Suddenly a little commotion outside, and we rushed to the deck to see looming up twenty feet from our bow an angry rock about fifty feet high, surrounded by breakers, and at the same time the boat gave a thud, we felt a slight shock, and a dull grating, and then we knew we were aground on the rocks. "All aft" was the first order, as the bow was crowded with passengers who had been straining their eyes for hours to get a glimpse of land. They came aft with a rush, and immediately were heard the other orders, "All hands on deck! Close the doors! To the boats!" in quick succession. In an instant the scene on deck became one of the liveliest activity. We felt in a few minutes that we were again afloat and free from the rocks. The coverings of the life boats were cut away and two sailors in each one stood ready to lower the boats when the word should be given....

Every one felt that it was a trying moment, not knowing what the examination of the boat might reveal, nor that in a few moments we might not be compelled to take to the boats for safety.... In a few minutes the word came up from below that the carpenter had examined the steamer and found no water in the hold. The "cutwater" only was reported broken in for a couple of feet.... We could get our bearings, catching sight of a lighthouse tower a little distance away, and knew we were near three small, rocky islands known as the "Cow, Bull and Calf," near the mouth of Bantry Bay. One of these we struck. To be sure we were now afloat, and our steamer uninjured—at least so far as we knew—but new difficulties beset us. We were still enveloped in a dense fog, our fog whistle out of order, and now one of the pistons became deranged in its packing.

We had backed out of the neighborhood of the island and were in broad sea, and had only now to fear collision with some outgoing vessel. Here we lay wallowing about in an unenviable state of suspense, shut in on all sides by the fog. About 10 o'clock the moon came out magnificently, the fog cleared, the lighthouse could be seen in the distance, and signal rockets to announce our arrival were sent up.... At 2 o'clock the steamer again started for Queenstown, about 70 miles away.... Miss C. says she is sorry to get off at Queenstown tomorrow. How dreadful! I am more and more sorry that she is so tall and I am so short. Such is life at sea.

Thursday, June 12. Reached Queenstown at 5 A.M., and saw the people landed by the tug. Everybody is disgusted to learn that Blaine and Logan are nominated.... We reached Liverpool about 10:30, saw its lights and smelled the smell of England. All baggage is carefully inspected for dynamite and so they stirred up our things in a most unceremonious way, these officials of Her Majesty. Found no contraband goods among our party except a song book containing many copyright songs, and these were promptly confiscated.

In a few minutes after landing we were all tucked in a four-wheeler bowling along the streets of Liverpool to the Northwestern Hotel. Our rooms are large, the beds plenty large enough for four—all England is famous for its beds—and everything has an air of substantial solidity with nothing for show. And so to bed *on land* for the first time in eight days. I braced myself before the wash-bowl as if I expected to be thrown from my feet by the next swell.

Friday, June 13. And this is old England! Its hedges, its trees, its beautiful green fields, its sheepfolds, its quaint country villages, its beautiful landscape scenery, of which the eye never tires—really like one vast landscape garden, with everything in the height of perfection of growth and beauty. And England in June!

Sunday, June 15. Morleys Hotel, London. I took the young ladies to hear Spurgeon. He is stout and thick-set with a German-English face and full beard. He did not fire up and sweep his audience, as I had expected. His preaching is free, almost colloquial in style, and all his body acts. Several times he almost raised a laugh.... The King of New Zealand was at the service with all his suite, and occupied prominent seats in the gallery.

Tuesday, June 17.... In the P.M. we all went to Parliament Houses. Had a letter to Mr. Kane, a member and a very nice gentleman. He took us into the gallery and pointed out Mr. Gladstone and Sir Stafford Northcote, these being the only notables present— Went from here to the National Gallery, where we spent the rest of the day. Saw for the first time good pictures of the recent masters, and some fair ones of the old ones. Was especially struck with the Horse Fair and a landscape of Claude Lorraine and some of Landseer's dogs.

Wednesday, June 18. Stopped at St. Bartholomew's at 1:30 to see Mr. Thomas Smith operate.... A small class of students in the amphitheater looked very green.... The surgeons are all very fine looking men. ... Was shown through the hospital after the operation ... a little disappointed in the whole thing.

Thursday, June 19. I spent the whole forenoon at the British Museum, an immense building filled with antiquities ... jewels, parchments, weapons, sarcophagi, etc., etc., until my eyes were tired, my brain weary and my legs! I would have been glad to exchange places with some of the comfortable, composed looking mummies we saw. I never realized before how large the world is, how many people have lived in it before us, and what a small place we (our city, our nation or our race) fill in it now. This is a great place to stop and soliloquize and ponder on past and future—if you have the time, but you don't.

Saturday, June 21.... To dinner again at the Grand Hotel, and to the Savoy theater to see Gilbert and Sullivan's *Princess Ida*.... We found many novelties— girls for ushers, all ladies required to remove their hats in the "stalls."... The opera was quite amusing and beautifully mounted.

Sunday, June 22.... Went to hear Joseph Parker at City Temple.... People were very ordinary looking class, much like those which fill Spurgeon's. It seems surprising that a man of Parker's power does not draw more from the higher classes. I was impressed now as never before how little standing socially any except *The Church* has here.... Mr. and Mrs. Isaacs surprised me by saying they have about decided to go to Paris on Tuesday, so we shall be together there for a few days. The young ladies do not suspect such a move. Had a call from Mr. and Mrs. Gifford in the P.M. and they have decided to meet me in Paris and go to Italy in company. I am delighted.

Paris, Tuesday, June 24.... Took a French breakfast and went out to get a first glimpse of Paris by daylight. Visited the Madeleine, Place de la Concorde, the Tuileries, and then spent the rest of the morning at the Louvre. Baedeker, our inseparable companion, tells us what the *important* pictures in a collection are. The Salon Carré contains about one hundred paintings, all gems. Enjoyed L. de V's Mona Lisa and Murillo's Immaculate Conception and Raphael's Madonna Jardinière. The first impression of Titian's Entombment was disappointing—shall visit it again.... I am disappointed in the looks of the people. The lower classes are small, and have a dogged, even brutal expression. The handsome French gentleman is a rara avis. The ladies dress better than in London. The young ones are quite pretty, the old ones fat and often bearded. The race looks deteriorated. Everybody goes to the Bon Marché, and so I went but bought only a few handkerchiefs and gloves. This store is vulgarly known as the "American Hearn."

Wednesday, June 25.... The galleries at the Luxembourg are filled with paintings, mostly of the French school and some good sculpture. But both were in the shameless French style....

Rome, Sunday, June 29. St. Peter's, the column of Trajan, the old Roman Forum, the palace of the Cæsars, the arch of Titus—think of it! It does not seem like a reality but like a dream from which I shall awake suddenly to find myself at 200 West 52 Street and that it is time to go to breakfast. I am staggered, overwhelmed; my adjectives are all used up, the English language breaks down, and I can now appreciate the old saying—"See Rome and die."

Tuesday, July 1.... Spent the morning in the Vatican galleries and Sistine chapel. Gave about an hour to the latter. It is grand, sublime, awful, and yet ridiculous in some particulars. Nearly broke our necks looking at the ceiling. It is a queer combination of heathenism and Christianity.

Wednesday, July 2.... Stopped in at some church, I have forgotten which, and saw Michael Angelo's "Christ and His Cross." Was not especially pleased. ... The fleas are getting very friendly.... The street scenes of Rome are growing familiar. The gaily decked horses and the donkey carts of the peasants, the long awnings overhanging the sidewalks, the "baby walkers," the little shops on the street, the dark-faced, light-hearted, happy people.... Have not heard a hand organ in Rome!

Friday, July 4. Pompei and Vesuvius—isn't that a pretty good way for an American citizen to celebrate the day? Up at six, we reached the base of a funicular in about four hours. Above here it is as steep as 45° and in some parts 60°, which is pretty steep I tell you. The railway was built only four years ago, and is about half a mile long. It looked shaky enough when we were halfway up and we were glad we had no ladies along to scream. I don't think we could have withheld one. The volcano has been growing more lively of late and made things quite interesting *for a novice* anyway. Above the railway we climbed about 100 yards to the "old crater." The guides offered to take us farther, but I thanked them *as I could see very well there.* All around us the vapor issued from crevices in the rocks. Every now and then, like an immense locomotive letting off steam, a large gush of steam would be sent out of the mouth of the volcano and molten rocks the size of half a man's body would be precipitated 300 or 400 feet in the air and fall with a thud a stone's throw away.... The descent we made with more confidence.

Naples, Sunday, July 6.... Jules Verne and family at our hotel. He routed me out this morning by mistake. A stout, jolly-looking man about 55, with a grizzly full beard....

Florence, Tuesday, July 8. Many artists copying are to be seen in all the galleries. By comparing the copies with the originals it is easy to see where the master shows his power. The copyists put everything into the picture except the soul which always eludes them.... We resolved to get away to-day at all hazards as we were afraid we should spend all we had. It is a great mistake to be poor if you are going to travel about these European cities. You do see so many things that would make nice bridal and Christmas presents. I am coming again when I get rich.

Bologna, Wednesday, July 9.... We drove around to the old university which has now 400 students, but in its palmy days had 10,000 and was the most celebrated in Europe. It was here that Novella d'Andrea, the great beauty, was once a teacher. She was so handsome she always lectured with her veil down or else behind a screen, so as to avoid distracting the minds of the students.

Venice, Thursday, July 10. "Every other city is prose, Venice is poetry." No noise, no street rabble, no horse cars, nothing that you see anywhere else. But fascinating as is Venice by daylight, Venice by night is trebly so, and *Venice by moonlight!!* Well, in the words of a great American citizen, *this takes the cake*. Who can describe the first evening in Venice? The lights along the Grand Canal, the hundreds of gondolas, threading about, each with little headlight, and one or two gondoliers, many in linen suits, sailor style, and straw hats, trimmed with blue, the boats of singers with lanterns, the pretty Italian songs, with stringed instruments as accompaniment, all to the delightful music of the plash of the oar of our own gondola, as we ourselves lie back on the cushioned seat, forgetful of everything save the present complete delight. The moon was full, and completed the scene when it came out of the clouds. It seems a toy city, a city for play, for music, for love, but not for serious work or sober thought. I don't wonder that these Italians fall in love at 15, and marry at 16. I don't see how, amid such surroundings, anybody can help falling in love with everybody else. It is fortunate for me I did not see a single young lady who could understand me or I might have declared myself forthwith.

Vienna, July 19

DEAR ONES ALL:

Well I have quite become settled in Vienna and like it very much, although the weather has been extremely hot.... I think I wrote you Dr. Griffith gave me at

Venice a letter to Dr. Cook, a friend of his who is here studying. I found he was from Buffalo, and had been here only six weeks, and had spent most of that time studying the language, as he knew not a word of German when he came. He was very kind and took me over to the Allgemeine Krankenhaus, which is said to be the largest hospital in the world. It covers eight blocks and accommodates 3000 patients at once.

Dr. Cook introduced me to several other American M.D.'s here, mostly from New York or Boston. I have found them all exceedingly kind, especially Dr. Coe, who has been here some time, and knows the ropes thoroughly. There is so much red tape about such a place that a man often has to spend a week, or even two, before getting to work at all. The boys, however, were kind enough to put me at once on the track, so that in three days I was quite up to snuff and had begun nearly all the courses I intended to take.*

The regular University year closed about the time I came, so that there are comparatively few students here now, only those doing special work, about fifty, I should say. But such a motley crew as they are: French, Italians, Russians, Portuguese, Brazilians, Japanese, Greeks, Germans and lastly the English and Americans. It seems like a veritable tower of Babel discussion to hear them all talking before the lecturer comes in. You think what a plain, clear, wholesome language English is, and wonder they do not all learn it, and stop their senseless jabbering. I can imagine that one coming here knowing nothing but his mother tongue might be well nigh distracted.

I felt quite curious myself to see how my German would go over here. Often, you know, it is one thing

---

* Obstetrics and pathology.

to know a foreign language while you are in America, and quite another to know it over here, where everything you get must come to you through it. So, I say, I felt a little anxious to see how I was going to make out. It has been twice as easy as I expected, and after French and Italian for so long it seems quite like coming back to my mother tongue.... I hope in a month to become quite a Deutscher.

But to get back to my story. The men all told me I would be much better fixed for my work if I could get a room somewhere in the hospital precincts.... After going the rounds and finding everything known taken I finally stumbled upon a little room which Frau Baumgarten said she would let for eleven guldens a month, or a little over four dollars. It is not large, but as neat as wax, and I find it very comfortable here.

I take my breakfast at a restaurant near by, and walk about five minutes to the "pension" for my dinner and supper. There we speak German also. The place is kept by a maiden lady of about forty, an old teacher. She is very fond of talking, differing thus, as you see, from most of her sex, and is good enough to correct us when we blunder, as we often do. There are at the table, besides Dr. Cook, two other doctors, one from Missouri and one from Boston, and a young Italian who is a transient. The meals are not elaborate, but still very wholesome, and I have no fault to find. Vienna is an expensive place to live in, however, board being nearly as high as in New York. This is due to the high rents, and those come from taxes, which are frightful. I was told that the owner of the building, which is new and modern, was obliged to pay one-half of his rent for taxes. So much for the maintenance of an Emperor and his court, and an immense standing army.

Vienna, as a city, is beautifully situated, and reminds me more of Paris than any place I have seen.... Beautiful music is to be heard on all sides here. I went the other evening to the "Volks' Garten" and heard Strauss's orchestra. They do play beautifully, too. So, all things considered, I think I shall enjoy my month's stay here very much. Expecting to be alone I have found instead more friends than at any other place.... There is very little prospect of cholera in Austria. You need not worry, for I shall make for Switzerland if the cholera should come.... What about politics? I think I shall vote for Cleveland. Will Curt run again? I do want to see you all, especially that baby. I take lots of pleasure in her picture though I should have liked it better if the hair had not been fuzzed.

With love to all,
Emmett

Vienna, August 3

Dear Ones All:

What can be the matter with your letters? I have had letters from my other correspondents regularly but have had none from you for a month. I do hope the monotony may be broken soon.... I am about through here in Vienna, and expect to leave to-morrow morning for Prague and Dresden, and to reach Bayreuth on Friday, August 8, to hear the last production of Parsifal at the Wagner festival. The advantages here are excellent in their way, but in very many departments by no means as good as the best in New York. Then, too, they are getting into a way of trying to see how many guldens they can make out of you. The German students are very disagreeable, as a rule. I should not care to spend more than three months here, if I had plenty of time at my disposal.... It is a great satisfaction, however, to come over and see just what Vienna is in a medical way. ...

. . . .

There may have been disappointment that European medicine was not as glamorous as he had pictured it. Perhaps he had anticipated too much. But a different side to the picture is revealed by the collection of books which he brought home. They tell a story of visits to libraries and bookshops, which were combed systematically for anything new pertaining to diseases of children: textbooks, monographs, graduation theses and periodicals—some in French like the treatises of Barthez and Rilliet and of Cadet de Gassicourt, but most in German. There could be no doubt that the German-speaking world was leading in the study of diseases of children. Austria had led the way in cultivating that field. The first pediatric journal had been started in Vienna two decades before; but the Germans were not far behind. A second journal, edited in Berlin, made its appearance in 1882. A society—the *Deutsche Gesellschaft fur Kinderheilkunde*—had been holding regular annual meetings for several years. A seven-volume treatise on pediatrics—beyond a doubt the most complete compilation in the world—had recently appeared, edited by Carl Gerhardt; a copy of that, too, was secured. The brief trip to Europe had opened Emmett Holt's eyes to the fact that pediatrics was a mature, recognized branch of medicine in the German-speaking world. American pediatrics was barely beginning, but the day was at hand when it too was to hold up its head.

. . . .

During the last few days I have been letting up a little on hospital work, and seeing something of Vienna. There seem to be no homes here. The people have rooms somewhere and eat at the cafés which are to be found on every hand. Here they lounge, drink beer and coffee and read the paper. The orchestra here has been running for a couple of weeks, and as I could get a good seat for about fifty cents I improved my opportunity. Their orchestra has about seventy-five pieces, and has the reputation of being one of the best in Europe.... This morning I started out with Dr. Cook to find a little Baptist Church, and after a long ride, and then a long walk we found it. It was off a court surrounded by tailor shops, where the men were at work, and occupied a little room only a little larger than the small prayer-meeting room in Webster. About fifty were there, and it was communion Sunday. The minister was a plain but earnest and quite intelligent man, and the whole service was solemn and had real religious feeling in it. It came down to my thirsty soul like a benediction, and I felt for the first time in weeks as though I had really been to church. Of course the whole service was in German, but I could understand nearly every word of the sermon. It did sound very odd to hear a man pray in German.

The men and women sat on opposite sides of the long narrow room, and during the hymn after the communion they joined hands across the aisle. After the service the brethren greeted each other with a kiss on each cheek, which is the custom here among all classes. The sisters did the same, but the brethren did not kiss the sisters, or I might have joined in this service, except that very few were either young or pretty. I had a nice chat with the minister. The chapel is prosperous, and they are to move in a few weeks into better quarters. You don't know how much I enjoyed the whole service. It is eleven o'clock now and I must get up early to-morrow. Good-night. With love to all,

EMMETT

Dresden, August 9. Dresden is lovely. The people here live in houses like good Christians and do not breakfast at one café, dine at another and get their supper at a beer garden, as do the people of Vienna. The Austrians are certainly a very inferior race, as a race.

Simplon, Friday, August 15.... Took a tramp from here back to the Hospice, three and a half hours—a good five-hour walk, generally reckoning. Very tired. Was within half a mile of Italy. At Hospice received by two monks, and conducted to the dining room and a splendid supper served forthwith, after which a pleasant chat with one, who spoke only French. Not forgetting to make my offering in the small box, I departed feeling that whatever might be said against the Catholic Church, certainly much must be said in its favor. I am sure I don't know when I have been better treated or more kindly than at the old Hospice. A rather lonely but a very delightful day.

August 16, Visp. Imagine my delight as I walked from the station toward the nearest hotel to see Squires and John at the window in early morning costume and hear them shouting to come up.

August 17, Gorner Grat.... The view is grand beyond description, Zermatt like a handful of blocks far below. A clear, bracing atmosphere which made me feel young again. Our blood tingles, we breathe quickly as we start to go up to Gorner Grat. We go by easy stages, and reach it in two hours, over 10,000 feet above the sea. From the summit of this, sitting on the

AN INNOCENT ABROAD

rocks, I am now writing. We are entirely surrounded by sharp, ragged peaks. . . . The stillness is solemn, impressive. One would be alone and meditate. Some white fleecy clouds float around the rugged Matterhorn in a most affectionate way. But it is dinner time and we have true Swiss Alpine appetites and must descend.

Later. We came down to Zermatt across the Gorner Glacier and Squires' bag had a narrow escape. The guide was carrying it by the strap which broke and the bag slid about a rod into a fissure which was all but wide enough to let it go to the bottom. It contained all of his tickets. . . . Squires lost part of his tickets on the mountain and left his umbrella at the hotel. We heard a lady had found some and were in hot pursuit all day, finally overtaking her at Visp. She had used the tickets, but paid him the equivalent . . . an exceedingly pleasant person.

Bruxelles, August 31

DEAR ONES ALL:

Since I wrote you from Lucerne last week, I have traveled so fast and seen so much that my head is almost dizzy. Whether I shall be able to give you any idea of where we have wandered remains to be seen. . . .

The ride from Schaffhausen to Strasbourg took us through the famous Black Forest and it seemed as if we were getting into Switzerland again. The railroad is the crookedest I think I ever saw. In making the descent from the mountain we could see several times our own track far below and had to ride miles before reaching the spot. I counted thirty-nine tunnels in one hour. I begin to think these people over here have almost as much enterprise as Yonkers in building railroads.

Strasbourg we found exceedingly interesting. It is a French city in language, habits and sympathy, but there is a garrison of 15,000 of Bismarck's best troops there to remind them that they belong to Germany. I don't wonder Bismarck wanted these Rhine provinces for the whole is like a garden.

Wiesbaden is one of the most popular European watering places. The springs here are hot, so that the water has to be cooled before you can drink it. They have a concert at the springs every evening and the correct thing to do is to bring your own glass to the spring, get it filled and promenade up and down sipping the water as you listen to the music and chat with your friends.

And what shall I say of the Rhine with its graceful windings between the mountains, the beautiful little villages along its course and its grand old castles which in the day of their glory capped nearly every prominent point in the view? ... The boys are in fine spirits. I hope to find some letters from you at London.

Love to all
Emmett

September 7. At sea.... Awoke about two A.M., the steamer pitching and dreadfully sick, as were also all the boys in the room.

September 15. Breakfast at Quarantine, landed by tender at Barge office at 8:30 and bade good-by to steamer friends, and "Took up the burden of life."

From a letter of Sabrah Holt to her son: "Did I tell you what Mrs. Ayer said? 'My, Emmett is getting rich, isn't he, to be able to go abroad so young!'"

VIII

AMERICAN PEDIATRICS

AFTER the return from Europe romance appears to have made rapid progress in the Sunday school class:

New York, March 4, '85

MY DEAR MOTHER:

To-night closes the longest and most anxious week I think I ever passed in my life. You little thought I imagine on reading my Sunday's letter of my state of mind. Or did you read between the lines and see the struggle through which I was passing?

I have been getting more and more certain of the fact that my feeling for Miss Linda Mairs was something stronger than a simple friendship, and at last it grew so oppressive that one week ago to-night—her twentieth birthday—I wrote her telling exactly my own feelings.... To-night it was decided. I am the happiest man in New York. Engaged! Only think of it! I can't realize it. I am afraid I shall wake up and find it all a dream. To think that the only girl I ever really wanted should fall in love with me.... What a wonderful Providence threw us together and under such peculiar circumstances. Only think of it—my thirtieth birthday! Truly your prayers for me have been answered.

My heart is too full to write. Oh, that I could see and tell you all about it.

It is late and I have time to write no more. Remember it is not announced yet and it is under *no circumstances to be mentioned outside our own immediate family.*

Yours with love,
EMMETT

Miss Mairs was from a conservative New York family with traditions that had to be satisfied. The following day Emmett received a formal note from his prospective mother-in-law.

15 East 57 St.
March 5, 1885

DEAR DR. HOLT,

What has occurred between Linda and yourself during the past week has been a great surprise to me. I allowed her to accept your invitations from time to time, as, from a knowledge of your associations and friends in New York, I felt justified in doing. It very recently dawned upon me that your attentions to her were becoming serious, and now you will see the propriety of making me acquainted with any of the particulars regarding yourself that it is proper for me as her mother to know. I think you will appreciate my feelings in the case, remembering that I have a double duty to perform to my fatherless children.

Very truly yours,
M. E. MAIRS

Dr. L. Emmett Holt
23 Park Avenue

The details of the interview are not recorded, but it appears that he was accepted and accepted unreservedly.

Sunday Evening
March 8, 1885

DEAR ONES ALL:

I presume you can guess where I have been spending the evening to-night. Linda wanted me to come to dinner and to tea both, but I thought it would be better not to begin too strong and so only accepted the latter invitation. This was the first time I had faced the whole family since the great event but I did not find it at all hard or embarrassing. All of them seem to be perfectly delighted.... I have only been up there six times in the past five days. Isn't that doing pretty well? The boys—her brothers—have already dubbed the library where we spend most of our time the "office." I wonder how people get along who are where they can't see one another except at long intervals.

Although our engagement is not announced, still the number of those who have been told confidentially is getting to be pretty large and we shall not try to keep it quiet very much longer. Squires and John were both very much surprised and seemed very much delighted. John was completely broken up to think I had got the start of him. Scarcely slept for a whole night and has been a changed man since. You need not be surprised at any time to learn he has been following suit.

We got through Sunday School pretty well to-day. I don't think that the other girls suspect anything, although they always study Linda very closely. I can control myself admirably, and no one would have imagined anything from my conduct I am sure. Last Sunday, however, while the thing was still undecided it was dreadful. Linda will substitute for another teacher for a few Sundays and will then have a class of her own, so she will probably not be in my class after this. It will seem as if two-thirds of the class had left, when she goes. I did not really know myself how much I had studied and worked to teach *her*....

I still find it very hard to realize and feel constantly as though there were danger of waking to find I had been dreaming. Don't think I shall love any of you any the less because of a new object of my affection. Rather the contrary.... When you get tired of hearing me sounding Linda's praises and extolling her virtues you have only to call *"time"* and I will stop.

With love to all,
EMMETT

The "great event" was duly appreciated in Webster. Eliza wrote:

Webster, March 11, 1885

MY DEAREST EMMETT:

The first thing upon my arrival at home was, *have you heard from Emmett? Do you know the latest?* Of course I was as surprised as the occasion demanded. Yet I have known all winter whither this "delicious drifting" was tending and have foreseen that presently the current would sweep everything before it. We are all so glad and so happy in that *you* are so happy.

It does seem funny to hear one who has always been so cool and calculating, who has always intended to make his matrimonial venture in the same way in which he would a business one, rave over his beloved like any of the rest of us. Curt hasn't had anything do him so much good since Carrie fell in love. You just ought to hear him go on. Lizzie and I have threatened to write to Linda to let her know what sort of people she may expect to meet. We have already taken her into our hearts. I shall love her if she is good to my little brother.... I want her picture; will you get it for me?

Has John succumbed to the inevitable fate?

With loving regards to her and ever the same love for you,

Your affectionate,
ELIZA

"I will not feel that she has robbed me of my place in your heart," wrote his mother, "but that God has given her a place a little nearer. I hope she will enjoy it for thirty years to come as much as I have enjoyed the thirty years that are past. This means more than you or she can understand now." Sabrah lived long enough to know that the marriage meant all that she had hoped.

Demoralization spread among the bachelors of the Flat. A few weeks after Emmett's engagement to Miss Mairs, John Calvert announced his engagement to her sister. Poor Squires was left to suffer endlessly from the remark of well-intentioned friends: "Too bad there isn't another Mairs sister for you."

"Squires—poor fellow!" wrote Sabrah. "Can't you hunt up a cousin or some other dear friend who is worthy of him? He is too good a fellow to be left out in the cold and too warm a heart to be chilled by the cold world as it will seem to him when he is separated from John."

In April of 1886, Emmett Holt and Linda Mairs were married. After a wedding trip taken by horse and buggy through the Shenandoah Valley, they set up housekeeping in a brownstone house at 15 East 54th Street, to which his office was moved.

The years to come were active ones for Emmett Holt—years of increasing family responsibilities, of a growing practice soon to be limited to diseases of children, of new clinical and teaching opportunities, of study and of writing. They were memorable years for medicine, too, and for pediatrics. For the renaissance of medicine that had been initiated by the discoveries of Koch and Pasteur in bacteriology and immunology was penetrating the minds of the profession. Each year was bringing fresh discoveries, and they were beginning to come from America as well as Europe. The laboratory studies were to be for many years yet the work of a chosen few, but the idea that came with them—that medical knowledge was no longer a fixed body of dogma, but a growing, living thing—this was appreciated by even the humblest physician. It bore fruit in a volume of clinical investigation such as had not been seen before. And with the growth of clinical observations came the need for new journals and medical societies. The new observations had to be presented and discussed.

The field of pediatrics was no exception. Others besides Emmett Holt were enthusiastically following it as a chosen career. More and more articles pertaining to diseases of children were appearing, scattered through various medical journals; it was only a question of time until they would demand an organ of expression of their own. The idea may have been in the minds of others, but it was a group of five young and ambitious New Yorkers who put it into execution. Just how the project was hatched is not recorded. No doubt there were many difficulties, not the least of which must have been to induce a publisher to embark on such a venture in virgin territory, but a publisher was found, and in January, 1884, the *Archives of Pediatrics* made its formal début. Its Editor-in-Chief was William Perry Watson of Jersey City, and his assistants were Andrew F. Currier, Henry Dwight Chapin, John Van Vorst, Jr., and L. Emmett Holt. Under the able management of Watson and his successor, Crandall, the *Archives* proved a success almost from the start. It published stimulating editorials, its editors abstracted the domestic and foreign literature conscientiously. From the year of its birth up to 1911 when a serious competitor first made its appearance, it carried the best new work in pediatrics that the country produced, and more than one British physician was inspired to publish in its columns.

The new journal had been engineered by a group of New Yorkers, but the young science was by no means confined to that city. There were kindred spirits in Philadelphia, Boston, Chicago, and elsewhere, but as yet they had no common meeting-place for discussion. A few years before, to be sure, in the sessions of the American Medical Association, the papers dealing with children had been segregated in a separate section, but there was as yet no organization of American pediatricians worthy of the name. The movement to form such a group began in 1887 at a meeting of the Ninth International Medical Congress held in Atlantic City, where the idea was discussed informally. It does not appear whether Holt was a party to these discussions or not, but in the following year he was one of a group of physicians who were invited to gather in Washington for the purpose of organizing an American Pediatric Society. There were forty-three of them in all—many of them destined to play parts of distinction in the development of that branch of medical science in America. From New York there were two veterans, Abraham Jacobi and J. Lewis Smith; there were several younger men—O'Dwyer, soon to become famous for his invention of intubation, Koplik,* Northrup, Chapin, and several others besides Holt; there were Rotch and Putnam from Boston. The Philadelphia delegation included Meigs and Pepper, Keating and Starr, authors of rising reputation of whom the first named was to contribute the first reliable analysis of breast milk. From Baltimore there were Booker and Osler, Adams from Washington, Forschheimer from Cincinnati, Blackader from Montreal and several more. The movement crystallized about the person of Abraham Jacobi, who was elected the first president of the newly formed society. Jacobi, then a man in his late fifties, was the outstanding personality of the group. Educated in Germany, he had come to the United States in 1853, but he had many contacts with the mother country and was well aware of the lead it had at that time. A picturesque figure with an unfailing sense of humor, he was above all a great-souled individual with a limitless capacity for human friendships. Jacobi has been called the "father of American pediatrics," and he lived long enough to be called its grandfather. His leadership, however, was not in the realm of scientific accomplishment. He himself made

* Discoverer of the spots in the mouth in measles that were to perpetuate his name.

no outstanding contributions to pediatric knowledge. He was not of the type of men who drive to achieve an ideal. With something of the philosopher in his make-up, his was rather the judicial type of mind, and one finds him in the early days of the society in the rôle of mediator between those with warring ideas.

The Society was organized with due enthusiasm and promulgated a constitution charging its members with the highest ideals in the pursuit of knowledge in their chosen specialty, with compulsory attendance at meetings, barring emergencies, and compulsory scientific communications at least every three years. There was provision for summary expulsion of members for "conduct unbecoming to a physician and a gentleman." The organization was destined to grow and to prosper, and it continued throughout Emmett Holt's lifetime to fulfil its function of bringing together in a very intimate way a group fired by a common interest.

The organization did more than stimulate its members as individuals. During its early years at least it sponsored a number of coöperative studies. The report of its committee to study the cause of scurvy presented evidence that made it impossible to doubt the efficacy of orange juice as a remedy. Another report on the value of diphtheria antitoxin was influential in overcoming the strong opposition to that agent.

There remained still another ambitious project to which the enthusiastic American pediatricians of the late eighties were to give birth—a four volume treatise written by various American authors and edited by Dr. John M. Keating of Philadelphia. Keating's *Cyclopedia of Diseases of Children,* which appeared in

1890, was an impressive production. It was certainly the most comprehensive work in English, but nevertheless it fell short of being epoch-making. It may be that it was launched prematurely; perhaps the contributors were not all selected with the greatest care, but the fact remains that the work was far from uniform in quality. It contains, for example, an extensive article, written in all seriousness, on the effects on children of maternal impressions during pregnancy, which must have seemed an anachronism to many even in that day. But there were many contributors to the *Cyclopedia* who were well selected and who put into it the best they had; one of these was Emmett Holt, who wrote the article on diarrheal diseases in infants. Into that article, really a monograph, went a wealth of experience, pathological and clinical, gained from seven years at the New York Infant Asylum. It presented a unique collection of well-studied cases. The foreign literature was meticulously covered, too. The greater part of the treatment was still devoted to drugs, but attention was also called, for the first time in the English literature, to a new treatment recently attempted by Professor Henoch of Berlin—the injection of salt solution under the skin to replace the loss of salt and water by the bowel in infants who were unable to retain fluid by mouth. The new treatment was epoch-making, but the greater part of a decade passed before it became widely used in America. It did not solve the problem of summer diarrhea in infants, but it saved the lives of countless young sufferers.

The years prior to the turn of the century brought other dramatic changes in pediatrics. Thomas Barlow of England pointed out to the medical world the analogy between certain painful swellings of the limbs from which infants not infrequently suffered and the scurvy which was so common among sailors deprived of a diet of fresh fruit and vegetables. Previously these infants had been regarded as rheumatic and had received local applications only; sometimes the swellings were opened by surgeons who were greatly dismayed to find only blood and no pus. But Barlow's observations left little doubt that these infants were suffering from scurvy. He painted the clinical picture of infantile scurvy much as it is known to-day and initiated the treatment of these patients with orange juice. The American Pediatric Society's collective investigation promptly confirmed the results, and its reports undoubtedly hastened the spread of the new treatment in this country. The mystic word vitamin had not been coined, but a deficiency disease in infants had been recognized for the first time.

Perhaps the greatest of the pediatric achievements of the nineties were the two major steps in the conquest of diphtheria. Diphtheria, in those days, was omnipresent, and no disease was more dreaded by parents. To watch the progress of laryngeal diphtheria to a termination in fatal asphyxia, quite powerless to check its advance, was the everyday lot of the physician. Diphtheria had ,taken Abraham Jacobi's only son. But there was one American physician who had an idea for preventing that fatal asphyxia.

Dr. Joseph O'Dwyer of New York was somewhat of a recluse and not well known to his colleagues in the city. He had conceived the idea that, if a tube could be introduced into the larynx and kept there, the air passage could be kept open and the larynx would not be obstructed by the diphtheritic membrane; the disease could then run its course with little risk to life. Day and night, in every spare moment, O'Dwyer worked upon his tube: he studied the anatomy of the larynx in the minutest detail, modified his designs again and again, tried different types of instruments for introducing and removing tubes, and after years of patient effort, trial and error, success was achieved. He perfected a tube which could be introduced into the larynx with ease, one which would remain there without being coughed up, and which could be readily removed when desired. The O'Dwyer intubation tube worked, and intubation soon became a standard medical procedure. O'Dwyer's achievement brought him the recognition of the profession, but the public acclaim he was not to enjoy, for he died a comparatively few years after his great invention.

The heyday of intubation has now passed, and the occasions for using his procedure are becoming relatively infrequent, but its value at the time can not be overestimated. In his native city the name of the man whose invention gave breath and life to many a child with diphtheria is all but forgotten, but in faraway Budapest a bronze tablet to him was erected on the occasion of the one-thousandth intubation performed in the Stephanie Hospital, and it remained for a Hungarian to write the history of intubation with an account of O'Dwyer's life.*

The second weapon in the fight against diphtheria

---

* Bokay, *Die Lehre von der Intubation* (Vogel, Leipsic, 1908).

was to come from the laboratories of Europe. The diphtheria bacillus had been identified by Klebs and Loeffler in 1883 and 1884. Its detection in the throat became a comparatively simple matter, and accurate diagnosis was now possible. But better was to follow. In 1890 Roux and Yersin discovered that these organisms accomplished most of their deadly work by a poison (diphtheria toxin) which they secreted, and in 1891 Behring in Berlin produced a successful antitoxin. Three years later the improved antitoxin of Roux was bringing about unbelievable results in the cure of that disease. In 1894 the first antitoxin was available in America, and in the following spring we find Emmett Holt reporting on its successful use before the American Pediatric Society. But, surprising as it may seem now, the new remedy was not accepted by the medical profession without a bitter fight. Dr. Joseph E. Winters was at this time professor of pediatrics in the recently founded Cornell Medical College in New York City. He was a forceful person and in consequence had something of a following, but he happened to be neither intelligent nor well read. Quite unable to keep abreast of the newer developments in medicine, he took refuge in opposing them. He denounced diphtheria antitoxin in no uncertain terms, denounced on every possible occasion, by word of mouth and in writing, the idea of introducing horse serum into human beings. Obviously something had to be done with such a stormy petrel. The American Pediatric Society decided to appoint a committee consisting of O'Dwyer, Northrup, Adams, and Holt to collect all the available data on the use of antitoxin and bring in an authoritative report. The brunt of the work fell upon Holt who was chairman. The channels of distribution of antitoxin were carefully followed, and letters were written to every physician who might conceivably have used it. During the winter of '95 and '96 the reports came flowing in, and by May first of the latter year there were 5,600 treated cases to be analyzed. To sort, tabulate and analyze the data was a gigantic task, and it consumed many midnight hours. There was need for haste, too. The official report was not due until the meeting of the Pediatric Society, the last of May, but there was to be a meeting of the New York Academy of Medicine in the middle of May to discuss the question of diphtheria antitoxin—Winters had been instrumental in engineering it—and it was necessary to have all the ammunition on hand. But Winters was not to be downed on that occasion.

"Winters' antitoxin meeting came off last night," Dr. Holt wrote to his wife. "He began at 8:15 and talked until nearly eleven o'clock. Did you ever hear of such an imposition? The meeting then adjourned the discussion of his paper. It was an awful outrage, and everybody, your husband included, was *mad*." But the success of the filibusterer was short-lived. At the next meeting of the Academy the discussion was resumed and the data obtained by the Pediatric Society's committee was presented. It was convincing. Winters continued for some years to teach against diphtheria antitoxin in his class-room until eventually he received a request from the medical school authorities to discontinue teaching that doctrine. But he was irrepressible on any topic and remained the *bête noir* on the New

York pediatric scene for many years to come—consistently on the wrong side of every important question. It was only in 1920 that his successor, Dr. Oscar Schloss, ushered in a new era for Cornell pediatrics.

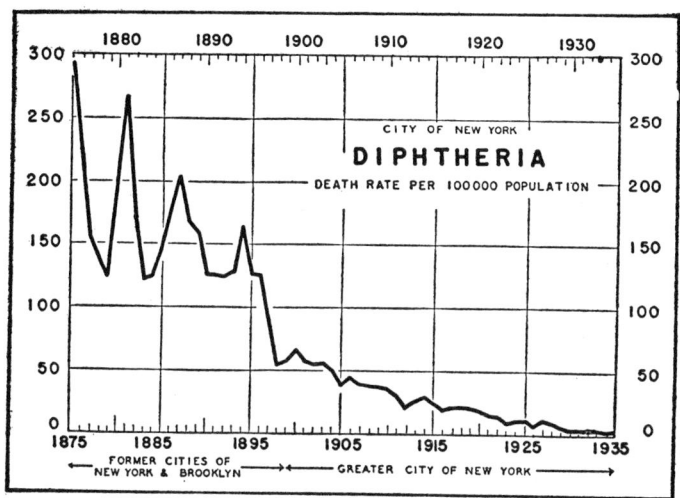

DIPHTHERIA MORTALITY IN NEW YORK CITY, SHOWING STRIKING REDUCTION IN MORTALITY FOLLOWING THE INTRODUCTION OF DIPHTHERIA ANTITOXIN IN 1895
(Courtesy New York City Health Department)

Diphtheria had received two major blows, and the death rate from it fell precipitously. The final wound—the development of protective inoculation against it—was not to come for another twenty years. Emmett Holt lived to see the death rate in New York City from that dreaded scourge fall from 200 per 100,000 in 1880 to 10 per 100,000 in 1923.

IX

CRUCIAL YEARS

PRACTICE was coming slowly at the time of Dr. Holt's marriage, but it was coming none the less surely. If he lacked some of the social graces of his more metropolitan colleagues—this upstate New Yorker with no small talk—he had other qualities that more than compensated. He was small in stature, but correspondingly alert in mind and body. There was a thoroughness about him—his searching questions and equally searching physical examinations—an innate honesty and a directness of approach that were disarming and could not fail to inspire confidence. And he had that even more important ingredient of success in practice—a keen understanding of human nature and an ability to manage people. Perhaps it was a mother filled with antivaccination propaganda, whose child needed to be vaccinated. He would listen sympathetically for a few moments while her colors were being shown. Then:

"So you're interested in this question of small-pox and vaccination, are you?"

"Yes indeed, Doctor."

"Then perhaps you would be interested in looking over these reports showing the incidence of small-pox in vaccinated and unvaccinated persons in the United States Registration Area."

Such data were always kept on tap at the office. The figures did their work without the necessity of argument. Nine times out of ten the vaccination could not be done too soon to suit that mother. The strong arm methods, successful in the hands of some physicians were never resorted to.

On one occasion the office door was thrown open to receive a new patient, an unhappy youngster of three or four who began to protest violently, to scream and hang back. A spanking was promptly administered by the mother which only increased the tumult and the protests. Dr. Holt watched the scene for a moment and then turned to the mother: "I have always noticed that spankings were most effective when they came as a rare treat."

Practice, with its successes and failures—in treating disease, in treating human beings under stress; it brought its rewards and discouragements, not always justly meted out—the lights and shadows that make up the life of the physician. There was the influenza epidemic of 1889, a busy time for all practitioners, which left many a vivid incident stamped on the memory. In later years he could recall one particular night call, after a strenuous day, to see a child just taken sick with influenza. It was 2 A.M. and at a distant uptown address; an only child; excited parents and relatives at the bedside and in their midst a precocious youngster of four, perfectly healthy. "What was it made you think this child had influenza?" "But, Doctor, she *said* she had it!" There were times when it required self-control to be tactful.

But the successes far outnumbered the failures. The waiting-room became more populous and the calls more frequent. The latter were soon made in a brougham drawn by two bay horses with a colored coachman on the box; the convention of the day demanded a frock coat, of course.

The time-consuming trip to Mount Vernon, which had been his pediatric education, now had to be abandoned, but the doors of hospitals in the city were beginning to open, and there was no difficulty in securing appointments nearer home. A small but active service at the New York Nursery and Child's Hospital was obtained. A more important opportunity was provided at the New York Foundling Asylum, a Catholic institution on East 68th Street. Here, as in Mount Vernon, there was overcrowding, inadequate nursing, and in consequence, disease in abundance. The attitude of the Church in those days was not as enlightened as it became a generation later. The doctrine that a body lost was a soul saved acted as an anodyne to the Church authorities, delaying many reforms which the attending physicians would have liked to introduce. But certainly none could have been kinder or more appreciative of the efforts that were made to care for their sick than were the good Sisters at the Foundling. It was a museum of disease in children, and here, too, was the opportunity to follow every fatal case to the autopsy table. It was the education of many a physician then and since.

There might be insuperable obstacles in the way of

administrative reform in the hospitals with which he was connected, but they did not find their counterpart in the quality of the service rendered. There the most exacting standards prevailed. Internes who were not willing to work and work overtime found that Dr. Holt's service was no place for them. Southerners found it difficult to obtain interneships, for he had discovered that few of them had ambitions compatible with hard work. One of his first internes at the Nursery and Child's recalls an incident that made a great impression on him. There was a rule of the service that any child admitted before ten o'clock at night had to be worked up before rounds the next morning, but the pediatric internes were somewhat harassed by having obstetrical responsibilities as well. On this occasion a child had been admitted at nine in the evening, but there had been two deliveries in the obstetrics ward that night, and the examination of the new pediatrics case was not completed when rounds commenced. There was a pause at the vacant chart and an inquiry as to what time the patient had come in. The time and the explanation were given.

"Doctor, you know the rules of the service, don't you?"

Nothing more was said, but for the remainder of his term of service, no night emergency was to interfere with the prompt work-up of a new case. Dr. Holt might be a hard taskmaster, but he was equally exacting of himself. The hospital patients were a responsibility equal to his private patients, and there was many a night emergency visit paid to the hospital.

The years brought new teaching opportunities, too.

The "quiz group" in anatomy had been supplanted by a teaching post at the New York Polyclinic Hospital and Medical School. The Polyclinic had been organized in 1881 and was largely the creation of one man, Dr. John A. Wyeth, a surgeon. He was a Southerner who had fought and practised his profession in the Civil War. A magnetic person with much of the traditional Southern Colonel in his make-up, he had married into one of New York's most distinguished medical families—the daughter of Marion Sims, the "father of American gynecology"—and he was well known and popular among the profession of the city. The Polyclinic was his brain-child—perhaps it was the forerunner of the "Medical Center" of our own day—a unit in which all the specialties were to be taught, not through didactic lectures, but exclusively from patients. This institution, however, was not destined to take a leading place in the city's medical life. The quality of its personnel was far from uniform, and it never succeeded in avoiding that pitfall which besets medical post-graduate teaching in general—the granting of diplomas with a bare minimum of training. But it did attract some men of ability and promise. Gibney, a Southerner and a Civil War veteran himself, was much drawn to Wyeth. He was appointed professor of orthopedic surgery, and during his first years in practice Emmett Holt had worked in Gibney's clinic at the Polyclinic. It was perhaps due to Gibney's backing that in 1891 Holt was made professor of pediatrics there, a post which he held until 1901 when he was appointed Jacobi's successor at Columbia.

Teaching was second nature to him. Whether it was

an elementary school at Wellsville, a group of young ladies interested in physiology while crossing the ocean, medical students, physicians, or mothers, he enjoyed it thoroughly. He had the gift of the born teacher of sensing the gap in the pupil's knowledge, throwing it into relief with a well-framed question and a poignant answer with just enough of the dramatic touch to impress it on the memory. There were many graduate students who felt the impress of his teaching during those years at the Polyclinic. But it was another institution—the Babies' Hospital—that was to be the real field for Holt's activities.

To have a hospital devoted exclusively to the care of infants and young children was an ambition cherished by many a member of that early pediatric group. It was a lifelong dream of Jacobi, never realized, one which was realized by Rotch only late in his career— and by a few of the others, but it was achieved by Holt fairly early in his life. To-day when institutions for children are combining with hospitals in other branches of medicine to form large medical units, this former thirst for separation is difficult to appreciate. But it must be remembered that the movement was really a revolt against the typical institution of that day in which a few cribs for children were placed in a corner of an adult ward, or even if they were sufficient in number to constitute a ward in themselves, were under the care of a physician whose chief concern was with adults. It was felt that only by segregating the child in an institution all his own could he become the center of attraction for doctors and nurses alike, and be studied and cared for as he deserved. This was a tenet of Emmett Holt's faith, and the opportunity to make it a reality came quite unexpectedly.

The Babies' Hospital, probably the first in this country to be devoted exclusively to the care of infants, had been founded in 1887. Two sisters—Drs. Sarah J. and Julia G. McNutt—had sponsored it medically, and it had been operated for a year. But the limited funds that had been contributed to it were soon exhausted. The McNutt sisters were unable to carry it further, and the hospital in 1889 found itself without funds, without an attending physician or a permanent home. The enterprise was in danger of being abandoned when Dr. Holt was called in. He took the hospital as it was, shaped it according to his own vision, and gave it life. From 1889 to 1923 when he left for China, he lavished upon it literally a parental care. It was in every sense of the word *his* creation—its finances, its bricks and stones, its administration, its medical policies, research and teaching. The first step was to secure financial backing, and it was obvious that no charitable institution could survive without the support of wealthy and socially prominent persons. His growing practice was beginning to bring him into contact with some of these. They were approached, and the idea of the new institution was "sold" to them. Carefully selected individuals were persuaded to go on the board of trustees. The contributions obtained were small at first, but the hospital was able to function in a modest way; it gained momentum as time went on. From time to time, particularly in its later years, it received substantial gifts, but its early growth and later sustenance were the work of an efficient money-raising machine which Holt organized—an enthusiastic board of women managers. He was a consummate master of the art of managing women, not only singly, but in groups as well. But before they could work they had to be interested, and interested they were.

The meetings of the women's board were held at regular weekly intervals, and they became essentially clinics for the education of the members. The mysteries of medicine always hold a fascination for the lay person, and what is more interesting for mothers than the mysteries about children? The talents which had held together the physiology class crossing the Atlantic were brought to bear effectively. He never made the mistake of demonstrating to the board a condition that, though perhaps of great medical interest, was incurable. That could cause only pain, pain which could not be translated into useful action. No, the story was likely to be one of an infant tragically emaciated on admission, of impossible home conditions, of a narrow escape from death; but it was invariably punctuated at the close by a beaming youngster about to be discharged. The women's board became popular; it increased in size, was divided up into committees and sub-committees. The board and the committees had to be given some sense of power—that was essential—but the facts were always put before them in such a way that the correct decision was invariably reached. The ladies loved it. It was their hospital and they worked for it.

The results of their labors showed in its material progress which was steady though not spectacular. Its first home was a converted dwelling-house at 657 Lexington Avenue, heavily mortgaged at that. The mortgages fell due at most inconvenient times, but they were paid off, and the hospital never again went into debt. It raised money for its expansion in advance. Within six years the house next door had been added, and in 1901 it achieved maturity in the form of a thoroughly modern seven-story building with out-patient facilities and laboratories, as well as beds. The new building was the apple of its chief's eye, and into it went no end of thought and planning. Hospitals in this country and the plans of those in Europe were studied in all details; calculations were made of the proper air space for each infant and what not, and there were innumerable consultations with the architects. But the final product was the last word in hospital construction and it served the city as a model institution for a quarter of a century.

Even in its new building the Babies' Hospital remained a small unit with only seventy-odd beds. It was the small unit that appealed most to Holt and in which he functioned best; one whose pulse he could feel, and all of whose details he could himself encompass. The group which operated the hospital—the superintendent, nurses, resident physicians, and even employees—formed an intimate family which was permeated with an *esprit de corps* impossible to achieve in any large organization. They were hard-workers, people who were willing to work more than eight hours a day to make things go, and enjoyed doing it. They gave of themselves without stint because the chief did likewise. Many of that group were women: the two superintendents, one after another, the pathologist and

THE AMERICAN PEDIATRIC SOCIETY
Lake George, 1905

THE BABIES' HOSPITAL.
1901

bacteriologist (for all but its first years), the two research chemists, nurses, of course, and the majority of resident physicians for the early years. Dr. Holt seemed to inspire in women a peculiar type of devoted service such as is rarely seen among men. It made for a high degree of efficiency—the service ran like clockwork—but the system was not entirely without its drawbacks. For one thing, it was based on a type of personal devotion that could not be readily transferred to some one else when he left town for his summer vacation. The service would go on out of loyalty, of course, but not quite with the same smoothness. Temperaments had a way of asserting themselves at such times, and more than once he was to return from his summer's vacation to find that two or more members of his erstwhile happy family were no longer on speaking terms with each other, over some minute or fancied grievance. The technic for resolving the difficulty was always the same. The grievances were listened to with a most sympathetic ear—one after another, with perhaps a tactful word of personal appreciation given in reply. Nothing was ever done about them, and nothing more was necessary. Once the pent-up poison was released, the machine functioned perfectly again, as before; the team was off on its winter's work, running smoothly in harness.

But the Babies' Hospital was more than an institution to give sick infants the best medical care. In a way that neither its women managers nor its trustees realized, it was on the firing line of the new knowledge. For at its head was one who was in contact with the new ideas as they appeared in this country, who read the foreign journals with care to learn the latest from German clinics or the significant observations from England and France. And in the wards of the Babies' Hospital the new ideas were promptly tested, to be adopted, discarded or modified as the case might be. Perhaps it was the new Henoch treatment for dehydrated babies with diarrhea, or the new diphtheria antitoxin; or at a later date the "protein milk" of Finkelstein and Meyer in Germany that was to become a conspicuous tool in the feeding of sick infants for a generation. The experiences at the hospital were conscientiously reported at medical meetings and in the literature, and made it a center for diffusion of knowledge. And the hospital made its own contributions too.

Dr. Holt's marriage had brought him into intimate contact with one person who became a particularly stimulating influence upon him along scientific lines— Dr. Christian A. Herter, who had married an intimate friend and relative of Mrs. Holt. Herter was a brilliant man with an extraordinary combination of talents. At the age of sixteen he was called by his father's death to accept important business responsibilities, in which he had shown an unusual aptitude. Within a very few years he had set his family's affairs in order and went on to pursue his studies. He had fallen under the spell of Welch and had followed him to Baltimore to work in pathology and bacteriology. He returned to New York and in 1889 joined the staff of the Babies' Hospital as pathologist. Herter was in many respects the antithesis of Emmett Holt. He was preëminently the scientific investigator. Although not one to overlook practical applications, should they appear, the practical applications of science were never for him the driving force as they were for Holt. The urge was a burning desire to answer philosophical questions, and science was a tool for that.

Not content with medicine, pathology, and bacteriology, he made himself a master of chemistry; studied protozoölogy, psychology. A restless spirit, highly introspective, he could find release in music, in philosophy, or beneath a sail, but there was no solace in religion. Yet the two men had much in common. They understood one another perfectly. They worked together on many an enterprise and remained close friends until Herter's death in 1910.

Herter was associated with the Babies' Hospital for a few years only. He went on to other fields of activity—to occupy a chair of pharmacology and to play a leading rôle in launching American biochemistry; but at that time his absorbing interest was the bacteriology of the digestive tract, and the digestive disorders of infants supplied an important part of his material. He was embarking on classical studies of a disease (intestinal infantilism) with which his name is still indelibly associated. Herter did the autopsies and the bacteriology for the Babies' Hospital, but there were few if any autopsies at which Holt was not present, nor was the latter to escape the contagion which fired his associate. One finds him in the laboratory at this time for more than routine autopsies— making permanent preparations of infants' stomachs from post-mortem material in order to measure the stomach's capacity at various ages and to determine how much a baby should be fed at a single feeding.

He might be lured into the laboratory but not for long. The laboratory was always interesting, but it could not compete with the immediate demands of a sick infant. He was to remain preëminently the clinician, but in his letters at this time one finds evidence of the irreconcilable conflict between science and practice. Another activity was competing with both.

X

TWO BEST SELLERS

BY a curious trick of fate, the early difficulties of the Babies' Hospital led to an undertaking which was to make the name of Holt known from one end of the country to the other. One of the largest items of expense in the hospitalization of infants is that of nursing care; it was an item of grave concern in those early days when the hospital was faced with mortgage payments. Only a few trained nurses were required for supervision and for carrying out medical treatments; the major portion of the work—the feeding, bathing, clothing, and caring for the linen—could be done by maids with less education, but they had to be paid, and the total expense was heavy. The happy suggestion seems to have been made by Mrs. Robert Chapin that the services of the nurse-maids could be obtained with a minimum of expense if they were given some sort of training and a diploma in lieu of pay. The idea was put into effect, and a training school for nurse-maids was started. The students were carefully selected and were given at first a four months' and later a six months' course of training with instruction in infant feeding, care, and nursery hygiene.

There was a real need for domestic servants who knew how to care for children. The graduates of the

Babies' Hospital filled that need, and the demand for their services soon outran the supply. They did not, of course, receive the training of a regular school of nursing but they were trained for that particular job, and well-trained. Teaching the nursery-maids was one more task which fell upon the hospital's attending physician, but for one who loved to teach, the labor was not a heavy one. To assist him he prepared a "Catechism for Nurses" in which were asked and answered the questions about clothing, bathing, feeding, sleep, fresh air, etc., that naturally arise in the mind of one having to care for children. There were twenty-three questions and answers, and they occupied most of four pages in a little pamphlet issued by the hospital. The nurses studied the catechism and when they graduated took it with them. There followed requests for copies from their employers and the supply was soon exhausted. It was apparent there was a popular demand for something of the kind. The catechism was expanded, and in 1894 *The Care and Feeding of Children* made its appearance. It was a modest booklet of sixty-six pages, carrying a graceful dedication to Mrs. Chapin as "the founder of the first training school for nurses of infants in America."

Probably no one would have been more surprised than Dr. Holt or his publishers had they been told that they were launching a volume that was to go through seventy-five printings, and which was to be translated into Spanish, Russian and Chinese. There had been other books, a number of them, but none that hit the nail on the head as did this one. In simple, direct language it asked and answered questions that mothers wished to know. Infant feeding was taken out of the realm of the mystic and brought down to earth. The feeding of that day was a complex business, confusing to many a physician who strove manfully to calculate formulas containing the proper percentages of protein, carbohydrate and fat; it was a system that could never be put in the hands of the public. Holt reduced it to a series of twenty ounce formulas—so much milk, so much sugar and so much water—with simple directions that any one could understand and follow. It was a service to the profession and the public alike.

The Care and Feeding of Children was well received. A reviewer in the New York *World* was moved to say: "If women were not permitted to marry until they could pass a fair examination in this short catechism of sixty pages the death rate would be decreased at least one-third." Its reputation spread slowly at first, but it gathered momentum, and before he realized it, it was in a fair way to become the infant bible of the nation. In time it was expanded to some two hundred pages and underwent twelve revisions during its author's life, but its essential qualities remained unchanged. The book became the mainstay of many a worried mother and exerted no inconsiderable influence on the profession as well, for the practitioners had to keep abreast of the pediatric knowledge which the mothers possessed.

Its success and the popular reputation which it brought might have inflated the ego of another type of person, but no one realized better than the author of *The Care and Feeding of Children* that it was not the product of a great pediatrician. It was an educational achievement, and as such brought him the satisfaction of a task well done in a field with a peculiar human appeal. Popular reputation was a responsibility which could be turned to good or bad account; it was to prove an asset in several of the undertakings of later years. Fame, however, was not without a few drawbacks. The first mothers whom he met who had raised "Holt babies" on the book must have given him a real thrill, but undoubtedly the first few hundred of these experiences were the best.

A more ambitious project than *The Care and Feeding of Children* was occupying the major portion of his spare time during the early nineties. Keating's *Cyclopedia* had been something of a disappointment to him. He was well aware that he knew more about a great many pediatric topics than did many of the contributors to that volume, and he was aware that he could write, too. He had felt his oats. He had a style that perhaps lacked literary finesse and polish, but it was a fresh, direct style that drove its point home. He could crystallize in a single pithy sentence a thought that would require a paragraph for others. The decision to write a textbook of his own seems to have come some time in 1890. It was six years before the work was completed, but it was pushed with zeal and enthusiasm. Into *The Diseases of Infancy and Childhood* went all his own experience and the experience of the institutions in which he worked—statistics from the Infant Asylum, the Foundling, the Polyclinic, the Nursery and Child's, and the Babies' Hospital. The statistics were worked through until a clear picture of the natural history of a disease was obtained—its origins, its symptoms, and its final outcome. And the foreign literature was combed, too—texts, periodicals and monographs. Certainly one of the outstanding contributions the author was able to make was a solid foundation of pathological observations. There were some physicians who believed that it was a mistake to offer pathological descriptions to practitioners of medicine. One of Dr. Holt's pediatric colleagues wrote a textbook of pediatrics which declared in its preface that it would not waste its readers' time with discussions of causes of disease or pathological descriptions, but would confine itself only to information needed by the practitioner—symptoms and treatment. That man made a bad guess, and his text fell flat. The practitioner wanted to understand disease as well as treat it, and besides he didn't like being patronized.

The pains of authorship are reflected in his letters to Mrs. Holt at this time.

I am afraid [he wrote in January, 1892] that I have been getting too selfish in my life, and in my strong desire to write a book and make a name for myself that I am doing so at the cost of something that perhaps I do not realize. I don't want to sacrifice every other interest in life to patients and medicine and my professional work. I am anxious to do my duty both to you and the children. But it does seem so hard to give all things their due place. I have resolved, however, to do better in this respect the rest of the winter than I have done so far. I want to live with the children more, and not simply board in the same house with them, and treat their colds when they have them.

Frequently, in other letters to his wife during those strenuous years, he came back to the subject.

June 27, 1892.... I received Archie's book * to-day with a card and his compliments. It makes a very creditable appearance. I wish mine were out. I really wonder sometimes if it will ever be a reality. I worked Scarlet Fever all the way down, and had Dr. Wollstein for three hours, and then my stenographer, so you see I am really doing business.

May 25, 1894. Dr. Cauldwell was in to-day, and when I told him I should finish my book this summer he said, "Where do you expect to be buried, in Greenwood or up the River?"

May 30, 1894. It is six p.m. and I have just awakened from a two hour nap made necessary by a somewhat late discussion with Rotch last evening on the subject of *books*. He is about where I am—perhaps not so well along—and if anything he is more nervous over his work than I am over mine. "These are *our* babies, Holt," he says, "and we are excusable if we do sit up all night to discuss them." Our books will both have merits of their own, and we both came to the conclusion that if we had gone in on a combine we would have swept the country before us. However, it may be best for both of us individually that we have done as we have. Rotch is a splendid fellow, and would insist that I tell him nothing about the views of my book, except upon points which he had already completed, lest there might be some "unconscious cerebration." He expects to work all summer at his, and I see

* Dr. Christian A. Herter's book *The Bacteriology of the Digestive Tract.*

TWO BEST SELLERS

that I must do nearly the same, but perhaps not quite so hard.

The struggle to produce a textbook might be a painful and discouraging one at times, but it was an educational one as well. It brought something of an encyclopedic knowledge of the subject as a whole, rounding out the gaps in individual experience. The necessity for taking a position in writing upon contentious questions serves to focus thought upon it, and is often productive of new ideas. It was an invaluable experience to him.

The *Diseases of Infancy and Childhood* made its appearance late in 1896. It was dedicated to Emmett Holt's first preceptor in the art of compiling and interpreting medical knowledge, "Dr. Virgil P. Gibney, as a tribute to his personal worth and high professional attainments, and in grateful remembrance of many acts of kindness." His pediatric colleagues were among the first to recognize its merits, and in the spring of 1897 Holt was elected president of the American Pediatric Society. The profession as a whole were not far behind. Rotch's text published the year before had jumped to the front, but Holt's soon surpassed it. Within two years of its publication its sales had surpassed those of any other pediatric text. It maintained a handsome lead against all comers throughout his lifetime, going through eight editions. It brought to its author a position comparable to that achieved by Osler in internal medicine. He was recognized as America's outstanding pediatrician.

XI

L. E. H. TO L. M. H., 1886-1902

Webster, N. Y., July 26, 1886

MY DEAREST WIFE:
The clock has just struck ten but all is still in the house as the grave, as all the others have gone to bed. I am taking care of Eugene to be relieved by Eliza about two or thereabouts.

I have had so much to do and think of that I have scarcely had time to get lonely until now. And I do want to see you *so much*. I hope you are not lonely and are well and as contented as possible. You have scarcely been out of my mind for an hour since I left. Yet somehow the separation does not have any of that bitterness that was so often felt a year ago. Have you found it so? I hope you have.

I have seen none except the family and the Doctor and done nothing except look after the patient and those about him.... Eugene has not been so well to-day. He is a *very sick man*... and unexpected complications often arise to turn the scale against such a patient.

I think my getting back on Wednesday extremely doubtful. They all lean on me and if I should return and he grow worse and die they would never get over it and I could never forgive myself. I wish you could be here, yet I know it is best you are not. My loss may prove Mother's gain and I am sure she will appreciate having her little girl to herself again. You see I can understand what a great privilege it is that she is enjoying....

July 27, '86

The unexpected has happened and the worst has come. I had barely finished writing when Eugene began to sink rapidly. All our attempts were futile; he passed away very peacefully at 6:30 A.M.

As I stood by his bedside this morning and saw Eliza with her heart almost bursting with grief, I realized as never before how inexpressibly dear you are to me and how it would almost break my heart to give you up and go, as she said, all through the remaining years of life alone.

You don't know how thankful I have been that I came. Eugene spoke of it a dozen times a day and it has been this morning a great comfort to them all, so they said....

Only think it was just three weeks ago that you and I went to Skaneateles to make our visit. How little we thought what the next few weeks had in store for us all. What a blessed Providence it is that hides the future from us.

Eliza and Belle will come to Webster to live, which will be a joy to Father and Mother. There are always some extenuating circumstances about every sorrow and grief.

I can hardly wait to come home. I do so long for a good talk with you....

Webster, N. Y., June 28, 1887

It is now past four o'clock and I can scarcely realize that twenty-four hours ago I was leaving the Dispensary and rushing to catch the 4:15 train. When I get here and settled it seems as if I had only been away for a few days, everything seems so much the same year after year. Coming up I had the river side, and enjoyed the ride very much. It was so beautiful and quiet and quite conducive to musing over past, present and future....

I found they scarcely expected me until the noon train, but Father, with his usual foresight, thought he would drive up, anyway, and I was very glad he did so. The weather is beautiful here, and they all seem very well and happy. The only drawback to our perfect happiness is the fact that you are not here. They all say it seems so strange to see me here alone. I hope it will not have to seem so again.

We had a lovely dinner, winding up with strawberry cake which was typical of those we enjoyed so much last year. I have been exercising mowing the lawn since dinner, and then took my nap. I am feeling better already for the change of air, and think my visit will do me good....

15 East 54th St., June 10, 1890

This is little Horace's birthday. Kiss the little darling for me. Your letter is just received. I am glad everything looks so bright and happy to you and hope it will continue so. I shall go up to Irvington again to dinner to-night, and to-morrow to drive with Dr. Gibney and dine at the Claremont (Grant's Tomb).... The Hospital moves to the country this week, so that will soon be beyond my reach and care. I have not been up to Irvington much this week, for although they are all kind still it seems very lonesome and forlorn there without you and the children.... I allowed myself to be persuaded into giving May some gratuitous advice about the baby with about the usual result. It will be some time before you catch me again. It is such a useless procedure to advise people who do not want to be advised and really does no good whatever. Except possibly to make them and yourself disgusted and uncomfortable. People must be allowed to run their own show in this world.... I hope you will get really rested while you are in Webster. Give them all my love, with a great deal for you....

The Manhattan Athletic Club, Oct. 2, 1891

You see I am getting to be quite a club man. I really find it a very comfortable place to get my dinner and write my letter in, by way of dessert. The cuisine is very good, and though I am generally alone I see friends here.

The weather has been charming for the past few days. I have ordered my winter suit of Bawden, and am already quite deep in practice. I think everything promises a very profitable winter, i.e., a busy one. I am meditating still on the question of dropping general practice among adults, and have concluded to go so far as to take no new ones unless they live reasonably near here, to do no more obstetrics, and to raise prices on old patients who live *very far* away. By these means I may be able to keep my practice down to the limit you would wish to see it.

... What you say about visiting home [Webster] oftener I feel is true, and I certainly shall go oftener in the next year than I have done in the past.

Don't get lonesome, kiss the children for me and tell Evelyn her moon flowers have climbed all the way up the rubber plant....

New York, Sunday, Jan. 10, 1892

Will it make you happy to know how much I have missed you to-day, and how really lonely I have been this afternoon? I realize very much more when I am here alone and the house is so still, how much of a place my dear wife and little children fill in my life here. I must confess that when they are here, and I know they are, I don't get nearly as much happiness out of my association with them as I ought, and as I might. It is only when you are all away that I feel how much is gone....

I am writing here with your tablet in my lap, sitting up in the big arm chair by the register in the library, and I have had nearly two hours of quiet for rest and reflection. I never seem able to get so much time when you are all at home....

Did you speak to the cook about staying?

Kiss the children for me. With love to Auntie....

>West Point, May 25, 1893
>[At a meeting of the American Pediatric Society]

I am sure you will be surprised when you read that it is only 7 A.M., and that I am up and dressed on the piazza writing. But the sun shone into my windows so early, in spite of green shades and blinds, that there was no such thing as sleep after 6 A.M., and after vainly trying for half an hour I got up, shaved, bathed and betook myself to the piazza to make sure of time to write to you before the men are up.

What a charming spot this is. You have been here, and know what the view from the piazza unfolds. I would verily believe I was in Europe, or some other distant place, instead of on the banks of the familiar Hudson. Only the rush of the railway trains seems to be homelike. Everything is so fresh, so green and so sunny this morning that if you were here (and awake) we would go for a lovely morning walk. I came up on the 4 P.M. train and met several men on the train, among them the renowned (?) Louis Starr of Phila. He looks like Osler and is quite chatty and pleasant. I was sorry I did not take the boat (not on Starr's account) for those who did had the enjoyment of a sail instead of a dusty ride. We have a large attendance here, the best I have ever seen. But ladies in the party are few. Mrs. Osler and the two daughters of J. Lewis Smith are the only ones I have seen....

The papers so far have been only fair, and the discussions long-drawn out, and as the President has asked us to give him any points about the conduct of the meeting I shall take him one side before the next session and tell him how to shut off the prolix M.D. who bobs up on all occasions and speaks three times on each topic. Blackader is much too kind and well-mannered to make a good presiding officer. It needs a mean man like your husband, who is not afraid of hurting feelings, to make a meeting interesting for the general audience by holding the debates down to the time and the topic in hand.

Every one says it was a most happy suggestion having the meeting here instead of in a city, and as that happy suggestion was mine, of course I smile but look unconscious.... Tell the children that I am going this afternoon to see the school where boys are taught to be soldiers, and I will tell them all about it, when I come next week....

P.S. Dr. Gibney went to the Chicago Fair, stayed one day, but it was so hot and uncomfortable and he was forbidden to smoke in one of the buildings that he and his wife decided when they reached their hotel to come back, which they did next morning. Isn't it amusing? The doctor really doesn't enjoy many things except work. I am afraid his bride must have been a little disappointed. You mustn't let your husband get in such a bad way....

15 East 54th Street, May 20, 1894

It is now 6 P.M. Sunday, and I have just awakened from my nap, and am sitting at my office desk shivering, for it has become all of a sudden very cold. We breakfasted at 9:15 this morning in honor of your absence, and I was down on time. Mr. Faunce was more than himself and preached most eloquently upon "Love believeth all things, hopeth all things, endureth all things." He began by saying that it was God's essential character. "God is love," not "God has love." He spoke of the various beliefs held by man in the past, that God was "power or justice," and gave a hit at Calvinism by the way. He thought this quarter of a century was learning how to do everything else but *love*. We were indebted to our parents and friends, who taught us to know; who furnished us with the materials by which we might gain a livelihood, or even achieve success in life, but we owed most to those— mother, sisters (and wife, he might have added)— who taught us to love. God's love was like man's love, only higher and better....

To go back to the time when you left on Friday. It came off very clear and pleasant in a few hours, so that I thought of you as having a comfortable ride. I found your telegram waiting for me on my return home before dinner, and was relieved to learn that no one had been sick on the way. It always makes me solemn to have you all go away at once, and I was quite unhappy until finally I buried my feelings in my work....

The house seems dreadfully quiet; as if twenty people had left, and no little man comes knocking at my door in the morning, calling "Poppyty!"....

May 22, 1894

Still it pours and pours. But you don't like weather letters so I will desist.

Curt has just dropped in for phenacetin for a headache, due I think to eating too fast. To-night he finished two large helpings of roast veal while I was eating *half* of my first helping. Such an example is doing for me more than all your warnings and imprecations. If you stay away long enough I am sure you will find me quite regulated in this respect.

Your nice long letter came this morning and brought a big ray of sunshine into the dining room when it came. How cunning of little Calvert! I think it is because all the "women folks" are too eager and can't wait to let him do what is natural to him. Lizzie wrote most enthusiastically to Curt about him, saying that he was without exception the sweetest baby she ever saw, not even excepting Alice when she was little....

Good-by dearest and don't get lonesome. The weeks will fly by only too quickly for Mother Holt, I know.

With kisses for the children and a great deal of love for yourself....

Sunday, May 27th, 1894

I received a note from Mrs. Rockefeller yesterday asking if I would go with them to the Hospital for the Ruptured and Crippled to-day. We went at 3 P.M. Dr. Gibney got up a singing service, which pleased the visitors very much. They were intensely interested and asked many questions about the children and the Institution which they inspected from roof to basement. They seemed exceedingly friendly and quite confidential in their remarks about Mr. Faunce and church matters. I didn't venture to ask John D. what his opinion of "Northern Pacific" was. I thought it might make him uncomfortable. Was I not considerate? They regretted very much that you were not with us and sent their love to you. They are really good people....

We had W.H. for a preacher to-day, but he ranted, and though he did say some good things there was too much W.H. in it from the beginning to end. He resembles Dr. X in the way in which he *forces himself* rather than his thought upon your attention. I should not care for him for steady diet. Mr. Faunce is good enough for me. Mother * was at church this morning; I found her in the pew when I arrived. She did not like the opening piece, which I missed; said the soprano "cried out of the depths" until she was thoroughly tired out with her screeching....

Last night I had an informal meeting of some of the Polyclinic men, who came together to discuss plans for the future. A new spirit of enterprise seemed to animate the men, so that I hope something may be done, for we were fast sinking into a condition of lethargy again. I think I shall retire from the office of secretary at the end of this year, as I don't like the little details which make up so much of the work of the position. The meeting broke up at 10:30 and I wrote an article on scurvy after that, but slept late this morning, and have had a fairly quiet day.

I am trying hard to get the book along as rapidly as possible in order that we may have some summer to ourselves this year. But there is much yet to do.

How would you like me to say good-by to the world

---

* Mrs. Mairs.

of books, autopsies and the "pill business" generally, as Kimball calls it, and loaf for a year and get rounded up a bit? I really think I shall have earned it when the present session is over....

May 30, 1894, Washington, D. C.
[Annual meeting of the American
Pediatric Society]

It is 6 P.M. and I have just awakened from a two hour nap made necessary by a somewhat late discussion with Rotch last evening.

... Adams had written me that he was to give a reception to the "baby men" at nine that evening and I was just in time. The sensation of the evening was an attack upon Northrup by Brown in Rotch's presence in which the former was accused of stealing other people's work and finally was called a *liar* outright. Northrup made no retort whatever, merely saying that he did not know at all to what Brown referred and the thing quieted down. Evidently Brown's blood was up with a little champagne to stir it. He is a hotheaded fellow and I think from what I can see and hear that there are two sides to the question. I am inclined to side with Northrup as I am very glad to do. I know you will be glad too to have Northrup vindicated. It has created quite a ripple of feeling in the Society and N. has very quietly said nothing when he had a good chance to say much against Brown.

The Adams family are all here. Mrs. A. said she would not leave after just getting in two new servants, a cook and a waiter. Dorothy is a fat chubby little thing of three now and the baby is too sweet for anything. He is large for his age and a docile sweet-tempered child with no nerves whatever apparently. His development is about like Calvert's except more robust.

How is our little man now? I hope he may get well and strong this summer.

... To-night will be the banquet of the entire medical Congress, including the members of all the societies which are now in session here. The speakers are to be Secretary Carlisle, Sen. Voorhees and others whose names I cannot recall now. Grover could not be obtained. I expect now to return Friday p.m. ... Goodby, dearest, I must dress for dinner....

15 East 54th Street, June 14, 1894

While I am writing this in the office at 8 P.M. John is stretched out on the sofa keeping cool, while Ed is entertaining us with more horse talk, which he picked up in Nashville, than I have heard in my life. Ed is in his most voluble mood, and you know how that is. We are really having a very comfortable time keeping bachelors' hall. We vote on the hour for breakfast, which now we are having at 7:30, and at night decide whether it will be ice cream or strawberries. I am afraid we will get spoiled. All the husbands got letters to-day but me. How is this? What have I done?...

Lakewood, New Jersey, April, 1895

This is but a line to let you know that we got down safely, and are very comfortably settled. We had nearly half an hour to wait at the ferry. Got our seats without trouble in the parlor car, and made a very short and easy trip here. Calvert was as good as gold, took no nap and made friends with some ladies in the car who had seats opposite, went over and sat on their laps and was generally cunning—laughed and frolicked in his most fascinating way. These ladies, I found to-night, were some singers who gave a concert here to-night with Tom Karl. The rooms were all ready and Calvert's crib even made up, and we were settled in a few moments....

How good it is to get away from the noise, the rush and the people! I have been revolving all sorts of plans for the future—when I am able to give up all but office and consultation work. I really *must* do more scientific work, and the time must not all go to calls.

It is now ten o'clock and I am beginning to feel the effects of travel, dinner, and change of air and will say good night to the sweetest wife in the world. God bless her and her dear little baby. With lots of love to you all....

15 East 54th street, May 17, 1896

It is nearly 7:30 and I have just been having a nice talk with the children. They have gone up to get ready for bed, and I will write my letter to you and retire early myself. Not for six months have I had so much leisure as to-day, and I have thoroughly enjoyed the children.

Three calls comprise the work of the day....

The children [Evelyn and Horace] are very anxious to know how Calvert enjoys the pigs, and what Baby Emmett says to the animals; also how he walks in his new shoes. So don't forget to answer in your next letter.

Give them all my love....

St. Nicholas Hotel, Cincinnati, June 2, 1898
[At a meeting of the American
Pediatric Society]

Yesterday was so full a day that it seems now that I have been here a week. I have just come up from breakfast preferring to rise early and take my coffee alone rather than wait for "the crowd," thus securing a few minutes to look over my address and write a line to you.

I sent you a Cincinnati paper yesterday with a notice of our meeting. We held our first session in the p.m.; 23 members are in attendance and about as many more visitors come to the meeting. Last evening the two local members here gave us a dinner at Chester Park, a suburb five miles away, where there is a sort of a high class summer entertainment place—a theater, roller-coaster, band of music, and an immense piazza where our dinner was given almost in the open air.

After our dinner we had the honor of meeting the medical profession of the city, about fifty or sixty of whom came out. They were a nice body of men, jolly, sociable and not too Western in their manners. My book and my official position * gained for me the distinction of being one of the distinguished guests and for an hour I felt quite famous. Especially when so many expressed the sentiment that they had never expected such an honor as shaking hands with me although so familiar with my writings. It seemed to me to be a huge joke—to witness the esteem in which I was held so far away. Really one must go away from home to be appreciated. Very many could not get over the fact that I was not six feet tall with a long beard and white hair, as their fancy had pictured me.... But the funny side is the one which appeals to me most strongly, I think. Some of the things said were simply killing.

This afternoon we are to be taken to the Rookwood (?) Pottery (if that is the way it is spelled). I wish you were going to be here to go. Next time you must certainly come for if they think me young what will they think of you?

* Dr. Holt was President of the Society that year.

Will Holt came in to see me yesterday and brought his oldest boy Walter. Will looks well and seems to have grown a good deal. His boy is a pale, skinny, nervous little chap of seven and not any too well behaved. Any of our brood would compare very favorably with him.

Good-by, dearest. I must go to work on my paper. With lots of love....

14 West 55th Street, May 29, 1902

I don't know when I have felt so badly to have you go off alone as to-day. I fear I have not been taking my share of the family burdens of late and that you, Dearest, have had too much to carry. In the future I am going to try and help you more, especially in the care and discipline of our little boys.

I felt awfully sorry to whip Emmett to-day but it was that or miss the train.* Had I had an hour's time, I am sure I could have managed it, but he was in his most obstinate mood and no ordinary measures would work. I am afraid that you may not find him easy to manage in W. but I am sure Horace will be better. If he is not send him straight back to the city and he can stay with me.

* It seems to have been on this occasion that the small culprit, far from cherishing resentment declared: "I don't love anybody in the world but Father."

XII

MEDICAL RESEARCH INCORPORATED

THE year 1901 found Emmett Holt in his forty-sixth year; he was a successful man by worldly standards. Practice had come now, all of it with children—all that he wanted—and it required an office assistant to help handle it. A succession of young men served in that capacity—La Fetra, Howland, Wilcox, Bartlett, Mason—men who later made names for themselves. American pediatrics had been existing only a little more than a decade, but it had passed the infantile stage. It was a recognized specialty now for young physicians to enter, and it was recognized by the medical schools, too. One by one the desultory lectures on diseases of children, given by a practitioner primarily interested in adults, were being abandoned, and full professorships of pediatrics were taking their place. In 1901, on Jacobi's retirement from the P. and S., now a part of Columbia University, Holt was appointed to succeed him, and in the following year, he was made a full professor.

He was back with the medical students again. Lectures at the old Vanderbilt Clinic in West 59th Street and clinics at the Babies' Hospital—they were vivid memories for twenty-one classes of students. Even a didactic lecture can be made interesting, if one has the gift, and an informal clinic with a small group can be more than that. He was a master of the art of teaching by withholding information—perhaps a history, perhaps laboratory data—that would give away the diagnosis. The students had to use their powers of observation to the utmost and to reason with a minimum of data. Then bit by bit the cat would be let out of the bag with new reasoning at each step until the final dénouement. The clinics were dramatic, and the lessons were not to be forgotten. There were tricks, too. Woe to the student who was misled into diagnosing an eruption as some contagious disease because he had been garbed in a gown and mask before examining the patient. He was likely to use his eyes more carefully in the future. But it was all good-natured. The clinics were fun for student and professor alike.

The year 1901 saw the beginning of another venture, a memorable one, of quite a different type. The turn of the century found America still far behind Europe in the field of medical research. Welch had made a beginning in Baltimore; the small group which he had organized was expanding, and some of his first pupils had gone to other cities, but the opportunities were small. There were pathologists and bacteriologists connected with the hospitals or health department laboratories, but they labored under a heavy and increasing burden of routine work. The staffs were small and the funds scanty; there was little time for original study. Europe had its Pasteur Institute, its Lister Institute, and its Kaiser Wilhelm Institute, but there was nothing analogous in America. The opportunity to establish such a project came quite unexpectedly.

Through the Fifth Avenue Baptist Church, which both families attended, Dr. Holt had become acquainted with the Rockefeller family. In November, 1900, on a railroad trip from Cleveland to New York he happened to encounter Mr. John D. Rockefeller, Jr., and they conversed at some length on the subject of medicine. Diphtheria antitoxin was then fresh in memory, and Dr. Holt went over in some detail the steps which led up to it, making the point that it was not a chance discovery but the result of patient and laborious work in which fundamental biological principles had been applied. The suggestion was made that what was needed to solve other pressing medical problems was men and resources devoted solely to medical research. It appears that the elder Rockefeller had had in mind the idea of giving money for medical research,* but it is certain that up to this time it had not taken definite shape or expressed itself in action. It was to do so now. There were further interviews and finally a dinner at Dr. Holt's home at which Mr. Rockefeller, Jr. and Dr. Herter were present and the project was developed in detail. At the close of the evening, Herter and Holt were asked to suggest the personnel of a group of physicians to direct such an institution. They named Welch, T. Mitchell Prudden, Theobald Smith, and Hermann Biggs. Mr. Rockefeller requested that they themselves consent to go on such a board. A few days later Dr. Holt received a letter

---

* Quite possibly he had discussed it with Mr. Frederick T. Gates, his personal adviser. The idea has been generally credited to Gates.

from Mr. Rockefeller containing the offer of $200,000 from his father for an institute of medical research.

The board met together for the first time in May, 1901, at which time Dr. Simon Flexner was added to the group. It was a distinguished company, that first board of scientific directors. Welch, then in his early fifties, jovial, obese, the beloved "Popsy" of the Baltimore medical students, was incorrigibly social; he might appear to be easy-going—a dilettante to the casual observer—but there was none who had more wisdom, or better judgment; he could look at problems with a complete lack of emotional bias. He had made his own scientific contributions—of the first rank, too —but more than that he had launched scientific medicine in America and was still to do more than any other individual to organize American medical investigation. Herter, quiet, reticent except among intimate friends, was quite the antithesis, a keen rapier-like intellect, but highly temperamental. Theobald Smith was every inch the investigator—a man who looked at problems from new angles; he was the first to discover that insects could be intermediate hosts in the transmission of disease. Of him it was said that American bacteriologists could be divided into two classes: (a) Theobald Smith and (b) all others. Prudden, the professor of Pathology at Columbia, who, like Welch, had drunk from the pioneer European springs, is a more shadowy personality. Biggs, silent and shrewd, trained as a bacteriologist, brought to the group the wisdom of a pioneer public health officer; and last there was Flexner, who was to become the managing director of the Institute—an aquiline intellect, with indomitable energy concealed beneath a suave exterior, but human withal; perhaps he was Welch's most brilliant pupil. Holt was the only clinician of the group; to it he contributed the point of view and the problems of the practising physician, and from it in return he gained something precious—an intimate contact with leaders of American scientific thought, a contact with ideas in the making as well as made. It was an intimate, congenial group, and, with one exception, its personnel remained unchanged throughout his lifetime.

There were practical problems to be faced from the start. Before the Institute could function it had to be incorporated under the laws of the State of New York, and to obtain a charter was not a simple matter. The public had become aware of the existence of animal experimentation, and there had arisen in New York a group of sentimental women who raised the hue and cry of "vivisection." Headed by Mrs. Diana Belais they swooped down upon Albany periodically demanding antivivisection legislation. Among their number was Mrs. John A. Mitchell, wife of the editor of *Life,* and that periodical began a series of cartoons depicting noble animals being tortured by physicians with ghoulish glee on their faces. The campaign lasted for about a decade, until a bored and enlightened public gently wafted it into oblivion. But the atmosphere was charged at the time the Institute had to be launched. Legislators were in doubt as to how deep-rooted the agitation was, and it was a question how they would react in chartering an organization that was to use the tool of animal experimentation. Certainly the application for a charter would have to be very tactfully worded. The exigencies of the occasion produced a happy thought. An institution to carry on experimental studies on "plants and animals" sounded much better than one which desired to indulge in animal experimentation alone. That no one had ever questioned the right of any one to experiment on living plants didn't matter. The document was rewritten with the plants in the foreground and the animals tucked away skilfully behind them. It stirred up no objections in Albany; the charter was granted, and the Rockefeller Institute became a reality.

The Institute began in a modest way. For the first few years it had no home and no permanent personnel. The funds that were dispersed were given as grants to a few individuals and institutions, but by 1906 it had a building at 66th Street and the East River, and was slowly accumulating a staff of workers. The original gift had been but an earnest of what was to come. As the possibilities for sound expansion became clearly outlined, the funds were forthcoming. The Institute grew; it added a hospital of its own, added clinical investigation to its functions. It outgrew its laboratories again and again, and finally added a branch at Princeton for the study of the diseases of animals. It encompassed the field of sciences that could contribute to medicine: chemistry, physics, general biology, and the pre-clinical medical sciences—anatomy, physiology, bacteriology, pathology, and pharmacology. Perhaps one could do anything with money; so it may have seemed to a bystander and so has thought many a philanthropist. But to a degree that few have realized, the success of the Institute was achieved by rigid adherence to a policy, a policy whose wisdom has not been appreciated by more than one foundation or individual of a later day—a policy of investing in men rather than in preconceived ideas. To pick men was the real work of the board of scientific directors—men of outstanding ability as investigators. Every institution of learning wanted men of that description, but universities were at a disadvantage in one respect—chairs had to be filled when they became vacant, and students had to be taught. The Institute was under no such pressure; it could afford to wait, to develop a particular line of work only after the ideal individual had been secured. And its bait was attractive—freedom from academic responsibilities and from routine work, and unlimited facilities for research. One by one leading men were secured: Samuel Meltzer, P. A. Levene, Alexis Carrel and Jacques Loeb came with the first decade; and there was Flexner himself. Others were to follow. There was little difficulty in finding younger men to work with these. The board of scientific directors, even if it possessed wisdom, was capable of human fallibility. There were mistakes, but not many; the batting average was extraordinarily high.

One more feature of the directors' policy is worthy of note. The research staff was left to pick its own problems—not perhaps the younger men, who needed guidance from their immediate superiors, but the mature minds. Not even the board of scientific directors in all its wisdom attempted to dictate to these men upon what they should work. It was a lesson that might well have been taken to heart by a later generation of philanthropists. Another quarter of a century was to see much of a different type of endowed medical research—the research project, coined in the mind of a highly paid non-medical director of a foundation, a project laden with gold offered to research workers in various institutions. The flow of gold can produce an appearance of activity in the hives, it can bring in a return of publications in scientific journals that will seem to justify to his trustees the existence of the originator of the bright idea. But it is not the method that will produce the significant research. The individual without scientific training can see a problem: any one who takes the trouble to pursue hospital statistics or public health reports can become impressed with the magnitude of a particular disease problem and can form the idea that it ought to be studied; but only the scientist himself can see that one problem offers the possibility of an intelligent solution and that another does not. The scientist must be left free to follow his leads, rather than be made the tool for the plausible thoughts of a layman. A first-class intellect, of course, can not be so bought, but there is tremendous waste in a system that puts the second-class intellects at the command of the money bags, working on the problems framed by the layman rather than by the first class scientist. The Rockefeller Institute's policy was the endowment of the first class intellect, and it brought an ample return on the investment.

The Institute did far more than furnish facilities for research to those who could use them advantageously. It set an example to the universities, showing what could be done in the field of experimental medicine. The movement made slow progress at first, but the example of Johns Hopkins was in time followed; schools of medicine raised funds, built laboratories, and provided salaries for research workers. In time no medical school could be regarded as first class unless it harbored laboratory and clinical investigators all along the line. It was a logical step. The ability to teach medical students and to advance medical knowledge might not always be combined in the same individual, but the teacher needed the intimate contact with those who were advancing knowledge in the field, contact under the same roof.

The Rockefeller Institute brought to Dr. Holt many stimulating contacts, but that was not all. It gave him the means of fulfilling one more life ambition—laboratory facilities for research in pediatrics. The laboratory had never been able to absorb him completely; it had never been able to wean him from the bedside, and it was not to do so now. But he had ideas, and he was now able to express them by directing others. One of the first grants the Institute made in the days before it had a building of its own, was to aid bacteriological and pathological studies at the Babies' Hospital. There were studies on the bacteriology of milk; on the bacteriology of meningitis and of infant diarrhea. Flexner had a hand in those undertakings; he had discovered the dysentery bacillus in adults, a few years before, but it remained to be determined how much of a part it played in the diarrhea of infants. The laboratories of the Babies' Hospital continued to turn out sound work in bacteriology and pathology, and when in 1911 its director turned to chemistry, the Institute supplied two chemists and a chemical laboratory that were to carry on for another decade studies in metabolism and nutrition that became lasting milestones.

One wonders what might have happened if Dr. Holt and Mr. Rockefeller had come back from Cleveland on different trains in 1900.

XIII

INTERLUDES

IT was nineteen years since he had been to Europe, and he was on his way there again in the summer of 1903, this time with Mrs. Holt and his son Horace. The trip takes form in letters, most of them written to his sister, Eliza. Eliza was now the sole occupant of the Webster home. Horace and Sabrah had passed away peacefully in their eightieth year, within a few weeks of each other. Tragedy had followed Eliza's steps; she was alone in the world, and her brother wrote to her at this time more fully than was his wont.

May 17, 1903, S. S. Zeeland
Dear Eliza:
It was hard to come away and leave all the dear ones behind. Calvert felt so badly he did not want to come to the steamer, but Emmett and the others all came, as well as the Calverts, Dr. Howland and others. We sailed at 10 o'clock sharp, a glorious morning.

Our passengers are very nice, not at all a fashionable lot, but sensible people like ourselves.... It seems still strange to have no responsibility for anything, and to be where one really can do nothing but loaf. My last week in New York was an awful one. A busy Monday morning; train for Washington, D. C., at 3 P.M.; read a paper there, and attended meetings on Tuesday and

Wednesday; Rockefeller Institute Director's meeting Tuesday evening, adjourning 1:15 A.M.; night train home Wednesday night; written examination at college on Thursday for 350 men, besides numerous appointments with patients. Thursday evening looking over examination papers till 2 A.M., and Friday doing all the *last things* that could not be done before. You may from this brief sketch imagine something of the great change to this delightful rest....

Must close now, the mail goes ashore soon. With much love from Linda and myself. Affectionately,

EMMETT

Berlin, May 31, 1903

Here we are settled after the long railroad ride from Amsterdam. It seems good to get to a place where we can speak the language....

... One of the most prominent Berlin physicians in diseases of children is Dr. Baginsky. Though I knew his writings well I had never had any correspondence with him, but intended calling on him while in the city. It chanced that on Monday he came to the hotel to see a patient and I sent my card to him. He received me like an old friend, and insisted upon all of us going with him in the afternoon to Saatwinkel, a forest of about half an hour's drive from the city.... He spoke English fluently, so we had no difficulty in conversing easily upon all topics. He knew my work and my professional standing in America quite as well as if he had lived in Chicago or Cincinnati, and was most cordial in every way.

The forest we visited was beautiful; all pines, very large, with a little lake close by. Mrs. Baginsky produced a large package of German cakes of various flavors, and coffee was ordered for all. So we had a nice little lunch, a ride on the lake, and what was more to us than either, an opportunity to see a characteristic German crowd on a holiday. There were fully 10,000 people on the two sides of the lake, and indefinite beer consumed. I saw *only one man* very slightly intoxicated. There was not a single policeman on the grounds; a more orderly, happy, contented crowd I never saw. Such a gathering near New York would have been impossible, with such order. On the grass we saw many children playing, and several times groups of men and women, not young either, playing blind man's buff. The German name is "Die blinde Kuh"—the blind cow.

We returned to Berlin in time to go to dinner at the Baginsky home. Only one other guest, a visiting cousin, was at the table, besides our family, Dr. B. and wife, and his boy, Horace's age. The boy knew only German and French, and after trying both on Horace with no success whatever, both boys decided to devote their entire attention to the business of the hour—eating, which they did most successfully but in silence.

We were quite taken by surprise when the boy was presented to us, to have him seize and kiss our hands in a most impassioned way. On rising from the table, all the guests are expected to go and shake hands with the hostess, as a sort of "thank you" for the hospitality shown. As we did not shake their hands, they proceeded to shake ours most heartily. After dinner we had coffee "in the garden." ... The people were most hospitable and it was with difficulty we could prevent them from entertaining us all the time.

(Dresden)

If anything we have enjoyed ourselves more than in Berlin. I called upon Dr. Schlossmann, with whom

I have had some correspondence upon medical topics, and he has done his best to make our stay delightful. Dr. S. is quite wealthy, and his wife belongs to one of the best families in Dresden. They have a handsome home surrounded by a large garden, and entertain in a very nice way.... They gave, for us, partly, and partly for another visiting doctor, a dinner party yesterday at 1:30, the usual dinner hour in Dresden. There were present Dr. and Mrs. S. (the latter speaking English fluently, her husband fairly), and Dr. Binet and his wife from Paris. He spoke English well, German fairly, but his wife only French. The party was completed by a Russian doctor and her husband, also a doctor. She, of course, spoke everything, as all Russians do, her husband only German, and Dr. Schlossmann's sisters from Hamburg, who spoke English fluently and French a little.

You can imagine the agony it must have cost the hostess of such a polyglot company to place her guests where they could understand each other, let alone entertain each other.... If our dinner with the Baginsky's is to be regarded as an experience this was even more. It was almost worth a trip across the water of itself.

After dinner we had coffee in the garden; saw the family of children in their playground. The Frenchman took some photos, and distinguished himself by doing some gymnastic feats upon the children's trapeze in a most childlike French way.

To-morrow we start on our way again and expect to spend a week going through a corner of Switzerland, after which we go direct to Paris.

Linda is waiting for this pen (the only one) and says I must stop writing, so I will bring this long epistle to a close....

Paris, le 29 Juin, 1903

DEAR ELIZA:

We have settled here at the Hotel Chatham, where I stayed when here nineteen years ago.... I have done something in a medical way during the past three days, while Linda and Horace have been shopping at the Bon Marché and seeing other sights. There is an American doctor, Dr. Magnin, practising here, who was with me in Bellevue in 1881. He has a fine practice here, and is able to give me cards of introduction to the specialists in children's diseases whom I wished to meet. Yesterday we went through the Salpetrière, a hospital for nervous diseases, the largest in the world; patients and attendants together number 6,000. We were shown the whole institution under most favorable conditions by the physician in charge. "We" includes, besides myself, Drs. Osler and Jacobs from Baltimore, my Paris-Bellevue doctor, and a few others.

Then Dr. Magnin gave us a most delightful luncheon at one of the most fashionable restaurants on the Champs Élysées. Ten were present, half of them being Frenchmen of the finest type. They were entertaining, courteous, refined, and spoke the language beautifully. Most of them knew a little English, and we all some French, while our host conversed freely in both languages, interpreting each party to the other when the point of discussion was not quite clearly understood. I have seen some nice hospitals here, and there is much to learn. Though many of these institutions are old and almost moldy, they contain the greatest aggregation of patients in the different departments that I have ever seen.*

---

*One incident which Dr. Holt forgot to mention was that after walking the wards of the Paris hospitals, as the custom was, at dawn, he fell asleep at the unventilated Comédie Française in the evening.

Welles, our college classmate at Rochester, is here, and we lunched with him at his home on Thursday and again to-day, after the service at the American church, which we all attended. Welles has planned for us a most delightful trip to see his country place near Tours, and make some automobile excursions in that neighborhood.

Paris is a wonderful city. Spending so much time here we will have to shorten up in England....

London, July 8

... We remained in Paris, seeing the sights and visiting the hospitals until July 2, Thursday. That day we began our automobile trip, of which I will try to give you some idea in this letter. M. Aboilard, an associate of Welles in business in Paris, with whom we dined at Welles' house on Sunday, placed at our disposal his auto, chauffeur, and entire outfit to make the trip to Welles' country place in Bourré, quite near the Loire and not far from Tours.... The machine was a "Mors," a 15-horsepower capable of doing 60 miles an hour, and quite new, having only been used a few weeks in Paris. The chauffeur was a steady Frenchman about 30 years old, with whom Welles and Aboilard had previously made long trips, and whom they knew to be perfectly reliable and well up in his business....

Our route lay through St. Cloud, Versailles, and then through the most beautiful farming country I ever saw in my life. This is the very garden of France.... Every inch of land seems to be cultivated and such neat and economical farming I never saw before. It was a constant delight to the eye to see such thrift and such order everywhere. At first the speed of the auto made us quite nervous, and fifteen to twenty miles an hour made us hold our breath when there were curves in the road, or hills, or many vehicles to meet or pass. Down hill we seemed to be going to utter destruction when just at the right moment the machine was held up in a style that was simply beautiful to see. Before we were through with our trip we bowled along at the breakneck speed of forty miles an hour, and got so we really did not mind it. That is the speed of an express train, and seems incredible to one knowing only American country roads, and American modes of travel on country roads. But here it is a different thing altogether. I never saw such roads as in this part of France. They were everywhere as smooth and hard as in the finest park at home. . . .

Welles' place is beautiful, situated about half way up a steep bluff, which is about three hundred feet above the valley, which it faces. . . . The houses (one quite new having been built about 60 yrs., the other "moderately old" having stood for at least 300) have the cliff at their backs, and this is made up of a very soft, white stone, which is not much harder than clay, and can be dug out with a pickaxe. These cliffs have been quarries for ages, or ever since Roman times, Welles said. All the buildings in this part of the world seem to be made of this stone. The quarries extend far underground, in places for miles, and are several stories in height. In the smaller caves wine is stored, and they take the place of a cellar generally. They also form Welles' stable, his store rooms, shop, reservoir, etc., etc. Whenever he wants more room for any purpose he simply adapts an old cave for the thing needed. . . . In many places the people live in them the year round, since they are "cool in summer, warm in winter and pleasant in spring and fall."

The day after our arrival Welles had us up early, and we started for a little spin about the country of the Loire valley. We returned about seven in the evening, having covered about one hundred and eighty miles and visited no end of interesting chateaux, ruins and old French towns.... It is simply amazing how the automobile annihilates distance. We would look on our map and see something interesting to visit about ten or twelve miles away, and we would decide to take this in; then we would whirl away for twenty minutes and there we were.... Even on Sunday Welles would allow us only a half-day of rest, and in the afternoon we took a short ride of about fifty miles to see some of the attractions near at hand.... In all we covered about five hundred and fifty miles without incident or accident....

. . . .

The trip brought other medical contacts aside from those at Berlin, Dresden and Paris. There was a return visit to Vienna where he met Escherich, its leading pediatrician, the discoverer of the colon bacillus, and his able assistant, Pirquet, who was about to begin classical studies of allergy that were to bring him fame. There was Emil Feer of Heidelberg, later a pioneer in Swiss pediatrics, Keller of Strasbourg who was blazing a trail in chemical studies of infants' intake and output, and other pediatricians of the German speaking countries. There was a meeting of the *Deutsche Gesellschaft für Kinderheilkunde* at which Holt was elected an honorary member. Perhaps the pleasantest of the gatherings was one in England:

The Peacock Inn, Rowsley, England, July 1903
We left Warwick Friday morning, Linda and Horace taking the train for this place, while I took

another back to London to meet my doctors for dinner. On the whole this was the most delightful social experience of my trip. We dined with Sir Thomas Barlow, and there were present, from London, Eustace Smith, Donkin, Lees, Coutts, Still and Goodhart, Ashby from Manchester and Thomson from Edinburgh—all men who were to a greater or less degree specialists in diseases of children, and nearly all of them authors of books upon the subject. The company comprise the most distinguished men in Great Britain in this department of medicine.

Sir Thomas gave me the post of honor at dinner, and all the men were kind and most friendly. They were very jolly and full of stories, and altogether we passed a most enjoyable evening. After dinner the first meeting of the C. C. C. [Children's Clinical Club] was called to order. This society is limited to fifteen members and meets three times a year. The meetings are very informal, and only one member not at the dinner attended. After interesting discussions introduced by the "provincial members," as they call those who do not reside in London, the chairman called upon me for a scientific contribution. I took about fifteen minutes in describing to them some of the work of the Rockefeller Institute in relation to milk and infant feeding in the New York tenements. They seemed very much interested and asked many questions about the work. They adjourned at eleven o'clock after what was to me the most delightful evening I had passed in Europe. These Englishmen are much like our own people, having only a slightly foreign flavor about them, which greatly adds to one's interest in them. For America and Americans they all seem to have a great regard, and were quite familiar with the good work and good workers of our side of the water.

INTERLUDES 155

This will be my last effusion. We expect to reach New York Saturday evening, August 1....

. . . .

Tradition was strong in the British Isles. There had always been individuals who had been interested in and had made outstanding contributions to knowledge of children's diseases at the bedside and in the autopsy room, but the consciousness of pediatrics as a branch of medicine in itself was only beginning to develop. The C. C. C. whose birth Holt had witnessed was a forerunner, one of two pioneer groups that were later to develop into the British Pediatric Society and the Section on Children's Diseases of the Royal Society of Medicine. The babies of London were still under the care of obstetricians and practitioners of internal medicine. A few of these were deeply interested in children, but a practice limited to diseases of children was unheard of in Great Britain. George Still, influenced in some measure by Holt's example, was the pioneer in taking that step. The Hospital for Sick Children at Great Ormond Street was in existence with traditions of its own, but it was nearly a quarter of a century before the children's wards in the great London hospitals were organized into pediatric services in which the babies would be looked after by specially trained men rather than by an attending physician interested in adults who rarely entered the children's ward unless it was to watch a Christmas party or to see some very unusual case.

The dinner in London was the beginning of several warm friendships. Still visited Holt later in America, and they corresponded with each other more than once. But it was John Thomson of Edinburgh who went straight to Emmett Holt's heart. A simple devout Scotchman with shrewdness and wisdom combined with a great soul, he could not be better described than by his epitaph: *"De rebus medicis, nemo sapientior; de rebus humanis, nemo humanior"*—"About medical affairs none more wise; about human affairs, none more human." Holt visited Thomson in Edinburgh some five years later. A photograph of Thomson hung on the wall of his New York office along with those of four other physicians: Walter James, Edward Trudeau, Simon Flexner, and Thomas Morgan Rotch.

The European contacts were renewed when he returned in the summer of 1908. They were always stimulating, and not infrequently they added a refreshing touch to his correspondence in the interim:

Budapest, the 25th March, 1908
DEAR COLLEAGUE:
In the property as the manager president of the Pediatric section of the XVIth International Congress of Medecine, which shall be held in September 1909 at Budapest, I apply to you dear Colleague, as to a famous celebrity of our specialty, already to-day, previously in confidential form, with a colleaguel request. Would you have the kindness—in the interest of a successful activity of the section—to advertise me friendly: the discussion of which special questions would you hold for particularly desirable in the transactions of the pediatric section? Please to inform me also kindly, if you would eventually undertake the care to report the theme, which you propose.

I mentioned already that this inquiry is previously

of intim character, and I would request you to direct your valuable answer, possibly till the end of May, to my above printed address.

Accept formerly for Your obliging complaisance my best thanks. I remain, dear Colleague, with the sincerest respects.

Yours,

PROF. DR. J. BOKAY

Europe might lure the Holts for an occasional summer, but there was an attraction for them on this side of the Atlantic that was hard to compete with, a camp on the shores of Upper Saranac Lake in the Adirondack Mountains that served as a summer home for twenty-six years. It was a beautiful spot—a point with a commanding view of the lake in its many moods, surrounded by wilderness and mountains. The drone of the outboard motor had not yet marred its stillness. After 1896 long summer vacations were spent there. It was more than a release from the confines and ugliness of the city; it was the real home of the family —an ideal place to bring up children. To one who loved law and order not even a vacation could be a casual affair. The days were planned for work and play; they were none the less joyful ones. One can picture them: hymn singing on the porch after breakfast; careful observations on the weather—the wind, the barometer, the extremes of temperature—all to be tabulated at the end of the summer; then the whistle of the morning steamer bringing the mail. Most of the mornings were given up to work. There were the books to be revised, journals to be read, manuscripts to be read and criticized, and no little incidental correspondence. But there was always an hour left to play tennis or swim with the children. There was work as well as play for the children, too, at least two hours of it. He was not one who believed that young minds should rusticate for three months without intellectual effort of some kind. With the younger ones it was the three R's or perhaps languages; with the older ones often some subjects of special interest: a chemist imported for a summer or two with an improvised chemical laboratory in a tent; another summer it was geology or perhaps painting.

The afternoons were spent out of doors with a round of golf at the Indian Carry Links across the water or else in work on the place—cleaning up the woods, making paths, revamping the tennis court. There was always some improvement under way. The vistas of the lake were carefully planned and cut. He took pleasure in surveying the shore line, calculating the weight of boulders, and one night, when mosquitoes made sleep impossible, he figured out that if a man could make as much noise as a mosquito, weight for weight, he could make himself heard from Upper Saranac to Albany. The day was an active one, but it was not complete without a peaceful half-hour in the hammock as twilight closed in. In the evening there were games with the whole family—cards or perhaps anagrams—and when the younger members had retired there was apt to be reading aloud by the fireside, rarely a novel, more often a biography or an essay; those of Samuel McChord Crothers were always favorites.

On Sundays the family went by rowboat to a small

island chapel to worship. Games were not played that day; instead there were rows or walks with the children and reading aloud to them. The daily routine was by no means inflexible. It was broken by occasional rough camping trips and many a day excursion by water; the Racquette River, the silent ponds and creeks covered with lily pads, were soul satisfying places. And there were mountain climbing expeditions; the trip up Ampersand had its itinerary all planned—the starting time, each point along the route, the number of minutes of rest allowed at such and such a brook— all with a view to a minimum of fatigue for the whole party. Upper Saranac provided friends too—a few of them; the Herter family across the lake was the star attraction of the early years, and many a visitor was to partake of the hospitality of Panther Point.

The summer months went all too fast, but they lived all winter long in the minds of the Holt family. It was then that Dr. Holt really had the opportunity to know his children; in winter he was perforce a more shadowy parent. He enjoyed teaching them to swim, to play tennis, golf or cards. The parental relation was a close one. It was before the days of child psychology, but was it needed by one who understood children? He knew the art of diverting them to avoid crises, and could usually avoid punishments. There was one occasion that nearly brought disaster to the household. Two small boys had conceived the brilliant idea of having a camp-fire under the front porch of the house; it seemed such a cozy, protected spot. The fagots were gathered, and the fire was well in progress before smoke issuing up through the cracks of the porch brought bustling adults to the scene who were just able to put out the fire before the building caught. But no punishment was to follow. It was appreciated that the act was one of ignorance rather than of mischief. The dangers of fire were carefully explained to the culprits, and that same afternoon they were conducted to a safe exposed rock and allowed to build and enjoy their camp-fire. There was complete understanding of the young child, but with adolescence came reticences that were harder to break through.

XIV

INFANT MORTALITY

IF the last two decades of the nineteenth century had witnessed a revolution in the science of medicine, changes no less dramatic were to follow in the early part of the twentieth. Blood counts and the microscopic examination of the blood films—the latter largely the contribution of Ehrlich—soon became as familiar a procedure to the physician as taking the temperature. There was the first blood transfusion done by Carrel at the Rockefeller Institute by means of an exceedingly delicate suturing of the donor's vein to that of the recipient; a baby almost exsanguinated miraculously brought back to life! It was a thrilling event for the medical world, but how much more so for those on the spot. Most of the common microorganisms had been discovered by 1902, but several important ones were to follow. The spirochaete of syphilis was discovered by Schaudinn in 1905, and upon its heels there followed two bull's eyes that ushered in a new epoch for that disease—the Wassermann reaction which made possible the diagnosis in the absence of symptoms, and salvarsan, the culmination of Ehrlich's work.

The pediatrician now had effective weapons to wield against congenital syphilis, and the disease began to yield. Its severe forms became rare; treatment became largely a question of treating the Wassermann reaction. The doctor could not do it all. His efforts had to be supplemented by social workers, by organizers of clinics for prenatal as well as postnatal treatment. The work of organization took time, but progress was steady if slow. The traditional taboo and American notions of personal liberty have prevented the 100 per cent job that has been done in Denmark and some other European countries where compulsory treatment has virtually eliminated congenital syphilis. The American parent is still free to have his syphilitic child treated irregularly or not at all, if he so chooses, or to have him treated by some of the cults that flourish among the less intelligent members of the population. But despite these limitations much has been accomplished.

The year of 1904 brought a deadly epidemic of cerebrospinal meningitis which focused attention sharply upon that disease. The meningococcus had only recently been discovered, but by 1907 it had met its match in the form of an effective antiserum, developed in Germany and perfected by workers in the United States. But success in the treatment of meningitis would have been quite impossible without a method of reaching the nervous system, of giving treatment at the site of the disease itself. The method preceded the discovery of the specific treatment by a few years, but it was an essential link in the chain. The brain and the spinal cord were dangerous places in which to fool around with a needle, and defied the approach of the physician who wished to examine the nature of the inflammatory processes which surrounded them. But a German physician, Quincke, discovered that in the lower part of the spinal canal the cord was less vulnerable, being protected by a relatively larger body of the surrounding cerebrospinal fluid. At this point the reservoir could be safely tapped, fluid could be removed for examination and drugs could be administered if desired. Quincke's procedure—lumbar puncture—was to become widely used in the United States, but not without taking at least one martyr for its toll. When first published it sounded like a rather heroic measure and was frowned upon by many a prominent physician.

A young pediatrician named A. H. Wentworth was the first to do a lumbar puncture in Boston. He was a man of much promise, and, as a laboratory and clinical investigator, was one of the first to sense the possibilities of biochemistry as a handmaiden of pediatrics. The puncture was successfully executed, but it was given rather unfortunate publicity. In the yellow journals and antivivisectionist pamphlets he was characterized as a doctor who experimented on his patients, a "human vivisector." With the support of the profession the storm might have been weathered. But that support was not forthcoming. Wentworth was roundly condemned by some of Boston's leading doctors. He was a ruined man. Virtually forced out of practice in Boston, his scientific career was ended and he retired to practice medicine in a small New England village. He lived long enough to see lumbar punctures become a matter of routine in every hospital of the country, but not long enough to recover from the shadow that had been cast on his professional ethics—a whispering campaign that followed him.

The misconstruction placed on new medical discoveries was not confined to Boston. Only a few years later it was New York, and this time with Holt in the storm center. Tuberculin—an extract of the tubercle bacillus—had been discovered by Koch some years previously. Heralded originally as valuable in the treatment of tuberculosis, it had proved a bitter disappointment, but a new use was discovered for it as a detector of the presence of tuberculosis. Pasteur's pupil Calmette found that a very small amount of tuberculin dropped into the eye would produce an inflammatory reaction in an infected person, and shortly afterward Pirquet of Vienna found that the skin would serve quite as well as the eye and was a safer place to test; a mere scratch of the skin, a little tuberculin rubbed in, and within two days if the subject were tuberculous a red spot would appear. Great was the surprise when Pirquet tests showed that nearly all adults in large cities were infected with tuberculosis; a minute latent focus of no practical significance in most cases, tuberculous infection did not mean active tuberculous disease. In the infant and young child, however, a positive tuberculin reaction usually meant recently acquired, active tuberculosis. The test proved to be an invaluable aid in diagnosis. Among the first Pirquet tests tried out in this country were some made at the Babies' Hospital. Somehow or other a reporter heard a garbled version, and there appeared in the Hearst press a lurid account of babies being used as experimental subjects, being inoculated with tuberculin germs under Dr. Holt's direction. The scoop was copied by other papers. Antivivisectionist pamphlets lost no time in making the best of such juicy copy, and *Life,* always ready to attack the medical investigator, put in its scathing comment. Even the European papers published garbled accounts, and from Germany and Switzerland as well as from all parts of this country came letters from physicians who could not understand what their colleague had been up to. The Wentworth episode, however, was not to be repeated. Having a reputation back of one was a help. A clear-cut statement was given to the press explaining the situation as it was; it was supported by editorials in the leading papers condemning the misrepresentation of fact, and with that the matter died, once and for all.

To the pediatrician the tuberculin test gave aid comparable to that of the Wassermann reaction in congenital syphilis. One could recognize the incipient case that had not frankly declared itself, could isolate it from a home where continuous reinfection might be occurring from an adult who might not even know he had tuberculosis. Indirectly, the greater ease of diagnosis in the highly susceptible infant was to help adult diagnosis. As a recent writer [*] has expressed it, "In the adult there is more than one way of recognizing tuberculosis; one may find the bacilli in his sputum or one may find tuberculosis in his baby."

Tuberculin did not conquer the problem of childhood tuberculosis, but it marked the beginning of a new epoch. Years were required for the knowledge to penetrate the medical and later the social conscious-

[*] E. A. Park.

ness. Only in very recent times has there been organized effort to discover and isolate the infected child and the child in danger of infection and to provide facilities for their care.

Diphtheria, meningitis, syphilis, tuberculosis: all had seen revolutionary events, events which were producing a rapid decline in the infant mortality rate. The pediatrician could view them with pride in his science, and his social aids none the less so. But probably the most significant achievement of the period was the conquest of infantile diarrhea. It was an appalling problem. Every summer, the death rate would mount to three or four times its winter level, and practically all of this was due to diarrhea. The attack on the problem was not one punctuated by dramatic episodes: it was an insidious campaign, lasting seventy years or more and waged simultaneously on many fronts.

There was the milk front. Much of the diarrhea of the early days was due to contaminated milk. The story of milk in New York City is an epic in itself. It has been graphically told by Hartley* and need only be touched upon here. The period from 1800 to 1850 had seen New York grow from a small town to a busy industrial center. The peaceful grazing cow had given way to the herd kept in the basement of the distillery, where the animals were fed on "distillery slop." They were milked by tramps who performed this service in return for a night's shelter. Conditions were filthy in the extreme. The animals were frequently diseased and rarely lived more than a year. The milk, besides being watered, was heavily contaminated, and the babies

* Hartley, *Essay on milk* (J. Leavitt, New York, 1848).

THE ROCKEFELLER INSTITUTE BOARD OF SCIENTIFIC DIRECTORS

Smith   Biggs   Flexner   Welch   Prudden   Holt   Herter

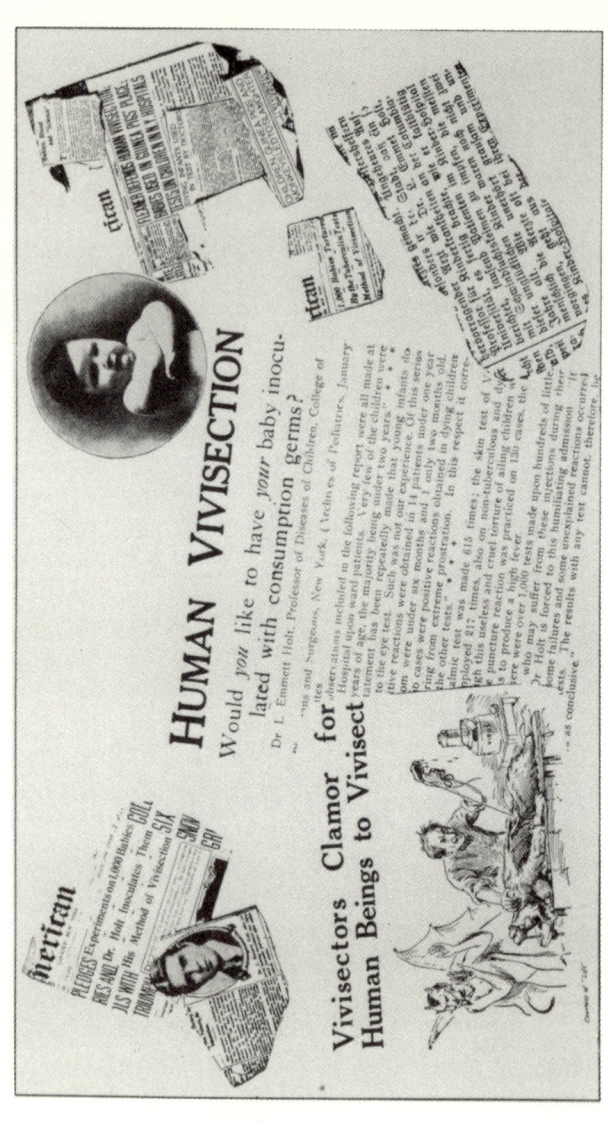

ANTIVIVISECTION PROPAGANDA
April, 1914

INFANT MORTALITY

fed on it died literally like flies. Year after year the infant death rate mounted until about the middle of the century the public consciousness was aroused. A death in his own family had stirred Robert Hartley to write his book. Frank Leslie took up the campaign, and the early issues of Leslie's weekly were filled with appalling disclosures of the milk industry. The milk profiteers and the politicians who were hand-in-glove with them were denounced in the pulpits of the city. The agitators stirred many a citizen, but they did not provide a solution of the problem. The advent of the railroads did that. First the Erie and then the other railroads brought milk from outlying farming districts within easy reach of the city. An enlightened public preferred the country milk. The distillery dairy was gradually forced out by competition, and by 1880 it had become a matter of history; the infant death rate had been declining for some years.

That had been the first round, the fight of a previous generation; without a knowledge of bacteriology to help them, they had correctly guessed the importance of clean milk; they had fought for it and had changed conditions for the better. Then came the era of bacteriology, and it was soon apparent that the problem was only half-solved. The milk of the suburban farmer was an improvement over that of the distillery. His cows were healthier and better fed, but at times they suffered from bovine tuberculosis, and he too could water the milk; his standards of cleanliness were usually rudimentary; the milk stood in open vessels unprotected from flies, was transported without refrigeration, and delivered in bulk in wagons with the cans exposed to the sun. The result was a high degree of bacterial contamination when it reached the consumer. Milk was an ideal culture medium for bacteria.

If it was a serious problem in public health, it was also a problem of immediate concern to the enlightened pediatrician of the early nineties who had to prescribe formulas for his babies. He could not conscientiously prescribe contaminated milk. Soxhlet in Germany had tried to solve the problem by boiling all milk fed to babies, but boiled milk was found to predispose to scurvy; it was feared that other valuable properties of milk might be lost by heating it. Soxhlet's method was not adopted in America. It was not until after the war that the practice of boiling milk and supplying the antiscorbutic vitamin independently in the form of orange juice came into use. Pure milk for patients was badly needed and there seemed no producer who would take the risk; all were sure that the added cost of proper refrigeration, a more intelligent milking personnel, and delivery in sealed bottles would be prohibitive, and that the demand for the product would be negligible.

In Boston a struggling company—the Walker-Gordon Co.—had been formed to fulfil the double function of providing pure milk from a model farm and also a laboratory where modified milk could be prepared according to a physician's prescription. New York needed exactly this, but the company was in no condition to extend its operations to another city, nor did bankers have the faith to finance the undertaking. In the end Herter, Holt, and one or two other physicians who believed in the idea put up the capital themselves; a Walker-Gordon branch was started with a farm at Plainsboro, New Jersey, and a milk laboratory in the city. The milk laboratory served its purpose for some years; as milk modification became simplified, however, its importance declined. But the real achievement was the production of pure milk as a commercial enterprise. The Walker-Gordon farm succeeded; in time it became a show place and an inspiration to other cities.

The movement for pure milk spread, and with it came inevitably exploitation—the producer with lower standards who would have the public believe that his milk was equally pure. He flourished for a time but not for long. In his wake he brought the medical milk commission. Henry L. Coit of Newark was its leading spirit. Milk commissions were formed in different cities and states; they met together and laid down rigid criteria for the production of pure milk: standards of cleanliness in the barns, health inspection of cattle, physical examination of employees, cleanliness of milking conditions, immediate cooling and bottling, and regulations covering the bacterial count of the finished product. One by one cities recognized the milk certified by the commissions. "Certified milk" became the protection of the public. In many cities it was the only milk that could be sold raw.

Certified milk solved the problem for those who could afford it; health department regulations had met the problem of watered milk; but the babies of the masses had still to be fed on badly contaminated milk, most of it still sold in bulk. It was here that a pioneer philanthropist came on the scene—Nathan Strauss, who organized a series of milk stations throughout the city where the babies of the poor could obtain good milk. It was not certified milk, but it was relatively clean and it was pasteurized so that most of its organisms had been destroyed. After 1911, when the milk stations were introduced, clean milk was available for New York's babies, rich and poor. There remained a "clean-up" job for the public health officers, to dry up the contaminated milk still sold. This was the work of a decade. First there came regulations for compulsory pasteurization of all but certified milk, grading it on its cleanliness. The producers saw the writing on the wall and climbed onto the "grade A" and "grade B" bandwagons as fast as possible. There were not many of them left to be checkmated by the final moves—the abolition of the sale of bulk milk in the city and of all grades below "A" and "B." It had taken the best part of seventy years to clean up New York City's milk supply but the task was now completed.

The milk front was only one attack on the problem; pure milk could eliminate one source of diarrhea, but not all of it. There was the pediatric front. Medical science had been making advances in the understanding and treatment of diarrhea and was still doing so. The discovery of the dysentery bacillus had shown that a large share of diarrhea was infectious in origin. A specific remedy was not forthcoming, but the discovery called the attention of the doctor to the need for isolation, to prevent the infection of one child from another, to prevent the infection of the adult who as an innocent carrier might convey it to other children. Somewhat later the profession began to realize that even the simple non-infectious diarrhea in which no pathogenic organisms could be cultivated from the intestine, was usually due to a "parenteral" infection—an infection in some distant part of the body, the eye, throat, ear or kidney—which produced a toxin powerful enough to damage the digestion. That gave one more reason for isolating babies with diarrhea and for isolating well babies from any infection whatsoever, no matter how mild. The pediatrician was learning how to treat the baby with diarrhea better than had his predecessors; he had learned the art of giving the disturbed intestine a preliminary rest, the futility of giving more food than the baby could digest; he had learned how to make feedings that were less upsetting to delicate digestions, how to eliminate the large curds of milk which were upsetting to the stomach, and above all he had learned from Henoch how to replace the precious water and salts lost by the body. The methods were continually being modified and improved upon.

There were many other forces at work in that period, reducing infant mortality in general and the prime cause of it, diarrhea, in particular. The public health nurse made her first appearance. In New York it was a pioneer spirit, Miss Lillian D. Wald, who organized a visiting nurse's service in connection with the Henry Street Settlement. Other agencies and the Health Department soon followed suit. Movements for better housing conditions made their appearance. The large orphanage which throughout history had unintentionally contributed so much to the mortality of its inmates had met its match in the person of Dr. Henry Dwight Chapin. In its place he organized the

Speedwell Society, an agency which arranged for the care of these infants in private boarding homes with an adoption bureau which often found permanent homes for them. No longer was the parentless infant to be exposed to the ravages of epidemics, and to succumb to the diarrhea to which they gave rise; he was to survive to find parental affection in place of brick walls. The Speedwell idea spread and more units were organized. The example of New York was copied in many other cities.

What part was Holt playing in the struggle? One finds him working simultaneously on many fronts—working to secure for New York City its first certified milk dairy, steering the young Rockefeller Institute to study the state of milk contamination in New York's tenements, serving on a committee of physicians to advise the Health Department on milk regulations and other matters. One finds him on the Board of Directors of the Henry Street Settlement, giving them a medical point of view on nursing problems, making a speech in Cleveland before a hospital association upon the infant's hospital and its needs. He was a prime mover in organizing the Association for the Prevention of Infant Mortality in 1911. For several years to come that organization served a useful purpose as a clearing house of information of what was being done in various cities by the pediatrician, the public health officer and the social organizer. After 1911 he was to be found in the laboratory, directing a study of the chemistry of diarrhea, measuring the elements lost to the body, coöperating with Jacques Loeb at the

INFANT MORTALITY

Rockefeller Institute in an effort to devise an ideal salt solution to replace that loss.

But his leading contribution was beyond doubt as an educator. Through the Catechism the mother was educated to know pure milk and to accept nothing less for her infant. Through the *Diseases of Infancy and Childhood* the practitioner was kept abreast of the movement; and there were the medical students, too. The P. and S. students were given a thorough course in pediatrics, certainly, but they were taught more than pediatrics. In a day when hygiene and public health were not a regular part of medical school curriculums, they learned in their pediatrics course the lessons of the fight against infant mortality, of the physician's responsibility to further maternal nursing, to secure pure milk for his community: these things and more they learned—and remembered.

The fight against infant mortality was a long one. It had its discouraging moments, too. For some of the early years the mortality statistics of the Babies' Hospital insisted in moving in the wrong direction. In 1900 when 145 babies died as contrasted with 114 the year before, there were criticisms from the board which brought the following comment from the physician in charge.

I am sorry to learn [he wrote] that this has been the occasion for some unfavorable comment, but am very sure that this increase is more apparent than real. We have received absolutely every child who has come to us without any regard to its condition. There are institutions in this city where patients are not allowed to die on the premises if it can be avoided. To accomplish this requires a great deal of chicanery. The cases are first culled with the greatest care, and then if they do not thrive they are promptly sent to other institutions. An excellent example of this has recently come under our notice. Of the eighteen patients first received in the hospital this autumn, sixteen came from other hospitals. ... It is not pleasant of course to have a dozen babies sent to us, as happened last summer, who died within twenty-four hours, but our reward may be to save the thirteenth. If we have a high mortality rate it is certainly to our credit that we take greater chances. Our usefulness cannot be gauged by our death rate. I am positive myself that the results for this year have been relatively much better than before.

If there were moments of discouragement, however, there were also lighter moments. Nathan Strauss, seeking for new worlds to conquer, had journeyed to Europe to spread the milk station idea. His efforts were sometimes misunderstood. From Heidelberg, Emil Feer wrote to his one pediatric friend in this country:

Heidelberg, 18 Jan. 1908
Confidential: Emmett Holt, Esq.
DEAR SIR,
I should be very much obliged to you for giving me some reference about Mister *Nathan Straus* from New York. This gentleman is here in Heidelberg since several months and has opened a laboratory of pasteurized milk.

I promised to him, to examine exactly his milk in the bacteriological and clinical way in my hospital and for the out-patients, but I told him, that only I and nobody else had the right to publish my investigations and to write over it.

Now, since Mister Straus is here, a great deal of newspapers in the country bring often popular treatises glorifying this man and his milk. This manner to make puffing advertisements seems to be not fair. Now several days ago a new advertisement was published in the newspapers by him or his friends, *publishing my investigations in a quite false way, without asking me for the permission!*

So I was obliged to forbid Mister Straus to call upon me farther and to refuse to continue my investigations about the pasteurized milk. I cannot allow that my name is abused for making a "Reklame" for Mister Straus and his milk.

Knowing nobody in New York except you, I beg your pardon, that I take liberty to adress to you my request to give me a *quite short information* about Nathan Straus.

I thank you very much before-hand for your kindness. Yours truly,

E. FEER

Prof. E. Feer
Director der Universitäts Kinderklinik

. . . .

Slowly, surely the efforts of many workers bore fruit. The rise in the Babies' Hospital's mortality in 1900 was only an eddy in the steady downward course of the figures for that institution. All over the city the infant mortality was declining. Down it came in the diseases which had been attacked in the form of a specific treatment or public health measures—and most surprising of all, down came the mortality almost as fast in the case of diseases about which nothing specific had been done. The health workers were receiving an extra dividend, for a vicious cycle had been broken. One disease decreased resistance to another, a successful attack on one was also an attack on the other, and some of the public health measures—pure milk, better nursing and housing—were directed against all diseases. Perhaps the most striking part of the achievement was the virtual elimination of deaths from summer diarrhea. In 1923 scarcely a vestige remained of that great rise in mortality that came with the hot weather; a year or two after Dr. Holt's death it disappeared altogether.

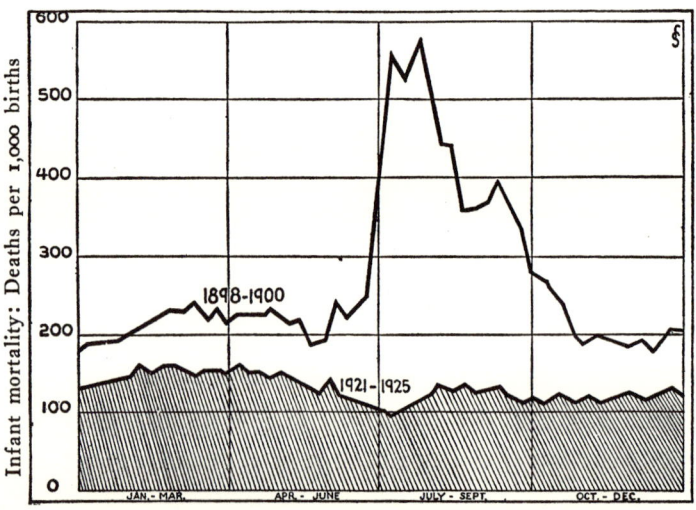

INFANT MORTALITY (BY WEEKS) IN NEW YORK CITY

The striking summer increase due to diarrheal diseases has been practically eliminated during the course of twenty-five years.

INFANT MORTALITY

The seemingly impossible had been accomplished, and it had been done in a period during which the city had grown to undreamed-of size, a period in which its density of population had greatly increased, and in which no checks had as yet been fastened on the great tide of foreign immigration. It was an achievement uncelebrated and unsung. There were no parades, flag wavings or speeches on the city hall steps to mark the victory that had saved the lives of so many of New York's young citizens. There was no awarding of medals, nor did the victors of that army organize a bonus

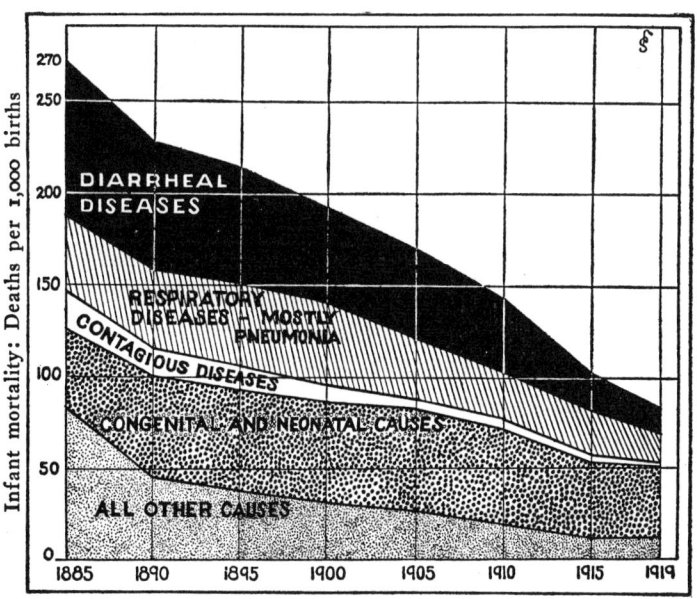

INFANT MORTALITY RATE IN NEW YORK CITY, 1885-1919
(Boroughs of Manhattan and Bronx)

raid upon the public treasury. The change had come about so gradually that in the minds of those engaged in it, it was taken for granted when it came.

What was going on in New York was in no sense unique. It was the same story, in greater or less degree, all over the country. Boston, Chicago, Minneapolis, Cincinnati, San Francisco, Richmond—all had their pioneer workers. No one could claim the credit for the movement; no one of them would have thought of so doing, but one wonders if any other individual did more for it than did Emmett Holt.

Was it worth while? Had the welfare of the race been lost sight of in the humanitarian appeal of the individual? Was the Spartan method of exposing the infant on a bare mountain top better suited to improve the stock by elimination of the unfit? The question is often asked. The human appeal would have been difficult to resist in any case, but the workers in that cause were doubly fortified with conviction that the race was in no way being attenuated. The sickly, feeble infant was in the overwhelming majority of instances the victim of circumstances rather than of any constitutional inferiority. The puny baby with marasmus, whose life for months might be hanging by a thread, could if he survived grow up to be as strong and sturdy an adult as the nation possessed.

XV

VIRGINIBUS PUERISQUE

IT was a strenuous life, New York even in the early nineteen hundreds. The family had outgrown the old brownstone house in 54th Street in 1897 and had moved to a more capacious one at 14 West 55th Street which served as home and office for more than twenty years. Perhaps the patients who waited in that rather somber downstairs hall wondered about the life that went on above the formal curling stairway, or the life of their physician after office hours; perhaps not. If those who wondered had followed their thoughts, they would have found a well-ordered household for both young and old. One could cover much ground in a well-planned day. Exercise was never neglected—there was always a horseback ride in the park after breakfast, and one great asset that Holt had was the ability to drop care and relax completely when a few moments offered. In the evening, with only ten or fifteen minutes to spare before dressing for dinner, he could lie down and fall asleep almost immediately and awake completely refreshed.

They were never a particularly sociable family. There were old friends, of course, and good ones too, but as time went on their social contacts were more and more with the people who were doing things in the world, rather than with the members of any particular social group. They were not the contacts made to launch a débutante daughter. Perhaps the children suffered in consequence, and perhaps they gained. It all depended on one's point of view.

New York was a fascinating place—none more so; it was filled with interesting people, but it was hardly a place for raising a family. The months between summers at Saranac were long ones. The problem was solved by a farm in the hills of Westchester County near Pleasantville, New York, where the family retired for week-ends. For the children it was a welcome contrast to city pavements and Central Park. There were horses, country to roam over, coasting and skating in winter, and all the interests of a farm and its animals. For Dr. Holt it brought back the simple life and many of the interests of the early Webster days. He delighted in planning the rotation of crops, the grafting of the apple-trees, and the diet of chickens. The fluctuations in the egg output of Holt hens were for years recorded in a little book, and one of the first functions after arrival on Saturday afternoon was the presentation of this document; there was rejoicing when the total was large and a corresponding solemnity and canvassing of remedial measures when it was small. One can picture the life there—a long Saturday afternoon nap on a porch overlooking the hills with their lengthening shadows, reading aloud before an open fire of applewood logs in the evening, and nights whose stillness was unbroken; on Sunday morning a tramp over the hills and fields, plans made for the coming week, perhaps a letter to an absent younger member of the family away at school or college, and a late afternoon train back to the city. Dr. Holt could never resist stopping for a half hour at the Babies' Hospital to see what had happened during the week-end and get primed for grand rounds Monday morning. The picture of Pleasantville would be incomplete without mention of the faithful hands that tended it—Fanny and James, an Anglo-Irish couple, products of an age that is past. They literally lived for the family, made the place the refuge that it was instead of the added care that it might have been. Pleasantville was a godsend. With it one could maintain one's perspective, could live sanely, even in New York.

In the fall of 1909 the family circle was broken by the death of Dr. Holt's youngest son, Kenneth, from pneumonia. He was a high-spirited boy of ten, the apple of his parents' eye. The scar was many years in healing, and it is reflected in many of the letters written at this time.

(To his son Calvert)

14 West 55th Street, New York
October 18/08

MY DEAR CALVERT:

How does it seem to be sixteen years old? Things move rapidly after that age is reached and soon you will have a vote. I wish you had one this year to cast for Taft and for Hughes. We are afraid H— will not get in though the latest reports are encouraging.

Shaw is doing very well as a chauffeur. With only two weeks of practice he handles the car very intelligently, always carefully—much too slow for Evelyn—but he is gaining in skill every day and will surprise you when you come home. When will that be?

We miss you *very much;* everybody does about the house. I am glad that you find school so interesting and like it so well. Do your best always. That is all that is asked of any of us. Be found upon the right side of every question which involves the order of the school, and be counted one who can be depended upon to do the right thing everywhere. Such a reputation is more to be prized than high standing in class work, although that is worth working hard for.

Remember your besetting sin, or rather fault, to talk too large and give your imagination full play, and be careful about your statements; it is better to be accurate than to be entertaining.

But it was not to preach or lecture that I started out when I began. We are all so anxious our boys should be *just-right* that we cannot forbear speaking to them about such things. Will you want any of your birthday money now, if so I will send it by Mother; the rest I will put in the bank for you. With much love,

FATHER

New York, Jan. 21, 1909

MY DEAR CALVERT:

I was very glad to get your nice letter. I think you have improved very much in your letters, and I have heard many people speak of them—Aunt Minnie, Uncle John, Aunt Katie, Dr. Faunce, and others. It pays to make an effort; to take pains with everything you do, for this helps much the next time. Your "B" list, which came to hand this morning, also made us very happy. Don't get discouraged, nor on the other hand too much puffed up, so that you think to get along without hard work. For I never have been able to do so, and few people can, not even T. R. . . . Emmett has been in the house for a couple of days with a cold, and we have had more time for billiards, as I have not been quite so hard worked as usual for this time of the year. E. has discovered several new games, which he is dying to show to you. We shall all go to Pleasantville this week. No one went last week. We hope for some fine coasting, as the crust is said to be hard. With lots of love from all, but especially from Father.

New York, Nov. 25, 1909
MY DEAR CALVERT:
I wish I could express to you how much pleasure and satisfaction your last letter gave to us. It is most gratifying to know that you are working patiently and with a purpose. Your reward will not be wanting, you may be assured. We all have our times of discouragement and despondency, but we must not let them overcome us, but conquer them; and then we grow strong. It is never best for us to have things go always for us and just to our liking. It is often the disappointments of life that really do us the most good. Every sorrow like that which we have had is meant to do something for us. It should make us kinder, more thoughtful for the happiness of others, and fill us with a resolve to make the most of every day and every year.

One great lesson which Kenneth should teach us all is courage and pluck. How much of both he always had. Think of these when you think of him, and try and have the same pluck in your work. While we remember him every day and almost every hour we must not grieve, but each of us try and do more for one another and those about us because he will not be here to do his part. Let us not be sad, but joyful for such a fine example as he gave us in many things, and thankful that God gave him to us for so many years. Be a friend to every small boy in the school, and make your influence felt for all that is good and true and noble. What we *are* is really very much more important than what we *have,* or even what we *know.* Character is above everything.

To-day has been quiet for us here. Mother has been sick in bed for a few days, nothing serious. Evelyn and Horace are in Irvington, so Emmett and I ate our turkey in solitary state, wishing, however, many times that you were here with us.

Real winter to-day. I suppose you got a touch of it in Pottstown. With a great deal of love from Mother and all the rest including Father.

Pleasantville, N. Y., January 23, 1910
MY DEAR CALVERT:

We are at the farm you see for Sunday—all of us now. But Emmett and I go down this evening and Mother and Evelyn will remain over night. It seems so lonely up here without Kenneth. At every corner one seems to expect his little red cap to appear which was always followed with his cheery greeting of halloa Father! In New York we don't seem to miss him so, but here every step about the place is associated so intimately with him. It is so hard to realize that we must now get on without him. But it is not good for us to grieve nor repine. If Kenneth's work is done, ours is not yet; and we must be up and doing, to make the most of the years and the opportunities that are still given to us.

We are glad of your letters always and enjoy them very much. Mother and I read them over more than once, you may be sure.

It was a keen disappointment to us that you failed in your algebra after going back.

I am glad you find your "Victor" so much company and an attraction to your room for your friends.

Do you see much of Duncan? He is a fine boy; I would cultivate him as much as you can.

I began this letter in Pleasantville and I am finishing it in New York now as Emmett and I have just come in from church. All send love with much from

FATHER

14 West 55th St., N. Y. May 6/10

MY DEAR CALVERT:

I have just come in and find them all in bed, so will seize the time to drop a line to you. I have been in Washington, D. C., for the past four days, returned last evening. I thought of you while passing through Philadelphia and wished I might have had time to run up to Pottstown and have a visit with you. But I was needed at home. Teaching had to be done and patients were waiting to be seen. It seems to me I spend my time in doing not what I would like to do, but what needs to be done. Don't fancy that cares will grow lighter when school days are over.

Well, we have bought the *Hankscraft* boat finally in spite of Emmett's forceful arguments. I hope it will turn out as well as Horace and Evelyn predict.

We seem a very much scattered family just now. Will it not be nice to be all together again? I long for the summer and the Camp, the woods and the Lake. I am afraid it will be hard to be back there tho without Kenneth who is so closely connected with everything there. With much love, my dear boy,

FATHER

(*To his son Emmett*)

New York, Jan. 19, 1913

MY DEAR EMMETT:

It has been like April to-day. Mother and I were in Pleasantville, and it was bright and sunny and no wind. The day was a joy and as we talked on the hills basking in the sunshine we thought how much we had to be thankful for in our children who are still spared to us, though we do miss dear Kenneth so much when we are at the farm. No interest in life begins to be so great as that which we have in you four who are to come after us, and take up our incomplete work and carry it on, much better than we ourselves have done it, we hope and pray.

While you are in college with so much to take up your time and your thoughts, don't forget at times to reflect upon the real purpose of it all. The opportunities of the present are great, those of the future I am sure will be even greater for those who will seize and use them. Last Sunday night I had a nice time talking to the P. and S. students at their Y. M. C. A. club. I told them that more men fail in a profession for lack of moral character than for lack of scientific training. I want to say the same to you. Keep your moral stands high. Marcus Aurelius, I think it was, who said, "One may live nobly, even in a palace." So I must say one may maintain high moral principles, even in college.

14 West 55th Street, New York, March 2, '13

MY DEAR EMMETT:

You will I am sure be relieved to hear that mother has rested very much better to-day and is gaining steadily. You must write her a little letter every few days while she is sick, for your letters are such a joy to her. They need not be long but write frequently. I in turn will keep you posted regarding her progress.

I am glad you are kept fully occupied with your work. You have always been very deliberate, not to say more, about your work and a little pressure to make you develop a more rapid pace, without sacrificing accuracy and efficiency will be of much benefit to you.

The worst of all things learned in college is a *bad habit of work*. I do not think you are as likely to fall into such habits as most boys, but a well-trained mind which will do your bidding, & do it rapidly & correctly, is really one of the chief things which a college education should give a man.

No matter what the task is afterwards you know how to tackle it, for you have learned how to think quickly and accurately. Just keep this point in mind in your study and see if you are schooling yourself to this sort of thing. To-day is my father's birthday. 94 years ago! It seems a long time ago. I have been thinking much of my own boyhood to-day and the old home at Webster, and the discipline and training which the country life of those days—50 yrs. ago—gave. I could wish that you boys also had something that is quite as good. My constant fear is that having been reared amid more luxurious surroundings, that these influences may tend to make you less self-reliant, less ambitious and independent in life than those which surrounded my own early life. See to it that they do not.

Well, I must close, my paper is full and it is nearly bedtime. Take good care of your body—do your intellectual work well—adhere to your high moral principles and may God bless you.

Your affectionate,
FATHER

(*To his son Emmett*)

New York, May 25, 1913

We were much disappointed for you in regard to the managership. But ... there are many other things in Harvard worth striving for. Don't forget the intellectual opportunities which are open to everybody who has the mind and the will to grasp and use them. These are things which in the end one finds more lasting, equally satisfactory and quite worth while. Pitch into your work of preparing for examinations and finish up your year with a good record in your college work. There is lots of time and many chances for distinction in other lines, also.

We were much amused at your crab-catching experience in the boat; too bad that fourth crew was given up. I am afraid that this family of Holts was not cut out for winning athletes. We must get our honors with our brains, if we win any. Everything is closing for the year here. My lectures finished two days ago, and now my examination is on, and I am amusing (?) myself in reading the papers. In the main they are good, and I feel rather pleased that the men who go out from P. and S. this year know so much of my special branch.

We are already making plans for the camp, arranging schedules for visitors, and ordering supplies from a certain Chicago catalogue house of which you may have heard.

February 7, 1915

You are, I am afraid, much as I used to be when I was younger in pushing the thing that you want to bring about a trifle too strenuously. I have learned, sometimes by sad experience, that we must not be too aggressive in this world. It tends to arouse antagonisms, and often leads to a misjudgment of one's motives and character. So take a kindly word of warning, and don't *push too hard* for what you want to do.

(*To his son Calvert*)

Panther Point Camp, July 9/19

DEAR CALVERT:

We are getting quite settled here at Camp and it's very natural to be here but rather lonesome; as yet we have seen no one on the Lake but Capt. John who is a little grayer as to hair, otherwise just the same.

It has been almost too cool nights so far and we have had a fire almost every night and needed it too. The days have been of the sort Mother likes to call the typical Adirondack days—ideally beautiful.

It is with regret that I think of you and Emmett working in the city, hot and dusty, when all this beautiful air, scenery, boats and swimming are being wasted apparently, yet I know that one cannot succeed either in business or in a profession and at the same time get the long summer's vacation when he is young that he is entitled to when older. So it makes me feel also very happy and proud to think of you two boys working your way up in life, patiently and without complaint, just as I remember I did when at your age I was doing the same.

The boats are running well, especially the *Comet*.

Baby Philip keeps us much occupied, almost too much in fact; if allowed he would soon become quite as tyrannical as the German Kaiser. We have enjoyed having him to ourselves, tho Mother will be very glad to see Evelyn to-morrow as he is beginning to get on her nerves a bit.

Lots of love from us both,   FATHER

14 West 55th St., New York, Feb. 2, 1920
MY DEAR CALVERT:

I received your letter this morning and was very glad to hear all was going so well with you. I can well understand what you say and feel about life in New York with its excitement and its rush. I feel it too and always have. But besides New York is a place of great opportunity, no other like it in this country in almost any line you can think of. My old teacher Dr. Anderson of Rochester of whom you have heard me often speak used to say to the young men, if you have got anything in you go to a big place to fly your kite, when you get your kite up in a great center it amounts to something.

I surely have had no reason to regret coming to New York and trying to fly my kite here. It was a little harder at first, but when the rewards came they were so much greater than would have been the case anywhere else.

We all ought to look at life as a great opportunity—the one and only chance we will have of making the very best and the most of ourselves. It is not simply fame or fortune that we should aim at, but at the satisfaction which comes and comes only from *something which is worth while really done well.* It may perhaps not make such a great difference exactly what the thing we finally decide to do is, provided it is doing something that the world needs to have done. It is the effect of our work upon ourselves that perhaps counts *more* than anything else. If our job makes us small, mean, and selfish, the sooner we get another one the better.

I don't want you to make a mistake in deciding what you are finally to do in life; but I am anxious that you shall get an experience which will give you a wide outlook and a broader vision. For this reason a trip to the great west seemed to offer some inducements. Get from it all you can in the shape of new views of life.

I think by this time you must have pretty nearly exhausted the possibilities of benefit—certainly of an intellectual sort—which camp life in winter affords, though the time and chance for thinking are most valuable.

Don't remain away too long or Mr. Tompkins may forget you. With much love,   FATHER

In the autumn of 1911 Dr. Holt was fifty-six years old. He had always enjoyed perfect health, but on this occasion disquieting symptoms pointing to the heart made their appearance. He consulted his colleague and personal physician, Dr. Walter B. James, and was told to take a complete rest. James was as able a clinician as the city could boast; he was professor of medicine at the P. and S., and together he and Holt had struggled with many of the problems of that institution. They were very good friends and often played golf together. James, of an old Baltimore family with aristocratic traditions, had a winning personality; with a keen sense of humor he was a delightful companion and raconteur. In later years when the New York Academy of Medicine needed a new home—particularly to house its library—and when there were insufficient funds available, Holt and James together visualized the enterprise as a project in post-graduate medical education, but it was James who staged the perfect dinner with just the proper amount of liquid refreshment at which the project was "sold" to the representatives of the Carnegie and Rockefeller Foundations. The two men appreciated and enjoyed each other, but they entertained somewhat different philosophies of life. Holt always felt that James, with something of the easy-going Southerner in his make-up, never took life as seriously as he should, never made the most of his really brilliant medical mind; he rarely wrote for the journals and wrote no textbook, and consequently failed to influence medicine beyond the local field as Osler had been able to do. James on the other hand felt that Holt took life too seriously, did not play enough, and missed many of the good things of life. On this occasion, however, James had the upper hand. He examined his friend's heart and was adamant in his prescription—nothing less would suffice than a complete rest and change of scene for four or five months —a trip to Egypt and up the Nile in a dahabeah. It was a handsome prescription, but once accepted it was accepted whole-heartedly. A party was made up—Dr. and Mrs. Holt, two of their children and a friend, and the Calverts.

They set out for Egypt in January 1912.

Dahabeah *Osiris,* February 3, 1912

DEAR CURT:

We are now just four weeks from home, and this is our fourth day on the Nile. How do we like it? Well, it is something indescribable. The *Osiris* is a house boat with commodious dining and sleeping cabins. We have a huge mast over one hundred feet long and carry an immense sail, sometimes two. But these sails we use only when the wind is good; most of the time it has been contrary, and so we have a tug to tow us. This is quite necessary in this part of the river, for the current is very strong and swift.

The life we lead is the laziest possible; breakfast at 8:30; get up on deck as soon after as possible, and spend the morning ostensibly in "reading up" places soon to be seen. But the views are too interesting, and we Oh! and Ah! to each other until our expletives and adjectives are all exhausted, and then we fall to kodaking everything which looks as if it would make a picture which would carry to friends at home some faint idea of the beauties which we are now enjoying....

Our party consists of the "dragoman," a Syrian by the name of Yango. Then we have a boat captain or "reis" and a ship's crew of a dozen (a cook, an assistant cook, a waiter and an assistant waiter).... I never before felt so much like an autocrat or czar for the entire ship and crew are at my disposal and we can sail or stop when and where we please.

When something interesting is reached we leave the *Osiris* and mount donkeys and ride in one long procession to the tomb or pyramid, as the case may be. With our entire party and "camp followers" we numbered last time twenty-one persons. You would smile, I am sure, to see J. C. mounted on a small donkey about as large as a yearling calf, his legs nearly touching the ground, leading the cavalcade across the desert.

Your appetite for ruins and hieroglyphics is at times more than sated, but for the scenery along the river, never. You could sit all day and watch the two shores, and find on one or other bank, or in the boats in the river itself, something of absorbing interest.

We sail only during the day. At night we tie up at some friendly bank, where the channel is close to the shore. Four stakes are driven into the ground, to which are attached the ropes which moor the boat fore and aft. Then the open front deck is enclosed with canvas and the sailors and crew sleep on the floor rolled up in their blankets. It gets pretty cold some nights, usually 50° or so; though this is an advantage as it conduces to early rising on the part of the Arabs. The neighborhood is not always the most reliable; and so a watch is kept all night, the sailors taking turn walking the deck.

Will you please send this letter to Horace?

Much love to all,
EMMETT

Dahabeah, *Osiris,* Feb. 14, 1912

MY DEAR CALVERT:

This is Valentine's Day but we would not think it from the weather. Yesterday it was 90° in the shade and we are all getting a nice coat of sunburn. Uncle John has a beautiful bright red nose and each one is decorated somewhere but we are all happy. Except for Evelyn I might say who has been suffering from an acute attack of indigestion and has in consequence missed two temples and much else of interest....

Our arrival in a village is a great event.... But the greatest excitement of all is selecting and mounting the donkeys. There are generally many more donkeys than are needed and the donkey boys get fairly wild as the critical moment approaches. They crowd and jostle one another and seem ready to tear each other's eyes out in their frenzy. Then a policeman appears with a large whip or cane which he plies about him vigorously, but never seems to hit anybody in particular. Finally we are mounted and stirrups adjusted and the boy proceeds to belabor the poor beast into his highest speed....

The donkey boys are very bright and quick witted. They have great trouble in fixing the relationships between us. Evelyn is generally taken for Aunt Minnie's daughter as they both have khaki dresses. Uncle John is sometimes looked upon as my father and Emmett as my brother....

We had been wanting some fresh fish for some days and yesterday morning a boat man was overhauled who had just caught a fine one weighing I should think about 15 pounds. We overheard the greatest commotion on the lower deck of the *Osiris* and rushing to the front saw Yango, the dragoman, Yusef, the head waiter, the cook, three or four of the crew and the fisherman yelling, pulling at each other, and at the fish, which the man was endeavoring to regain hold of and go back to his boat. If they had been Italians, knives would have been drawn in no time. But this was simply a little by-play to get a few more piastres. When these were forthcoming all was serene....

You are a dear boy and your letters have made us very happy. Don't get discouraged with school studies but keep steadily at it and your reward will surely come. Good night and much love, FATHER

The Fayum, March 18

DEAR CURT:

If you will get out your atlas you will see that the Fayum is an oasis about forty miles from Cairo. Well, that's where I am just now, in camp on the desert, on the rim of this oasis. On one side I look out on an indefinite expanse of sand and low rocky mountains, on the other the broad green plain covered with wheat, clover and beans. Like Abraham I am sitting in the door of my tent in the cool of the day, and there is much in our experiences of the past few days to remind us of Bible scenes and stories. We left Cairo, or rather the Pyramids, for a camping trip to this oasis, this being one of the thing travelers are advised to do. This is really camping de luxe. There preceded us on our way the caravan consisting of ten heavily laden camels which took tents, bedding, provisions and all our belongings for a week's journey....

We eat a cold lunch by the way and ride about five hours, mostly on a walk at a four-mile gait, before reaching our camp for the night. This we find quite luxurious. We have six sleeping tents, a large tent which is our dining room, and another not quite so large which is our kitchen. Our sleeping tents have iron bedsteads, rugs on the sand floors, wash basins and pitchers, and really everything needed for comfort. Our dinners consist of four or five courses served by two waiters. So you see one can camp like this indefinitely and not get homesick.

We break camp in the morning about eight o'clock, and it is a marvel to see our tents come down and everything folded up into the smallest possible space, and then lashed securely to the backs of camels. Each takes a small wagon load, five to six hundred pounds is considered not too much for a good-sized animal. They are not pleasant, and growl and snort a good deal when they are being packed, and sometimes they have to be helped up with their bulky loads; but when once on their feet they seem able to go on, swaying from side to side, at a three-mile gait for an indefinite time. At first we found them rather tiresome to ride, as their movement keeps the rider bending at his waist at every step, and their eternal bobbing is monotonous. But one soon gets used to it, and for a long pull most of us now prefer the camel to the donkey....

Each camel has a man or boy attached who cares for the beast and drives him. Some of these boys are very small; one of ours looks not more than eight, tho he is said to be twelve. (There is no Child Labor law in Egypt.) His devotion to his camel and the reciprocal affection is amusing to see. Helluaneah (the camel) and Sakleh the boy at all times wish to travel together and the boy is usually just behind holding to the camel's tail which he can barely reach. He is missed immediately if he disappears and the beast will not go again until Sakleh takes his place.

The nights are cool, so that we need heavy blankets, and a hot water bag besides. By ten o'clock, however, the sun is high enough to be felt forcibly, and by noon it is hot, and we gladly seek the shady side of a projecting rock or cliff, when we halt for lunch. When no such shelter affords we stretch ourselves out on the sand and rest or sleep for an hour before we resume our march. Generally we travel about three hours in the morning and two in the afternoon, so as to reach our camp about five o'clock. Then we get a cup of tea, play cards or read, or take a walk till dark, and have our dinner at half-past seven and go at once to bed; but, alas, not always to sleep, for the unmentionable insect known as the flea has discovered our whereabouts, and at night it is his time of activity. This is the one drawback to Egypt. Even in our best hotels we are sometimes attacked.

We had a little excitement one afternoon by reason of missing our camp. I have said that the caravan follows us as we leave in the morning, and as they go much slower soon falls far behind. When we stop for noon rest and lunch they pass us, and are all in order when we arrive at the end of our ride. Generally camping places are well defined, and as the same trip is made often about the same places are chosen for stops. One night our camp was not in the expected place, and for more than an hour we could not discover where it was. This was in a rolling country, with many small hills and valleys. Runners were sent out on foot in various directions; while Fadlalla took our strongest camel and started off at a rapid pace in another. We fired off the gun and scanned the horizon in every direction for any sign or signal of camp or men. It was finally discovered about six o'clock, much to one side of the usual site, greatly, I may add, to the disappointment of Emmett, and the girls, I think also, who had pictured the romance and excitement of being lost in the desert for the night. The rest of us, however, did not feel the need of any such thrill, and were glad to get to cover, as a strong wind was blowing, and it was none too warm....

By this time no doubt you are thinking of Webster. It will be a disappointment not to see you when we land. All send love.

Your affectionate brother,
Emmett

Naples, March 30, 1912

My dear Calvert:

Back on European soil again you see! Spring is just beginning. The wistaria is out in full bloom and all spring flowers are coming on very rapidly. Every evening we are serenaded by guitars and vocalists—chiefly airs from the old Italian operas.

Mother has been taken in charge by a fat cabman named Tomaso, whose stand is just in front of the hotel. He speaks a little English, which is more than most of them do, and he drives her through all the interesting streets and points out all the sights with the greatest delight. Yesterday he passed a gentleman, very much dressed up, in a carriage, and Tomaso informed her he was "going to be matrimonied." ...

I have visited some hospitals here, and seen some interesting men, but their buildings are not very good. I wanted to see the medical school, but learned that the students, because of some grievance, had *been on a strike* for two months past. You might suggest this up at Horace Mann when things do not go to the liking of the students.

I am sorry you have been lonesome, as I see very clearly by your letters you have, but you will appreciate us all the more perhaps when we do come. When you feel homesick or lonesome plunge into your work with all the force you can command, that is the best cure I know.

All send love with a great deal from me to my dear boy Calvert.

Your affectionate,
FATHER

Perhaps the prescription was an unduly radical one, perhaps it was just what was needed. At least as far as the results went it justified itself, for with one brief exception the heart gave no more trouble for almost twelve years.

XVI

NEW VISTAS

EMMETT HOLT'S lifetime had seen American pediatrics develop through several eras. From a dark age in which tradition reigned unchallenged, in which only a rare individual made a new observation, it had emerged into the sunlight where even the humblest practitioner had the courage to observe and record his clinical observations and to suggest new interpretations. Pathology, bacteriology, and immunology had come to throw light on processes of disease, and they in turn had been translated into a virile public health movement. The decade following 1910 saw a new handmaiden, chemistry, come to the aid of the pediatrician; saw the foundations laid of a new science, experimental nutrition, from which practical lessons were learned about the feeding of children.

Holt's pupil, John Howland, was the real pioneer in launching the chemical era in American pediatrics, and perhaps he did as much as any one to turn his former chief in that direction. Howland had an unusual combination of talents. He was a native New Yorker but with a solid New England background. With a rugged frame that suggested the New Hampshire hills, he had been a star athlete at Yale. A brilliant conversationalist, interested in everything under the sun and with an entertaining anecdote about almost everything, he was always a social favorite. Coupled with intelligence these were qualities to make for success in almost any field of endeavor, but there was in addition a drive that would not be satisfied by climbing existing ladders, an imagination that carved out new paths to be followed. He had begun his pediatric career in the early nineteen hundreds as Holt's office assistant, and for a time he followed the beaten track —practice, the study of disease in hospital wards and the autopsy room, teaching on the staff of the P. and S. He assisted his chief in the work of revising the *Diseases of Infancy and Childhood,* and from 1911 on was a recognized co-author in that undertaking. But his real urge was not that of a compiler of knowledge. He could recall one Saturday afternoon in the early days of their association when, the morning office hours over, he had promised himself to take in a championship tennis match at Hoboken. After lunch, just as he was about to leave, the suggestion came from Holt that they go down to the office for a bit and see what could be made of the data on the weight of the thymus gland which he had gathered from four hospital services. Howland's heart sank, but it was almost a royal command. The data were transcribed; columns were added up; averages and means were calculated; the weight of the thymus was analyzed by age, sex, race, previous state of health and what not. The afternoon wore on, and the tennis match retreated into the dim distance; it was six o'clock when they finished.

Statistics were meat to an orderly mind like Holt's; to Howland they were chains, necessary at times perhaps, but to be avoided if possible. Practice, too, was a necessity; there was no other livelihood for a pediatrician then. He was an expert clinician, and patients were devoted to him, but though clinical medicine made a strong intellectual appeal, the solution of the human problem was never for him, as it was for Holt, the fundamental driving force. Resentful of the time consumed by problems of managing human beings, he longed for an opportunity to study disease in the clinic and laboratory without interruption. It was the laboratory experiment that could lure him to work nights and all odd moments in the face of an active practice. Under the stimulus of Graham Lusk he constructed at Bellevue Hospital a calorimeter in which the energy requirements of an infant could be measured and infant feeding placed on a secure scientific basis. It may have been Lusk's influence, perhaps the influence of a year spent at Strasbourg where pioneer chemical studies of the metabolism of infants had been made for a decade, but at any rate the idea became firmly rooted in his mind that the chemical approach was the one that ought to be followed by the pediatrician, that there was many a first class plum to be picked by climbing that tree. Howland struggled along for some years, but in 1912 his opportunity came, a call to Johns Hopkins to take charge of the country's first full-time department of pediatrics. A salaried post, relieving him of the necessity of practice, it permitted him to pursue disease into the laboratory—particularly the chemical laboratory—and to steer younger men to do likewise. He seized it, and the plums began to fall thick and fast—but that is another story.

That Holt had hitherto been insensible to the possibilies of the chemical approach to disease can hardly be imagined. No one could have been an intimate friend of Herter and remained so, nor could one who followed the German literature of the period. One who did not foresee the possibilities of chemistry would hardly have made the effort to teach it to his children at an early age in the Adirondacks. There can be no doubt that he was sympathetic with the ambitions of Howland but had not been stirred himself to follow them. But there was an afternoon in 1910 when he and Howland were having a medical argument in the course of which the younger man brought forth definite chemical evidence to bear on the point in question. Finally, Holt said: "Well, that settles it. I see that we have got to go into the chemical laboratory."

Once the decision was made, the project was put into action without delay. With funds from the Rockefeller Institute, the Babies' Hospital was equipped with an up-to-date chemical laboratory and a staff of two trained biochemists. It was not the type of organization to develop younger pediatricians to go and do likewise; that was Howland's contribution—modeled on the German University clinic. But the Babies' Hospital team—Holt, Courtney and Fales—was an efficient unit for carrying on work. His task was largely that of planning the work, the greater part of interpreting the data when they came through, and of writing the papers; the actual determinations were done by the others. The problems were usually discussed in detail with Levene or Van Slyke of the Rockefeller Institute, who collaborated in some of them. Their counsel was invaluable, but the guiding hand in most of them was that of Holt.

From 1911 to 1923 the chemical laboratories of the hospital turned out a series of solid contributions. There were balance studies—the intake and output of nearly every chemical substance for which an analytical method was available were measured in health and in disease. The influence of different types of feeding on the absorption of this or that was measured. There were the first reliable analysis of the minerals of human milk, some of the earliest essays in blood chemistry of infants, comprehensive studies of calcium metabolism and of fat metabolism. Some of the ground had been covered before but not so well; much was virgin territory. The observations may not have shown quite so much originality as those of Howland, but they were solid building stones, and they counted. There were not many men who at fifty-five, their careers made, could pick up the tools of the coming generation and use them forcefully and effectively: at least there were not many of those older physicians who had grown up in an atmosphere of clinical and pathological observation and description, who did—not even Osler, who was only four years Holt's senior. It required a freshness, an adventurous and youthful point of view.

Holt and Howland remained in close touch with each other even after Howland left New York. They corresponded almost continuously. It might be some matter connected with the textbook—a passage which one or the other had written being submitted for criticism, or something pertaining to the new *American Journal of Diseases of Children* of which they were both editors (the old *Archives of Pediatrics* had become inadequate for the load), but often enough it was a thought about this or that pediatric problem, clinical or laboratory. They spoke the same language.

The science of nutrition had been growing surely and steadily. Calories, proteins, carbohydrates, fats and minerals—they were its tools; they had been worked with for a generation more or less, and it seemed as if not many more years would be needed before one knew all about them and could combine them in suitable proportions to secure optimum health and growth. Who could have foreseen that the second decade of the century would see that science burst all its bounds, that before long scarcely a year would pass without some new essential food constituent being discovered? Some of the new knowledge was of purely academic interest, but some had a profound influence on the practice of pediatrics. Sparks have a way of starting in unexpected corners, and one of these was Thomas B. Osborne, a chemist at the Connecticut Agricultural Experiment Station, spending his life in the tedious work of preparing chemically pure proteins from vegetable and animal sources. The medical profession paid no attention to Osborne's work, saw no possible practical applications in it, but he worked on, and in the course of years he had prepared in pure form the proteins of wheat, corn and many other grains, the proteins of egg and, notably, those of milk. Then with his associate, Lafayette B. Mendel of Yale, he began a classical series of feeding experiments on rats. The animals received no natural foods; they were fed only on the pure chemical substances. All of them received adequate amounts of protein, carbohydrate, fat and minerals; they received sufficient calories, but on some diets they gained weight and grew normally, while on others they did not. In due time the answer was forthcoming. The proteins were not equally valuable as foods; some of them contained amino-acids that were essential for growth, whereas others contained little or none of these. One by one the "essential amino-acids" were identified. Lactalbumin, the chief protein of human milk, was considerably richer in some of these important substances than was casein, the chief protein of cows' milk. That was a finding that struck home to Holt; it explained some bitter experiences he had had in using the Rotch formulas in past years—letters from past patients who would say: "Dear Doctor, We tried the formula you gave us for several months and the baby did badly. Finally in despair we moved to the country, bought a cow and fed the baby whole cow's milk. She improved at once and is now blooming." Rotch had been afraid of the high protein content of cows' milk, had insisted that it should be diluted until its percentage of protein did not exceed that of human milk, but he had not known that the quality of the cows' milk protein was inferior and that he was diluting it too far. His dilutions worked for most babies, as there was a fair margin of safety, but not for all. The pediatricians had followed Rotch for two decades—not blindly, for the dilute formulas were obviously more digestible, but unaware of their drawbacks; they were now to learn how to have their cake and eat it too, how to improve the digestibility of the cows' milk without resorting to a dangerous degree of dilution.

The feeding experiment with a small animal like the rat offered great advantages over the slower process of trial and error with feeding the human species that had characterized pediatrics through the ages—a process that too often gave equivocal results, that might require a generation to learn a lesson that a subsequent generation was as likely as not to forget, and in which complicating factors were always throwing one off the track. With the rat one could set the stage, could control conditions and make them sufficiently rigorous to insure a clear-cut answer to a question; one could use large numbers of animals to eliminate the chance complication, and the results came quickly. Of course one had to be cautious in applying to man the results obtained with the rat—in the last analysis it was the baby that counted—but with a definite answer for the rat, it was not so difficult to determine its applicability for the child.

The use of the small laboratory animal was not original with Osborne and Mendel. It was merely a tool which suited their purpose. The same approach was being used by other workers in that field—a method that proved invaluable in the discovery and elucidation of those mysterious substances, the vitamins. There were two of those curious deficiency diseases known at the time: scurvy, the bane of sailors, now recognized in babies also, which could be cured by the addition of a minute amount of some factor present in orange juice; and beri-beri, a disease of the Orient, found among those whose diet was largely polished rice, and cured by the addition of rice polishings. They could be cured but not understood—not until help began to come from the experimental animal. A Dutchman, Eijkman, working in Java, had been the first to produce a deficiency disease in animals; he had produced typical beri-beri in the pigeon, had cured it with polishings of rice. He had provided a method by which the distribution of the vitamin in nature could be studied and by which its chemical nature was eventually to be revealed. Beri-beri was not an American problem and Eijkman's work created little stir in this country; but it came nearer home when in 1911 two Norwegians, Holst and Frölich, produced experimental scurvy in guinea-pigs, providing a means of studying that disease which was to be equally productive. Curiously enough, the third deficiency disease to be recognized was discovered in the experimental animal before it was known in man. E. V. McCollum, an agricultural chemist, who, like Osborne and Mendel, was feeding rats on purified diets, made the observation that on certain diets they developed sore eyes which could be cured by the inclusion of a small amount of certain animal fats in the diet. The rat disease, xerophthalmia, remained a laboratory curiosity until the time of the World War, when a shortage of fats in Northern Europe was followed by curious ulcers of the cornea in infants and young children. It was Bloch of Copenhagen who identified the new disease with the xerophthalmia of rats and applied the proper remedy. Other vitamins were to follow: it was only a few years later that an efficient team of workers in Baltimore, Park and Shipley from Howland's department, working with McCollum and Simmonds, carried out classical researches that brought rickets within the fold of the deficiency diseases, and identified a new accessory food factor, vitamin D, which would cure it. And the following decade gave birth to still more vitamins.

Holt did not join the growing army of animal experimenters, but he was greatly influenced by them. One finds him toward the end of the decade drawing the metabolism experiments to a close and pursuing the feeding experiment in the young human animal even with its obvious limitations. One finds him studying the growth of children in an institution whose diet was accurately known and making comparisons with other groups on a different dietary; searching for the ideal food requirements of children by a detailed analysis of the dietaries of a large series of outstandingly healthy children. The Holt-Fales standards that resulted from that study guided many a physician and health worker in later years. But above all he was conscious of the fact that the newer knowledge of nutrition was slow in being appreciated, in being applied.

To those who live in an age when vitamins accost the eye on the pages of magazines and daily papers or from the walls of trolley cars, when they are wafted over the air between the strains of symphony concerts and jazz, it may seem difficult to believe that there was a period when these dramatic discoveries went almost unheeded, but such was the case. Osborne and Mendel complained bitterly that the pediatricians, that group in the medical profession that should be most interested in following their work, paid no attention to them, that with the exception of Holt and Howland no physicians wrote for their reprints, corresponded with them, or came to see them. Perhaps it was this goad which sank home, perhaps it was unnecessary with one who had the instincts of the teacher so deeply ingrained. At any rate one finds him at this time writing, speaking before pediatric groups on the practical applications of the vitamin studies in nutrition, giving a comprehensive review of the subject in the Lane lectures at San Francisco and expanding them in the form of a new book—*Food, Health and Growth*. The period required for the dissemination of the new work was a surprisingly short one.

If there were new fields opening with the years, they took none of the greenness of the old. There was always the new patient whose problem was a challenge to the practitioner, the new class of students to stimulate the teacher, and the hospital with its manifold clinical problems and the ideas engendered by them could never be less than a fascinating place. The story of the Babies' Hospital of that decade would not be complete without mention of the part it played in the solution of one clinical problem, that of pyloric stenosis.

Congenital hypertrophic stenosis of the pylorus—to give it its full name—was a rather rare condition manifesting itself shortly after birth, in which a knot of contracted muscle prevented the food from leaving the stomach, with rather disastrous results. It had been described a century before; it kept turning up occasionally in the post-mortem room, but was regarded as one of those rare curiosities about which nothing could be done. It was generally ignored in textbooks and in the contemporary pediatric literature. But early in the new century it had attracted the attention of that canny

Scotch observer, John Thomson. Thomson had defined the clinical picture of the condition, had written a classical description of the symptoms: the characteristic projectile type of vomiting, the small hard lump which could be felt in the upper abdomen, the waves crossing the abdomen from left to right which could readily be seen with the proper lighting. Probably Holt had read Thomson's papers, and there can hardly be any doubt that when he visited Edinburgh in 1908, they discussed pyloric stenosis. At any rate, the staff of the Babies' Hospital became acutely conscious of the condition, and it became recognized with increasing frequency. To recognize it, however, was not to cure it. The mortality was very high, and the surgical procedures available in those days were long and were poorly tolerated by new-born infants. But better days were soon to come. An infinitely simpler operation was developed. Like so many other ideas, the Fredet-Rammstedt operation was born in France and developed in Germany, but it worked and worked like a charm. The surgeons of the Babies' Hospital—Dr. William A. Downes and Dr. Richard Bolling—were among the first to try out the new operation in this country. The results were dramatic—babies at death's door restored to perfect health within a few weeks. They were presented at medical meetings—the technic and results of the operation, the equally important post-operative medical care—and before long the Babies' Hospital established a reputation for the treatment of these "pylorics"; in they flowed from all over the city, from Long Island, New Jersey, upstate New York, and New England. A condition that a few years ago had been a rarity now filled the infants' wards. The two surgeons now had an experience of several hundred cases apiece back of them; the operation which at first had required half an hour could now be done in seven minutes; the experience in the medical care was helped by the swelling numbers, and as a result the mortality came down, down, down, until from more than 50 per cent it was reduced to something like 4 per cent. The pyloric babies were the Babies' Hospital pride, a pride that was not confined to the medical staff but was shared by the nurses, the nurse-maids, the superintendent, the telephone operator. They were all a part of it. There was an *esprit de corps* that is possible only in a small institution. They all knew the symptoms of the disease— the Women's Board of Managers knew them well. Even the elevator man knew them. On his vacation in Atlantic City, he noticed in a side street a baby on a porch vomiting in a projectile manner. He immediately went up and told the mother: "Mother, your baby has pyloric stenosis. Take the next train to New York and take him right to the Babies' Hospital if you want him to get well. I'm only the elevator man but I know." The advice was heeded in part only. The baby was taken to a Philadelphia Hospital, but the diagnosis proved correct.

The mortality from that disease had been tremendously decreased. It had been more than decimated, but it could not be obliterated entirely. However, there were very few mothers now who could write to Dr. Holt:

You will remember me as the mother of the poor little stenosis baby who made such a gallant fight for her little life at the Babies' Hospital last May. Ever since that tragic time I have wanted you to know that her father and I did appreciate your interest in her and your great kindness to us. The bigness of your sympathy and the wisdom of your counsel were a source of strength and comfort to us then, and have been ever since. I was unwilling, however, to write you until I could say that I had got hold of myself again, and was able to go about my life's duties in such a spirit as you would approve.

XVII

CHILDREN OF TO-MORROW

DR. HOLT had been deeply stirred by the World War from its beginning. The entry of the United States into the conflict in 1917 found him, perhaps for the first time in his life, resenting his sixty-two years, as one by one the younger men about him went into the service. The spirit that was sweeping the country had caught him, too, but the opportunity to serve was not to come in the form of a commission as medical officer.*

When the figures for the selective draft of 1917 began to come in, it was found that an appallingly large number of men—nearly one third of those examined—were physically unfit for service. The causes were numerous: defects of various kinds, chronic diseases often unsuspected by the subject himself, but beyond all expectation was the frequency of rejections for underheight and underweight. Perhaps the health of the nation had deteriorated since the days of the hardy pioneer; perhaps the physically unfit had always been there to sink or swim as best they could, overlooked by the historian. Certainly the nation had never been combed over with such a fine-tooth comb before. How-

---

* He was offered a major's commission in the medical corps, but declined it.

ever that might be, that large proportion of the physically unfit was not pleasant to contemplate either in time of war or peace, and it set many people thinking what could be done to remedy it.

There was one obvious approach. There was no doubt that the roots of many of these disorders lay in childhood and adolescence; the possibility of recognizing them then and correcting them before it was too late lay open. There was no accurate information as to the health of the nation's school children. School health examinations were sporadic and, as a rule, superficial. The infant, and the child in industry, had been for some years matters of public concern, engaging the attention of both private and governmental agencies, but the school child as a public health problem had not yet been conceived of. That was a fruit of the United States' entry into the World War.

In the autumn of 1917 the Association for Improving the Condition of the Poor conducted a survey of the health of public school children in New York City. Some 170,000 children were given physical examinations, with the finding that approximately one child in five was suffering from a serious degree of malnutrition. This state of affairs was not confined to New York. Similiar conditions were found in other cities, nor did rural districts make an appreciably better showing. Stimulated by the A.I.C.P. survey a group of seven New York pediatricians * formed a "Committee of War Time Problems in Childhood" of the New York Academy of Medicine. There was no indication at that

* H. D. Chapin, R. H. Dennett, S. V. Haas, R. S. Haynes, L. E. Holt, C. H. Smith, H. B. Wilcox.

time as to how long the war would last—it might be for another four or five years or even longer. These individuals felt that their most patriotic contribution would be in an effort to conserve the future man power of the country by a concerted drive to improve the health of school children. The means discussed were three: (1) adequate physical examinations; (2) adequate school lunches; and (3) education of the child himself in matters of food and health. It was decided to make a trial of these on a small scale. With the cooperation of the A.I.C.P. and the People's Institute a "Food Scout Demonstration" was carried out in Public School 40. The results were most encouraging; they showed that with the proper technic the problem could be met. The New York experiment stirred up interest elsewhere. In February, 1918, Commissioner Caxton, the Federal Commissioner of Education, called a conference in Atlantic City "to consider ways of establishing health and health habits as part of the education of school children." Franklin K. Lane, then Secretary of the Interior, became interested, and conferred with the New York group. It was his suggestion that the Committee on War Time Problems be replaced by a national organization consisting of physicians, educators, social workers and public spirited men and women from various parts of the country to carry on a campaign that would bring to all the country's school children the results that had been achieved in Public School 40. The suggestion was approved. On March 5, 1918, Dr. Holt received a letter from a subcommittee empowered to act on it. In speaking of the proposal to organize such a national committee it stated:

It has seemed to us that this end may best be accomplished by the appointment of a chairman with free powers to organize his own associates. We also feel that there is no one who possesses, with the capabilities for filling the national chairmanship, the respect and esteem of everyone throughout the land, in all walks of life, as do you. Therefore with the utmost earnestness we urge you to accept the position and do appoint you to it, according to the powers conferred upon us. . . .

Whatever coöperation and assistance we or the members of the committee as a whole can render you is yours to demand.

We are, very sincerely,
Roger H. Dennett
Herbert B. Wilcox
Royal S. Haynes

Dr. Holt did not accept the position at once. He hesitated to assume a new responsibility of such magnitude. With an active medical practice, teaching, research, hospital work and other medical ventures he was more than an ordinarily busy man. However, these things would sooner or later have to be turned over to others. He had carried pediatrics through the descriptive stage; the advance was now fast becoming the province of the laboratory, where younger men with better training than he in the fundamental sciences could take the lead. The new project made a great appeal. It seemed so well worth while. The field was almost virgin territory, and it was true that he could give it what younger men couldn't. After a week of hesitation he accepted the post, and for the next four and a half years of his life he gave the Child Health Organization the best that he had to give.

It sprang into being almost overnight. A night letter stating the objectives of the proposed campaign and containing an invitation to join the National Committee was sent out to various prominent people who might be interested in the venture: Ex-President Theodore Roosevelt, Charles W. Eliot, John Dewey, John Spargo, Dr. William H. Welch, Dr. Simon Flexner, Dr. Hermann Biggs, Dr. Thomas D. Wood, Dr. Victor Heiser, John Finley, William Wirt, Felix Warburg, Ray Lyman Wilbur, Owen Lovejoy, Samuel McC. Lindsay and a number of others. The response was immediate. Some lent their names, and others offered and gave freely their time and advice. The National Committee met soon afterward and the organization got under way.

How was the task to be accomplished? Propaganda to educate parents and even children themselves had already been tried extensively. There were numerous schools with medical inspections, with courses in physiology and hygiene, physical education, and domestic science; yet these measures had failed. The attempts at parental education were too often in conflict with lifelong inherited prejudices on bringing up children. The medical examinations were usually cursory, attention being focused on contagious diseases and physical defects rather than on malnutrition and what might lie back of it. The teaching of physiology and hygiene—limited almost entirely to older children—was textbook teaching of the driest sort; it was unrelated to the child's daily life and made no appeal. Domestic science courses were concerned with the technic of cooking rather than with what or how to eat, and as for physical education, the emphasis was all on athletic prowess for the few rather than health for the many. The Child Health Organization decided to strike at the heart of the problem: to advertise child health by appealing to the child himself. If the children themselves could be effectively reached, the interest of teachers and parents would soon follow. But if the appeal was to be effective, new means would have to be employed, and the best that human ingenuity and talent could devise were needed.

As so often happens, the occasion brought out the talent. The story of the Child Health Organization would be most incomplete without mention of two women who had a large share in contributing to its success—Miss Sally Lucas Jean, its director, and Mrs. Frederick Peterson, its oft-time hostess, in whose house it took form. Miss Jean brought to the organization a mind that never tired of devising new and original ways of interesting children, with an unerring instinct for their psychology. Mrs. Peterson shared with her an enthusiasm that was contagious. She, too, had a genius for originality in methods of appeal, and the gift of writing verses that were to carry the truths of health to young minds far and wide. Of course there were others, too.

The younger children were perhaps the more difficult to reach. On them didactic instruction would be entirely wasted. Health had to be made a game or introduced as a diversion. Comic characters were found to be very effective here, and the C.H.O. developed several of them. There was "Cho-Cho," a professional clown who would intersperse his feats and drolleries with suggestions about proper food, sleep, and fresh air. There was the "Health Fairy," a nurse in disguise, who told fairy stories to children in which the principles of health were in the background. There were also a magician and a ventriloquist who, after capturing their young audiences, could drive home a few truths about how to be healthy. The technic of impressing the young has survived in the familiar "Popeye" of our own day, but it was new then. The comic characters toured the country, visiting schools, exhibitions, county fairs—any place where children were gathered together, and their success was phenomenal. Among other exhibits developed was the "Healthland Flyer," a model railway carrying passengers and stopping at such suggestive stations as "Milkville," "Toothbrush Junction," etc. Before riding on this each child was required to be weighed and measured and was told whether he was up to normal weight or not. With the exhibits and characters went literature—posters, nursery rhymes and jingles—to supplement and keep alive the interest in health. It was attractive literature, well written and illustrated, so good that it couldn't be thrown away. There was "Cho-Cho's" alphabet written by Mrs. Peterson, which began:

> A is for Apples and also for Air
> Children need both and we have them to spare.

It hit the spot and had to be reprinted again and again. One insurance company distributed a million copies, and it was translated into French by request.

For slightly older children different methods of appeal were employed. The school was used as a medium for reaching them, and the desire for organization and the spirit of competition were made use of. Health clubs were organized requiring the performance of health "chores" and with periodic inspections; their constitution was a document prepared by the C.H.O. called the "Rules of the Game"—a few simple maxims on what is a desirable regimen in the way of eating, sleeping, cleanliness, and personal hygiene. Probably the most successful method used at this age was the height-weight competition conducted by the school itself, with rewards for the greatest gain or improvement. With a skilful teacher it was not difficult to make health "the thing," and once this state of mind was attained it was easy to gain the coöperation of the unfortunates who were below par physically and who were as a rule only too eager to emulate their fellows.

Children in the higher grades were quite capable of understanding most of the problems of public health—the necessity for quarantine against contagious diseases, for vaccination, for a pure water supply, proper sewage disposal, etc. But the aim of the C.H.O. was to get away from the didactic course in hygiene, and to present the information in an incidental and interesting way. Why could not many of these subjects be introduced as stories? What could be more thrilling than the story of the conquest of yellow fever or malaria? Were not the heroes of medicine—Harvey, Jenner, Lister, Pasteur, Walter Reed—of as great importance to the world as the political and military leaders whose doings fill history books? In connection with the building of the Panama Canal was it not interesting to know that the Americans succeeded where the French had failed because General Gorgas knew how to protect the workers against the mosquito? Matters of public health could be used as subjects for debate, or for English composition; they could be brought into courses of history. Competitions for health posters and health plays could be introduced into courses in drawing and dramatics. And why not in mathematics, too? Could not the traditional A, B and C of the arithmetical or algebraic problem be employed as profitably in calculating the relative cost to a community of improving its water supply and the alternative, the cost of a typhoid epidemic, as in some of the varied economic ventures in which this historic trio had always delighted? The ways in which older children could be given a proper background of health information seemed endless. In time the results would tell, for these children would be the voters of to-morrow.

Of course the C.H.O. could not carry out these measures on a large scale. But it could stage demonstrations in enlightened schools, showing what could be done with proper methods of attack. It could stage conferences of educators at which these newer methods were described and discussed, and by indirect methods create a demand for its goods among educators. The results were not long in coming. From all parts of the country came demands for "Cho-Cho," for posters, for literature. Letters and personal visits from school teachers and principals who wanted to learn the best ways of appealing to their pupils began to swamp the office.

From forty-nine foreign countries came requests for advice and information. Many things were easier when people came to them for advice. One could not go to an unknown school and say to them: "You must have better physical examinations for your children." But when the principal came asking for help, it was easy to point out what had been accomplished by school X through adequate physical examinations.

Although the children themselves and the school teachers were the C.H.O.'s chief target, the public at large was not neglected. Editorials describing the child health movement began to appear in various newspapers; probably few of the readers realized that they were stimulated by the organization itself. None of the tools of modern publicity was neglected in this campaign to sell health to the country as patriotism and Liberty Bonds had been sold during the war. The magazine article presented a problem. An article by a physician, particularly a well known physician, would be far more effective than one from a professional writer, but could it be done without incurring the criticism of self-advertising? Dr. Holt decided that it could be done, but not by himself alone. A group of fifteen or twenty pediatricians was organized, each one of whom wrote a popular article for the *Delineator* on some aspect of health or disease in childhood. Not a word of criticism was forthcoming.

But the path of achievement was never free from thorns. Money had to be raised for all these undertakings; it had to be done entirely on the strength of ideas, before tangible results could be shown, and it had to be done almost entirely by the responsible head of the organization. The enthusiastic producers of new ideas often produced them faster than the growth of the budget. To curb impatience and keep the organization on a sound financial basis was a painful necessity.

To Miss Jean he wrote:

August 24, 1918

I have been much concerned since my visit to New York about the finances of the C.H.O.

As you are aware, with funds in hand and in sight, at our present rate of expenditure our money will be used up in two or three months and I am loath to make plans for the future without a better basis of support than is now in sight.

During the last few days I have signed and mailed about forty letters to various rich men who are philanthropically inclined.

These letters were prepared in the office and were very strong ones, and will bring results if any appeal for our work will. But until we do get more money it is folly to make arrangements with Washington, which will involve an enlarged staff, new responsibilities and greatly increased expenses.

To begin and be obliged to quit after three months is a situation not pleasant to contemplate.

Our publicity has been so good that we have created a demand for our goods that we cannot by any possibility begin to supply. My experience in life has taught me that it is not difficult to secure a wide market for things that are given away whether this be literature or advice.

It is because I am so deeply interested in the work of the C.H.O. that I do not want it to be a Jonah's Gourd. But we must cut our garment according to our cloth, and keep our expenses within our income. Not to do this is to court disaster.

. . . .

There were other troubles, too. Secretary Lane had promised support on many occasions, had promised that the Department of the Interior would print and distribute the C.H.O. literature. It was done eventually, but there were delays that seemed interminable. "I fear," Dr. Holt wrote to Miss Jean, "that he forgets about us the moment we leave his office."

Even such an estimable character as "Cho-Cho" gave trouble. Warming to what he felt was the most worthwhile effort of his life, he began to grow in self esteem, and discarding his carefully learned lines he began to improvise, regarding himself as a real authority on diet, hygiene, and even the morals of childhood. Eventually a new "Cho-Cho" had to be found.

On one occasion an affiliated committee got out of hand. A nucleus of opposition to the publicity program had developed, and at a meeting from which Dr. Holt was absent it became vocal. It was the feeling that the organization was going in for froth rather than substance. Some of Miss Jean's pet proposals were in danger of being voted down. In despair she telephoned Dr. Holt that he must come down at once. He came and presented the matter in a somewhat different light. The publicity measures—the clowns, prestidigitators and nursery rhymes—were only the brass band. The real objectives of the organization had by no means been lost sight of, and the more substantial if less dramatic part of the program was going forward in an orderly fashion. The interest aroused in health education was being followed up, and steps were being taken to supply the demand for this new commodity. The C.H.O. literature was helping school authorities to extract funds from recalcitrant politicians for better school lunches, for better physical examinations, for better health teaching. The demand for better health teachers, too, was being met. Teachers College had been induced to offer a course in health teaching, the first of its kind; other universities were following suit; prizes and scholarships for initiative in that field were offered by the C.H.O. The day was carried, and the committee worked in harmony thereafter.

There was the problem of contributions from commercial interests. Once an association of milk dealers sent a contribution "in payment of work done by your association in advertising milk." A somewhat pungent reply was drawn up and submitted to Dr. Holt.

It really seems to me [he commented] that you have been almost too stiff in your letter to the treasurer. Our position has been made quite clear in the early correspondence, and I think it would be a serious mistake to quibble over the wording of their letter. We know that they are actuated by motives of self-interest only, and I have no doubt they charge their contribution up to advertising expenses, which from their point of view it really is. I am not one of those who look upon such contributions as "tainted money." We have assumed no obligations to them; that has already been made quite clear. We are only incidentally helping their business, but they are far-sighted enough to recognize this. We have their good will and coöperation.

I would hesitate to jeopardize either by taking a position which would seem to impugn their motives. I think it is best to let the matter pass.

. . . .

The C.H.O. weathered its problems and went on its way, and the rapidity with which its message spread was astonishing. What were the factors responsible for its extraordinary success? They can easily be overlooked. Personal devotion to a cause and energy to follow it through are essential ingredients of success in any undertaking. A less obvious point which was borne in mind by the C.H.O. from the beginning was the policy of putting out nothing but the best in the way of literature and propaganda. Pains and expense were not spared to secure literary and artistic talent, for the children must be so fascinated and intrigued that they could not throw the rhymes and pictures into the scrap-basket. No literature was allowed to circulate until it had been submitted to the most rigorous criticism that pediatrician, nutrition expert, educator and professional advertiser could give it. Another point that should be stressed is that the C.H.O. for the four and a half years of its life remained a *small* organization. In spite of the national scope of its program and the national committee that stood back of it, the work was done by a very few people; one man could know it all and direct it all down to the smallest detail—and one man did. It was the type of organization which Dr. Holt found the readiest tool to work with. It was responsive to the helm: errors could be corrected and new ideas put into action without delays and without red tape. "What fun Holt is having with that new toy of his," was Dr. Welch's comment from Baltimore.

It was fun. His other activities were not dropped by any means, but there was no doubt that the child health movement came closest to his heart. All his personal influence was thrown into it. We find him making speeches to women's clubs, stressing the part that women were playing and could play in the movement; to students of hygiene and public health, showing how the education of the young would influence the health legislation of the future; to nurses, school principals and other groups.

The "one-man organization," however, had its weakness. It always needed the presence of the one leader to carry it along. Dr. Holt probably realized in 1922 that he would not be able to do so very much longer, and he sought for some younger man to whom to turn over the reins. There seemed to be no one available. The onerous task of raising money had devolved almost entirely upon him, and without a person of his prestige at the helm it seemed likely that the funds and the work would be seriously curtailed. Some more permanent solution would have to be found, and eventually was found.

The Association for the Study and Prevention of Infant Mortality which had been started in 1910 had continued to function. In an unobtrusive way it had played an important part in the movement to reduce maternal and infant mortality. It had been responsible for numerous mortality studies, had collected and stimulated others to collect accurate statistics, and by its meetings, literature and personnel service it had been an educational force, aiding communities and public health officials in solving their problems. It had inspired and guided many a "better babies" campaign. This organization, too, had felt the impress of the War. Dr. S. Josephine Baker, its president, had presented a strong report on "lessons from the draft," had been instrumental in extending its activities to include the school child and changing its name to the American Child Hygiene Association. The Association had had its financial problems to wrestle with, but an era of prosperity was dawning. After the war the American Red Cross had come to its aid with substantial contributions. In 1920 its diplomatic secretary, Dr. Philip Van Ingen, became aware that the American Relief Association, organized for the relief of the children of war-torn Europe, had completed its task abroad and yet had large unexpended funds; it was still under the control of Herbert Hoover, then Secretary of Commerce. Dr. Van Ingen succeeded in interesting Mr. Hoover in the American Child Hygiene Assocation; he was elected its president, and the A.R.A. funds thus became available for the benefit of American children. The American Child Hygiene Association seemed a safe home for the C.H.O. The ideals of both organizations and many of their objectives were the same. They had coöperated to prevent duplication of effort. Mr. Hoover had achieved a reputation as an administrator. His presence assured financial backing and he was interested in the C.H.O. with its newer methods of approach. Proposals of marriage were made, and in January, 1923, the two organizations were fused into the American Child Health Association with Mr. Hoover as its president. Dr. Holt remained as vice-president, but he served for a few months only before leaving for China in the autumn of 1923.

The new Association functioned for another twelve years, continuing the activities of its two predecessors. The work of promotion had been largely completed, and although efforts along this line were continued, the all-important task was that of educational guidance for schools. The word health became almost a drug on the market, and a more subtle literature was developed in which this word did not appear at all. The organization branched out into new fields: radio talks to educate the public, research in standards of measurement for children. Then came financial difficulties, the depression, and the end of the A.R.A. funds. It was finally dissolved in 1935.

The task was not completed by any means. There were plenty of underprivileged children, plenty who were neglected medically and whose education in the field of health was still deplorable, but the Association could nevertheless disband with pride, for the situation had greatly changed for the better. Others in great numbers had taken up the task. Many an agency to combat disease had come to appreciate that the child should be the center of its program. States and most large cities had established bureaus of child hygiene. And lastly a paternalistic federal government—to counterbalance many of its sins—could point with pride to the great increase in the appropriations and activities of its two unwedded agencies that had in large measure taken over the activities of the A.C.H.A. —the Child Hygiene Division of the Public Health

Service and the Children's Bureau of the Department of Labor.

Child health is now a recognized career—for physicians, for nurses, and for educators; it attracts about the same proportion of leaders, would-be leaders, followers, and well-intentioned obstructionists as does any other branch of human endeavor. But those who enjoy its benefits to-day should not forget their debt to the pioneers of the post-war years who did so much to put it on the map.

XVIII

CANNES, 1919

DOCTOR HOLT was to play a part in yet another public health enterprise which had its origin in the Great War. It was a bold enterprise, and it was destined to bear fruit, even if the fullest hopes for it were not to be realized.

The signing of the Armistice in 1918 found the Allied Nations equipped with efficient and highly developed Red Cross relief organizations. To Mr. Henry P. Davison, the man who had played the leading rôle in building up the war organization of the American Red Cross, the prospect of disbanding such agencies—altruistic in their endeavor and backed by popular support—seemed quite unthinkable. He sought for new fields of activity to which the Red Cross might devote itself in times of peace. What greater field was there for a humanitarian agency than that of public health? Mr. Davison conceived the plan of uniting the Red Cross organizations of the different nations into an international body, which could attack systematically the problems of public health.

It was a magnificent idea—the Red Cross as the human welfare department of the new world organization—and no time was lost in putting it into execution.

In February, 1919, there was formed in Paris a "Committee of Red Cross Societies" composed of representatives of the American, British, French, Italian, and Japanese organizations. Later on this Committee was to be transformed into the "League of Red Cross Societies," and the other nations were to be included.

An undertaking of such scope must have an intelligent and well thought out program. The best medical advice was needed to formulate it. In April, 1919, the Committee therefore called together at Cannes a conference of men outstanding in the fields of medical science and public health to formulate its program. It was a distinguished gathering—these fifty-odd delegates from America, from Britain and the Dominions, from France, Italy and Japan. It represented the fields of public health in which the Red Cross might be expected to engage. There were public health officers, pediatricians interested in child welfare, experts in tuberculosis, tropical diseases, public health nursing, etc., and representatives of the Red Cross. There were nineteen Americans in all, and probably the most distinguished of them was Dr. Holt's friend, William H. Welch, in his seventieth year, now director of the recently organized School of Hygiene and Public Health at Johns Hopkins. Among the others were Hermann M. Biggs, Health Commissioner of New York State; Richard P. Strong, director of the Harvard School of Tropical Medicine; and Edward R. Baldwin of the Trudeau Sanatorium representing tuberculosis. Child hygiene was represented by four delegates: Holt from New York, Hamill from Philadelphia, Talbot from

Boston, and Lucas from San Francisco. The Red Cross was represented by Livingston Farrand, director of the American organization.

The American delegation, with one or two exceptions, set sail from New York on the *Leviathan* early in March, 1919. The story of this trip comes out vividly in Dr. Holt's letters written to his wife:

S. S. Leviathan
March 16, 1919

I am going to write you a line a day—a sort of diary of our trip to send when we reach Brest.... I am glad you did not come, so far as comforts are concerned. No stewardesses, no hot water, and cold water only at limited hours are among the things in which transport ships differ from ordinary passenger vessels, but by no means all the differences. The *Leviathan* has been stripped of everything in the way of luxury to make her a Navy ship. The Navy men are very kind and impress us all with their intelligence and courtesy to their men under them. Very different from the discipline on German ships—but yet discipline is by no means lacking.

To our party of doctors Mr. Henry Morgenthau has been added; he is a special Red Cross delegate and will remain for the R. C. Congress to be held at Geneva when our Congress closes. It has been arranged, since we have so much to discuss, that we hold a business session every day from ten to twelve to get our ideas formulated and get a vision of the whole movement which is contemplated by the R. C., which is really nothing less than an international welfare work, affecting health, education and industrial conditions, and thus bringing the nations more closely together than could be done by any political agreement and association.

Last evening we met Secretary and Mrs. Daniels and had a long talk with them in the dining salon after which we were all invited to their apartments—the royal suite on the steamer—built I understand for the Kaiser. We found the Secretary very affable and Mrs. D. really quite delightful, a simple, natural, motherly individual without a particle of affectation and with a warm Southern manner. Altogether we were pleased with our first acquaintance. The Secretary does not strike me as a man of great ability but like an average Southerner of intelligence—not unlike Mr. J——....

March 17

Favorable weather continues.... More and more evidences as time goes on that we are on a transport, not a passenger ship. No such thing as a deck chair is to be found. We can walk at will, but there is no place to sit out even for an hour. The steward informs us the allowance of towels is two a week, reminding me of the Providence boarding house rules: towels changed Wednesday and Saturday....

Sunday service at 10:30 was interesting; the singing was good; the service conducted by the chaplain and a fifteen minute address by Secretary Daniels which was really good. I don't know but we shall get quite to admire him—at least we have come to respect him....

An interesting evening in the smoking room when Mr. Morgenthau told us all of his experiences in Constantinople with the German ambassador, Wangenheim, giving a great many details not contained in his book.... Their [the Germans'] treachery and villainy seems almost beyond belief....

A two hour session discussing the Red Cross mission.... The discussions are most interesting and are participated in by all, though Dr. Welch and H. M. do most of the talking. Still Dr. Biggs and I do now and then get a chance for a word. The others have little to say as yet. We are really having a very good time and I am beginning to get used to my hard bed and sleep better.... As we come to study the work projected by the Red Cross on an international scale, the more clearly does it appear that such an organization with a purpose truly altruistic may accomplish far more to bring the different nations to an understanding and a sympathy with each other than a league of nations which is purely political and whose final decisions I fear will satisfy nobody. Mr. M. quoted Mr. Wilson as believing that such a league would not endure more than twenty years.... We find our problem opening up a great many questions of world-wide interest. I hope we may be able to contribute even a little toward the solution of some of them. By the time we reach Cannes we shall by discussion have at least clarified our own vision very much.

March 21

So many activities yesterday I did not get time to write. We are now having two sessions a day which consume about three hours in all and require no little preparation in the way of material for discussion.... Mrs. Daniels invited us to tea two days ago and both she and Josephus improve steadily on acquaintance. They were anxious to know something of the work we were doing and asked us to hold our morning session in their apartments.... Our topic at this session was the Child Welfare program upon which Hamill and I have been working hard for two days past. All seemed much impressed with the presentation, which, however, did not satisfy me. Dr. Welch thought we made such a strong statement that this would doubtless be one of the first pieces of work to be undertaken by the Red Cross, if they finally decide to enter the broad field of public health work.

I exhibited some of our Child Health literature in which the others were much interested and I presented Mrs. Daniels with an autographed copy of the Alphabet which she admired very much. You may tell Mrs. Peterson when you see her....

I never saw time pass so rapidly on shipboard as during this trip. We really have no time at all for just enjoyment except at meals. We have a square table for eight; Dr. Welch and Mr. M. face each other, I am next, then Drs. Biggs and Baldwin; next to Mr. M. sits Col. Russell, then Hamill and Talbot. I have never seen Dr. Welch more entertaining and he and Mr. M. are both full of stories. Besides this we have much serious talk—political and otherwise. The Secretary likes to stop at our table on his way from the dining saloon —and chat.... He certainly grows upon us, and he is a much more able man than I gave him credit for being.

March 22

Well, I have bought a fountain pen—not a good one you see, but it may serve the purpose to write my diary letter. I am afraid the details of our trip may not be as interesting to you to read as they have been to me to write.... Yesterday the announcement came at dinner that a general meeting was to be held that evening in the dining saloon. Besides the Secretary, members of the medical commission were to be heard from; Mr. Morgenthau said that Dr. Welch, Dr. Biggs and I were scheduled to speak. I had but a few minutes to collect my thoughts before the meeting was to begin. Captain Phelps presided and after the Secretary made some general remarks Dr. Welch told in twenty minutes what the medical men had done in the War in camp at home and abroad. Dr. Biggs spoke upon the economic importance of public health work and the necessity for it now in the countries which had suffered most.

I discarded my notes entirely... and talked for fifteen minutes regarding the importance of Child Welfare work and some of the plans which were being outlined if this was to be taken up by the Red Cross. Dr. Hamill, a prejudiced listener, I am sure, was kind enough to say that I made the best talk of the three. I did not agree with him. It was hard to follow men like the others but the audience was attentive and many afterwards professed themselves much interested and impressed. On the whole I had reason not to be ashamed of my effort and think as so often happens an extempore affair is much better than one for which too much preparation has been made....

My address last night brought in the usual number of greetings from members of the crew, officers, passengers and Y.M.C.A. workers whose children have been brought up on "the book." I am afraid I shall never be able to get away from it, but would like to be remembered for something more....

I have just read over this letter and find that it contains considerable matter that is repeated. So I fear it will require considerable editing before publication, i.e. being read to the rest of the family. But I hope it contains enough of detail for you to get an idea of how we have passed our week. But it does not tell how much I miss you all and how glad I shall be to be back home again....

Just now we are entering the port of Brest which on a sunny day would be a glorious sight, swarming as it is with transports, battleships and smaller craft of every description. We are sorry to disembark ... certainly it has been one of the pleasantest of voyages ... lacking only the presence of the family to make it perfect.

Paris, March 24, 1919

Well here we are in Paris most comfortably even luxuriously housed at the Hotel Wagram.... Mr. Morgenthau's knowledge of the ways of European travel, the magic word "Ambassador's party," and the influence of the Red Cross united in securing for us the best accommodations to be had en route from Brest. It's great to travel here and be looked after. Mr. M. arranged everything for our departure and everything here was prepared by Red Cross officials. I never saw Paris look so dismal as on our arrival early this morning. The rain was pouring, it was cold and decidedly unattractive, but things look better now we have breakfasted.... It seems about time I should be getting letters from home but I realize I must wait several days.

March 28th

So much has taken place since I wrote last that I fear I shall not be able to record it all.... We had our first interview with Mr. Davison yesterday and another this afternoon from which we have just returned. We find that his conception of the work to be undertaken by an international Red Cross differs in some very important respects from our own as formulated on board ship. The final decision will doubtless be a program different from both and better than either.

We all dine with him to-night at his hotel and continue our discussion as we wish to get our own program fully worked out before meeting the other groups at Cannes....

Mr. Morgenthau has been out all the morning and brings us the latest news from the Peace Conference. He had a long talk with Col. House, Henry White, Hoover and others, and has even seen Mr. Wilson. Things at the moment are in a very critical condition, and as Mr. M. said, they are all fairly quaking in their boots as to what may happen. It is expected, however, that a couple of weeks will clear things up and that all will come right. At least that is their hope. France is obdurate for reparations. Germany is literally starving. The whole east is ready to burst into a flame of revolution and no one really knows what change in the destinies of the world may be brought about by the events of even a few days. Food and transportation facilities are what are lacking most just now. A picture of the situation in Germany has just been shown us by Welch in a report given him by his nephew obtained from two officials just returned from Germany. I will write this on a separate sheet. It should be regarded as confidential....

Report on Conditions in Germany

The Boche is a savage in victory, a sycophant in defeat, a disgusting boot-licking crawler. There is not a spark of morality or character left in this generation. From being over-disciplined they have reacted to extreme license. Dissipation is rife in the big cities, drinking, dancing, etc. The poor are starving, the rich are hoarding food.

The Germans attribute all their trouble to Pres.

Wilson and to America entering the War. Great bitterness is shown everywhere. Last month the feeling reached a white heat. Women of the better (?) classes jam you in the ribs muttering "Verdammte Amerikaner."

The Kaiser whom they expected to lead his army and die fighting at its head is despised for deserting the cause, the army, the people and even his sick wife. Ludendorf barely escaped a mob by fleeing to Sweden and is now in hiding. Hindenburg is the only one who had the courage to face defeat and is still trusted.

Bernstorff is now in charge of American affairs at the Foreign office, but the American commissioners refuse to meet him officially or speak to him.

At Hotel Adlon, the American headquarters in Berlin, are 100 of our men occupying the second floor under the protection of the Ebert government. There are machine guns manned day and night on all the other floors of the hotel and at many of the windows. Machine gun fights in the street are of constant occurrence and one must be watchful. The Spartacists are increasing rapidly in numbers. The people are against Ebert and more loyal to the old régime. The present government must fall and a more radical one replace it. Germany encouraged Bolshevism up to the time of the Armistice thinking it would jump Germany into France and Italy; now they see their mistake. Though officials admit their army must have surrendered in three weeks, the people still claim the army unbeaten.

Germany is now preparing an elaborate Bill of Claims against the Allies, tabulating everything—loss of life, of arms, legs, fingers and wounds; also injuries to the health of the population; lowered birth rate—all these in Germany and adjacent countries of the Central Powers. These latter are laid up against the

British blockade of foodstuffs and to *their* prolonging the war and putting Germany in her present economic condition. They claim now that to return in materials and machinery what they stole from France, Poland, Belgium and Serbia would cripple their own business recovery. (Can one conceive such reasoning?) On every side is evident the absolute lack of character and the moral degeneracy of the people. Conditions are now chaotic. In Berlin men prefer idleness to work; one out of employment because of cessation of the war get 8 marks a day; hence why work except for exorbitant wages?

Prices of everything are soaring out of sight. One portion of chicken costs 200 marks; one suit of clothes 1000 marks. Even the rich mothers say they cannot get food for their children. There is no nickel, leather or rubber left in Germany. The few taxis left run on steel tires. A headwaiter who was given half a cake of soap showed his gratitude by bringing a beautiful inlaid cabinet the next day.

The Bavarians are better off—the Spartacists are in general control. They seize all the food and clothing which they then distribute only to those who will join them, hence they recruit rapidly.

The overthrow of the Ebert government is predicted in sixty days unless food reaches Germany in quantity.

. . . . .

March 26

Mr. Davison's dinner at the Tour d'Argent, one of the old French restaurants with a history going back more than a century, was a great success. In a room smaller than our dining room we had a long table for twenty-one placed cornerwise to get into the room. It was most intimate and it was with an undertone of real religious fervor that the present chaotic condition of the world was viewed, and plans discussed for relief on an international scale. Mr. Davison's own interest and one might almost say consecration to the cause is surprising. He is a big man—that was already known—in affairs, but he is a big soul as well, and the group of men he has gathered about him here at Paris headquarters is of a quality that makes one proud of his fellow countrymen. Mr. Olds of St. Paul, one of the most prominent lawyers in the northwest, Mr. Cutter and Mr. Burr, bankers and business men in New York, are types—all have given up large affairs at home to come here and work for nothing but love. I take off my hat to the foreign organization of the Red Cross.... One wonders what the ultimate effect will be on the men who have given up things of great importance to come here and do relief work. The general impression seems to be that many of them will never be satisfied to go back to the old game of making money, having had a taste of a deeper joy and a larger satisfaction. Some of them talk quite freely on this subject. They have had a vision of greater interest and greater usefulness and will not be content to take up the old life again.... I won't say more of their work here lest I may be accused of being enthusiastic, and that would never do after what I have thought and said regarding the Red Cross.

To-day we are to be shown some of the activities in the city outside the central office and will lunch at one of the canteens. To-morrow we pack up and leave for Cannes....

It is really great fun traveling and being taken care of—a new experience for me.... Must close to catch the mail steamer. I am feeling very well; food plenty and excellent.

Cannes, March 29, 1919

I wish you might look over my shoulder as I am writing and see the glorious view which my window offers. A bright morning, clear sky, warm sunshine with the blue Mediterranean lying directly in front and not one hundred yards away the bay of Cannes flanked on either side by mountains which extend quite to the sea—such the picture you would get. The bay has many small boats, some with dark red sails like those we used to see at Sainte Marguerite. The contrast of this scene with Paris—cold, rainy, bleak and cloudy—makes it seem like a different world, and already our spirits rise with the change of surroundings.

... We are luxuriously housed at the Carlton, the best hotel in the place. Hamill and I who still stick together have a suite of rooms furnished in the French style with big windows facing the sea.... We get on admirably as roommates. He is most orderly and always considerate.... Our formal conferences do not begin until April 1st, so we have been allowed two days' holiday by Mr. Davison who came down with us.

March 30

I was interrupted in my letter by a telephone call from the office stating that we were to be ready in fifteen minutes for a motor trip.... The Red Cross has a number of motor cars here and we filled three of them and started for Nice and Monte Carlo. We went on the upper Corniche and returned by the lower road. It was hardly recognizable as the same drive we took in 1912 on that cold cloudy rainy day. Our trip was perfect and such views of the sea, the snow-capped mountains, the nearer hills and the beautiful villas, I never expect to see again.

The Davisons have a villa here and Mrs. D. and

the boy who was injured in the aeroplane accident are spending the season. I went in the car with Mrs. D. who you may remember is Mrs. Gibney's cousin and suggests her in many little ways. She is most interesting and I enjoyed the day very much.

We had lunch at the hotel at Monte Carlo opposite the Casino and then all except the two who were in uniform (Drs. Strong and Russell) went in to watch the play for half an hour. To me it was a pathetic sight, fully half of those at the tables were women, a number of them in mourning, and several looked over 65 years old. Few if any looked to be of the wealthy leisure class who were playing for fun, but for all it seemed so serious, so earnest as to be very depressing.

We faced a strong wind on our return ride, so it was well we had plenty of wraps.... I was put in a closed car and felt I had almost the best place in the party.... I have not yet become accustomed to having special concessions made to me because of years and my gray hair, but I suppose I might as well....

The women's fashions here and in Paris are much more extreme than in New York where they were certainly bad enough. The dresses of the fashionable barely come below the knee and would be quite appropriate for bathing suits....

Have just come in from a long chat with Leonard McAneny. He hopes to get home this month, I wish I might too. Travel is interesting, mighty interesting just now, but I begin to long for a few days of quiet at Pleasantville where I fancy you must be at this minute. I am sure I was never cut out for public life; there are no charms for me like those of home....

I will close this now and send it on tonight. Am feeling fine—no colds, no indigestion....

>   Cannes, April 2, 1919

So much has happened in the last two days that there has been very little time or opportunity for writing.

When the Conference organized yesterday Dr. Roux, head of the Pasteur Institute, was elected President, Dr. Machiafava of Rome, Vice-President, and I found myself slated for the office of general secretary of the whole show. This is hardly a sinecure when there are usually three meetings a day to attend, elaborate minutes to write during the sessions, which must later be copied by stenographers, translated into French, then manifolded and mimeographed so that each delegate may have a copy. I have a French and two English stenographers at my disposal as well as other assistants who lighten somewhat the labors of my position. But the duties keep me pretty busy as you may well imagine. I am indebted for this honor to Dr. Welch who has worked with me as secretary so long at the meetings of the Rockefeller Institute. Dr. W. is chairman of the Executive Council which runs the whole conference.

There are now in attendance some 50 delegates, 19 American and the rest about equally divided between the British, French and Italian. Only one Japanese has put in an appearance; he speaks French and so is able to keep in touch with the discussion. The foreigners are a fine bunch and comprise many of the most distinguished names in modern medicine. The meetings are most interesting as a study of national character as well as of individuals and medical science. They are held in French or English, and are translated into the other language by Dr. Rist. He does it admirably—often making a much better speech than the original one....

I find my French rather weak, but it begins to come back little by little. In a month under compulsion I think I could stumble along very tolerably.

At lunch to-day I sat with Mr. and Mrs. Morgenthau and one of the nursing delegates, the Comtesse Roussy de Sales, a woman with an English mother, a French father, born in New York but living in France for the past 25 years. It is hard to know what to call her she is so cosmopolitan, highly intelligent and with delightful manners. She is very high up in the French Red Cross and has had charge of a hospital with 2000 beds right behind the front. Our other table companion was Dr. Linsley Williams of New York, just back from several weeks with the army of occupation. The talk you may well imagine was interesting—even thrilling.

W. says the Germans are suffering badly for food; the poor starving. There is no clothing but old things made over, all new garments of paper; shoes with wooden soles and paper uppers; no woman allowed to possess more than two dresses, etc. They still believe that England brought on the war by coaxing Russia to begin it. They were told in December 1914 that their army was occupying Paris already. Most of them begin now to hate the Kaiser, but do not know whom to believe or to trust. They are a sorry lot. As for their resuming the war! there isn't a ghost of a chance of it. Economically they are simply down and out, and all the more intelligent ones are slowly coming to realize it. They have not in their hospitals rubber enough for drainage tubes, no gloves for operations, no hot water bags. Without soap for two years their linen has gone to pieces from being washed with other chemicals. The reporter who comes in for a day and sees only the few people fairly well dressed upon the streets and gets a fair meal (at enormous cost to be sure) at his hotel gets a poor and very faulty idea of things.

Williams and his men personally examined 2500 school children, measured and weighed them. Such a collection of things as they were wearing as clothing would amaze you. Well, enough of the Boche....

Events other than those of the conference there are none. Our only diversion is being photographed which happens several times almost every day. It's time to close and dress for dinner, so I must stop for now....

. . . .

The Conference was not without its tense moments. If the European members were caught unprepared with programs, the Americans were too well provided with them. Unaware of the plans being made on the voyage over, Mr. Davison had entrusted a certain Dr. S.— an American already in Paris—with the formulation of the official program for discussion. The result was a document containing, to be sure, many of the same ideas as the ship's program, but couched in most uninspiring language. Mr. Morgenthau had insisted that the ship's program should be a warm and inspiring document. Mr. Davison, however, felt that he could not gracefully decline to accept Dr. S.'s program, and the ship's program was consequently scrapped. It had, however, been shown privately to a few of the English delegates.

At the opening session no sooner was the official program read than one of the English delegates rose and requested that the program prepared on ship be also read. When this was done, another English delegate moved that this be made the official program of the Conference. The situation was embarrassing, but it was saved by Dr. Welch who suggested a committee to combine the best features of both programs. The final product was almost word for word the ship's program.

. . . .

Cannes, April 6

Three weeks yesterday since we sailed from Hoboken and as yet not a word; we are all getting hungry for home news; I myself am very hungry for some. I have finished a short letter to Emmett and have now a quiet hour on Sunday morning to talk with you all. The day is simply perfect; like our best days of early May in Pleasantville. The conference has no meetings to-day and the members have gone on a motor trip, but I decided to take advantage of their absence to write and read.

The beauties of Cannes grow upon me, but like all places at the sea it needs the bright sun to make it appear at its best. I wish you were here; a row or a sail on the quiet bay would appeal to you....

The conference goes on well and on the whole increases in interest as the days pass and the men get better acquainted. I like them all, especially the English delegates with whom naturally we have most in common. The French here are fine and the Italians especially fine.

We meet each morning at ten o'clock for a two hour session. I, as secretary, sit at the table with the President, the Vice-President and Mr. Davison.... The first thing is always the minutes of the previous day's meeting in which I have to summarize the discussion of that session. This is no easy matter, and it takes me after the session fully two hours to write out the reports which must then be typed and then put into French. The members have been kind enough to say that my minutes were good; but it takes time and effort to make them interesting. I find I can write better under pressure. Then comes lunch for which we are all ravenous as we get nothing but a roll and cup of coffee for breakfast.

In the afternoon I write my minutes while the others chat or walk. Then come section meetings at 3:30 or 4 and at 5 o'clock daily a meeting of the Executive Council at which I also must be present and whose minutes I must write up. They are fortunately not very long ones. Then a short walk, a nap if possible and dinner at eight o'clock. After coffee there are usually some committees or special conferences and those who have none may play a couple of rubbers of bridge. I am often of this group. We go to bed late and rise late. Such is our day and they are much alike, though filled with interesting discussions and experiences....

...We caught a Tartar yesterday in Dr. Pinard of Paris who at our section meeting insisted on talking all the time in most rapid French, gesticulating excitedly and quite broke up the meeting. In consequence we had to refer our report to a special group who worked until after midnight upon it. These French are funny; he was only in earnest, but seemed in a fury. He is quite an old man and we had to give him his say. Besides, he occupies a very important position in Paris and throughout France. Still these are minor annoyances and nothing in comparison to the pleasure one has in meeting some of the foreigners.

...Yesterday afternoon Biggs and I were invited

with Mr. Morgenthau to tea at Lady Waterlow's. Here we had a chance to meet some real royalty. The Duchesse de Vendôme, who is a sister of Albert, King of Belgium, Princesse de Bourbon, daughter of the Duke of Vendôme, Lady Burghcleve, and others. They were all most cordial in manner and we chatted most informally about everything. Albert's sister is a fine woman and looks very much like his picture. The Princess was seated next to me at tea and was interested in telling me of her two year old son of whom she is very proud. She looks like a handsome English girl of twenty-five. All the ladies were beautifully and very properly dressed—not at all in the prevailing extreme French style we see so much of at the hotel.

Lady W. was a Miss Hamilton of San Francisco, one of the rich families of the '49 group I guess. Her husband was Lord Mayor of London. She has been much in Royal society in London and Europe generally; was intimate with the Kaiser's sisters who had paid her long visits here at Cannes. Knew Wilhelm himself very well and told us lots of interesting gossip about the Hohenzollerns. Prince Henry, the Kaiser's brother made, you will remember, a tour of England in a motor in the early summer of 1914. Lady W. was with him on this trip. Now it is believed he came as a spy.... Well, I guess you have had enough of Lady W. and her place....

April 8

... The past two days have been really strenuous ones, but the Child Welfare report was made at this morning's session, and now that is off my mind. You may be interested in knowing something of how it was received. Drs. Biggs and Welch were good enough to say that it was the best report thus far presented and all the speakers praised it warmly. Sir Arthur Newsholme, the Chairman of the Section on Child Welfare, told the Conference it was really *my* report in which they all concurred most cordially. I read it to a crowded room—the largest attendance we have had at any session yet, and the interest in the subject was very great. I never expect again to address an audience so distinguished. Had you been there, I think perhaps you too might have been a little proud of your husband in such a renowned company. The whole thing seems to me quite absurd when I think of it, that I should be preparing and presenting a Child Welfare program which, to use the words of Ivy Lee, the publicity man of the Conference, "they will shoot out all over the world."

Well, some queer things have come to me in life; these things don't please my vanity. I think they rather make me feel humble and quite undeserving. To have been here at this Conference is something to be remembered as long as I shall live....

. . . .

The Cannes Conference closed on April 11th, although the secretary and a few others had to stay several days longer to "mop up" and get the reports in final shape. The two weeks had been strenuous ones, but the delegates had the satisfaction of accomplishing what the Conference had set out to do. Mr. Davison was more than pleased with the results. The international program for public health had been mapped out, and there remained only to put it into action.

And what was this program? An international Red Cross body, not to replace but to guide and develop the national societies. In its hands was the expert information compiled by the sections of the Cannes Conference—methods for the control of tuberculosis, malaria, venereal diseases, plans for developing public health nursing in different countries. The section on preventive medicine had outlined the share that governments should play in the promotion of public health: desirable health legislation and how to obtain it, the health organization of a state, methods of controlling epidemics, etc. In the Child Welfare report were to be found many of the ideas which activated the C.H.O., but the program was more comprehensive. It was a program of medical supervision by means of clinics, welfare stations, and visiting nurses, beginning in the prenatal period and carrying the child through school and the industrial hazards. And all along the line it was a program of education—of the parents, of the child himself and of legislators. Publicity was of course an essential for the entire Red Cross undertaking, and the publicity section of the Cannes Conference had made its plans for this.

In two particulars the Cannes policy deserves special comment. One was the stress on avoidance of too much organization machinery, which might impede action. Another was the realization that it would be unwise to attempt a rigid standardization of health enterprises in all countries. Customs and modes of thought were different. One could perhaps aim at certain standards, but one must proceed tactfully by developing the best in the way of tradition and custom which existed in any country.

Three weeks after the close of the Cannes Conference, the "League of Red Cross Societies" was formed in Geneva. And then came a real difficulty. A competent director had to be found. The post demanded a medical man with experience in public health administration. It demanded other attributes but above all a man of initiative. Upon this point depended the future of the whole project—whether the League was to become merely an international bulletin board or a creative force. The man was not to be found. Many of the Cannes delegates would have qualified admirably—several were in fact offered the position—but none were willing to leave their tasks and opportunities at home.

Before a suitable director could be found valuable time was lost, and in the meantime had come the fiasco of the United States and the League of Nations, and with it the idealism born of the war received its death blow. The doctors and the Red Cross officials did not quarrel as did the statesmen, but the psychological moment had been allowed to pass, and the enthusiasm for international coöperation was lost. But not entirely lost. The League of Red Cross Societies still survives and performs valuable, if little known functions. It maintains its international bulletin board where those who desire can obtain all information about methods of disaster relief, health education and health legislation, public health nursing, protection of immigrants, etc. Instead of five it recently numbered nearly sixty member nations, and it has started many Red Cross activities.

The Cannes Child Welfare program is not being "shot out all over the world," but it is still tacked to the board, and the education of the child has found expression in a new Red Cross development, the Junior Red Cross, which aims to develop in school children ideas of health and of doing for others at home and abroad. Letters and contributions of school children, manual and financial, go to needy children in other lands. All this is handled by the Red Cross League. Perhaps the League has not taken the initiative in public health as much as it was hoped it would. But its activity is steadily growing. Its ultimate future can not be foretold.

The fullest fruits of the Cannes Conference were, however, to grow from an offshoot of that gathering. While the doctors were working on their program on the sunny Riviera, the diplomats were busy in rainy Paris thrashing out the details of the Covenant of the League of Nations. Mr. Morgenthau was in constant touch with both groups and divided his time between them. The ideas that were debated out at Cannes thus found their way to Paris, and in the Covenant, the original draft of which had contained only a sentence or two about health, there was finally embodied the provision for the Health Organization of the League of Nations, much as it exists to-day. It is this organization which has led the way in handling the international public health problems. We owe it many things. For the first time in the world's history it is possible to obtain accurate information about disease in any country. A standard terminology in reporting diseases and deaths has been practically accomplished. An active intelligence service follows the spread of epidemics, and broadcasts this information speedily. It is now possible to pool international resources in curbing an epidemic which may be for the moment confined to a single country. A nation, no matter how low its finances, may by appealing to the League obtain medical talent—the best available—to solve some national problem, either in the form of a medical commission or in the coöperation of scientific research at home. The League commissions on malaria, smallpox, tuberculosis, the protection of women and children, opium, etc., have not solved these problems, but they have done much to eliminate the national barriers which impeded their solution. International coöperation, even among physicians, has been difficult at times in the past. A bureau to standardize methods of diagnosis, the potency of drugs, quarantine regulations and countless other matters, has been a great advance.

The stepchild has grown faster than the natural child. He has taken many of the latter's toys away from him, but perhaps after all there are some things which are better done by governments than by private agencies. The main thing is that there is no quarrel between the two organizations; they have been too well reared for that. They work side by side coöperating to the best of their ability, and perhaps the gentlemen of the Cannes Conference can feel in both of them a just pride.

XIX

REWARDS

DR. HOLT returned from Cannes in May, 1919. He was to have four more years in New York—active years. But his physical strength was not all that it had been; it had to be husbanded carefully. Up until now each year had brought new activities and interests, and inevitably increased burdens. The period for gradual retrenchment had come. The lithe figure no longer ran up-stairs to catch a bite of lunch and return to the office. The stairs had been replaced by an elevator, and the house which had been the Holt home for more than twenty-five years had given way to an apartment. Patients were seen now only three mornings a week. Diversions, too, had to be less strenuous. Golf was played but rarely, and the links could not be hilly ones. And the week-end retreat at Pleasantville was appreciated more than ever now.

(To his son Calvert)

Pleasantville, Feb. 21/20

MY DEAR CALVERT:
Picture us sitting here by the fire in the living room, Mother reading the paper, Bozo lying at my feet happy and contented but with an odor which indicates the need of a good soap and water bath.

We have just come in from a long tramp over the hills. The crust is so hard we can walk on it, tho the snow is from one to two feet deep on the level and shows no signs of melting as yet.

No autos have run here for over two weeks. We get two sleigh rides every week we come up and thankful that we still have other means of transportation than a gasoline car.

Just now we are expecting Uncle Ed who is coming up alone to spend the day and night with us and have a taste of the country in winter which he loves so much.

Your account of your work is most interesting. Certainly you will get a new view point of life which is a valuable thing for any one. You can also get a sympathy with the railroad worker and his job which could not be gained in any other way. Of course we would not want you to spend the rest of your days (and nights) in firing a locomotive, but it does please us that you have found that you can do it, and do it well too.

I have done a good deal of hard physical work in my day and I am thankful for the experience.

To achieve mastery over ourselves is really the most important thing to have gained in life, and when this is once done, all other conquests by comparison are easy.

Here comes the sleigh with Uncle Ed and so I will finish this.

Write us often if but a line.

With much love,
FATHER

14 West 55 Street, New York
March 10/20

MY DEAR CALVERT:

Your letter written in commemoration of my birthday was duly received and very much appreciated.

These recurring anniversaries do make me reflect upon the years and wonder if we have made the most out of them for ourselves and for the world. The world needs us all at this time when selfishness, graft and greed are so common and so *universal* I had almost said. It seems to me I never knew a time when *greed* was so rampant as it seems to be now, almost everywhere.

Some time I hope we in this country may wake up to the fact that he serves himself best who serves his fellow men best. Really that is the only thing which in the long run is really worth while.

It is to me a source of satisfaction to feel that I have done a little, but oh, so little compared with what remains for the generation to which you children belong to do. Things are changing very fast in these times and the wealthy privileged few are not going to have so rosy a path as they have had for the last forty or fifty years. Every one will have to do something to justify his existence.

You knew I presume that Emmett had got his appointment at the Presbyterian Hospital.

I am feeling very well; get my ride indoors every morning and am teaching as usual three times a week. Dr. Haynes is now back from Europe and will relieve me somewhat in the spring days when I get real lazy.

Did I write you that the Child Health Organization got a contribution from the Carnegie Corporation of $10,000 and one from the Commonwealth Foundation for a like sum? This with the $10,000 from the Red

Cross makes it necessary for us to raise but $20,000 for the year which I think will not be difficult....

With much love,
FATHER

(*To his son Emmett*)

New York, March 21, 1920

MY DEAR EMMETT:

Your birthday yesterday was not forgotten, though we did not send you any reminder. This is a great month of anniversaries. You are now just twenty-five years old, just my age when I graduated in medicine forty years ago. How well I remember that week! Our year closed in March, just about this time. I had many ambitions, but hardly expected a realization of so many of them as circumstances have made possible during these years. Without Mother's help they would never have been. How much I owe to her I can never adequately express. May you be as fortunate in finding some one to help you realize your ideals as I was.

I often wish I could bequeath to you the result of my forty years' experience in medicine, so that you might be able to begin where I shall leave off. But I am afraid it might not prove the blessing that one might imagine, for it is one of the rules of life that it is our own experience which develops us, and not that of others, who would fain give it to us.

I still hope that you may begin practice before I retire altogether, for I am sure there are ways in which I might help you a good deal. Though I am impressed with the fact that the medicine of the future is to be very different from the medicine of my time.

Wonderful changes have taken place during these forty years; such great ones have I seen that I am at

CANNES CONFERENCE
1919

DR. HOLT IN CHINA
1923

times almost tempted to follow Uncle John's example, and write my reminiscences along the lines of his *Men Who Have Meant Much to Me*.* In the last number of the *Unpop* Mr. Henry Holt has been giving some very interesting ones of his, which we have found most entertaining. I am afraid, however, that my "R's" would find a very small audience; so I think I will postpone their composition until I find nothing useful that I am able to do....

(*To his son Calvert*)

Pleasantville, N. Y., March 5, 1921

MY DEAR CALVERT:

I have had a great many nice birthday presents in my many birthdays, but none I think which gave me more pleasure than your letter. I suppose there is nothing in life which gives so much satisfaction as appreciation by those we love or those whose good opinion we value.

Children bring problems to parents as some time you will know for yourself. But ours have brought comparatively few; and as the years have gone by, they have brought us with each year greater satisfaction.

I hope when you reach the age of sixty-six years you may have a son to write you as fine a letter as the one you have written me, and that your home and your life may bring you as much joy and as much satisfaction as mine have brought me.

With much love to the best of boys,

FATHER

* The reference is to Dr. John B. Calvert's book of that title.

(*To his son Emmett*)

Washington, Conn.
August 3, 1922

MY DEAR EMMETT:

I enclose a card to the Asst. Librarian of the Academy which will enable you to get anything you want there.... Well, you will have only one month more at the Babies' Hospital. I fear you have not got as much out of the service as you expected and I greatly regret that I have not myself been able to give you as much as I had hoped I might. I am sorry that in all probability I will never have another chance to hand on to you somewhat from my experience, such as it is: But so it is in life—its greatest opportunities are too often not seen until they have passed. I blame myself much more than I do any one else.

Working with Dr. Howland I am sure will be very pleasant and stimulating, and I know you will make the most of these advantages. I hope you will not lose interest in the clinical side of pediatrics, for it is only its practical application which justifies research according to my way of thinking.

You are, I hope, taking some time to go over the *Care and Feeding* for desirable changes, for those which must be made must be ready in October.... The camp is not yet rented, so you and Olivia may have a chance to go up there for part of your vacation.

With much love,
FATHER

New York, March 25, 1923

It was interesting to have your paper appear in the same issue of the Journal with mine. The "father-and-son" golf tournaments have become quite an important sporting event in this region. But I think intellectual associations more worthwhile....

. . . .

In 1923 he was sixty-eight years old. The professorship at Columbia had been resigned two years before, after twenty-one classes of medical students had been steered along their path. There had been a dinner on this occasion—a memorable one for him—for there were gathered together not only the present staff of the Columbia department, but others from afar who had worked with him at one time or another, come to pay homage to the retiring chief. But if the old activities were curtailed it was only that they might permit him to devote himself more fully to that new task for which he seemed to be so uniquely needed—the Child Health Organization and its program. The teaching responsibilities had passed on, to one of his pupils, but the born teacher remained. As likely as not a week-end in Pleasantville would find him instructing a newly acquired daughter-in-law in the mysteries of finance.

Some of the old tasks could be turned over to others, but even that was difficult. The Henry Street settlement had refused to accept his resignation from its board. From other organizations resignation was not to be thought of. There was his alma mater, Rochester University: he had been one of its trustees since 1902 and had given its President, Rush Rhees, constant advice in regard to its scientific faculty, its buildings, commencement speakers, and candidates for honorary degrees; also advice in regard to its investments, the most opportune times for approaching prospective donors, and so forth. Rochester had not remained the small college of President Anderson's day. It had grown with the city, and had received generous support from citizens to whom it was an object of civic pride. It was now in a fair way to become the fifth richest university in the country, and it was embarking on a new development, financed in part by the Rockefeller Foundation, that came very close to Dr. Holt's heart—a modern medical school. It was very important that this should get off to a good start. The credit for bringing this project to fruition belongs to Mr. Abraham Flexner, and its subsequent development was largely the work of its first appointee and dean, Dr. George Whipple. Nevertheless there were many problems arising while it was being hatched in which the advice of Holt who knew both the medical and the local problems was helpful.

The New York Academy of Medicine had, on two occasions, offered him the highest honor it had to bestow: the presidency. But each time he declined. It was not his job, and it needed some one with more social gifts than he to make a good presiding officer for such an august body. He insisted that they reëlect Walter James.

The meeting of the American Pediatric Society in 1923 at French Lick Springs was another memorable occasion for him. To be elected its president for a second time was an honor that had been granted to none save Abraham Jacobi. The Society had altered considerably from its early days. A bare handful of the original group of enthusiasts were now left. Rotch had died some years before. At his death Dr. Holt had written to one of his own children: "We had been

REWARDS

close friends for forty years. Some day you will know what that means." The kindly and ever courteous Blackader, now eighty years old, no longer came to the meetings. New blood had come in—clinicians of a younger generation, men whose interests were centered in laboratory investigation: the Society contained the best of them. But it was somewhat of a motley gathering, for among the men of promise who had been taken in during the years were a number whose promise had not been fulfilled. They were growing old without ideas to contribute; modern medicine had passed them by, but an unfortunate rule of the Society, later happily abrogated, insisted that those who would remain members must speak periodically, and speak they did. The program was a curious mixture of the best of the modern, and the past making a pitiful attempt to be modern. Much of it would have irritated the stern critic of Dr. Knight in 1878 or the slightly more tolerant listener to the eloquence of Dr. Pinard in 1919, but not so the Holt of 1923. For with the years had come a certain mellowness and tolerance for the shortcomings of others. These were his friends, and even their foibles were dear to him. The good papers of the meeting shone all the more by contrast: the others furnished a chance for relaxation and occasionally a touch of the comic. But there was nothing of the comic in the president's address: "American Pediatrics—a Retrospect and a Forecast." He compared the program of 1896, when he had been president before, to that of the present session. Then there had been only one paper portraying the results of a laboratory investigation. Now they filled half the program. Laboratory medicine and preventive medicine were coming into their own. But what of the future? Must the three fields—that of the experimenter, the health expert and the practitioner of clinical pediatrics—keep on diverging until they became quite separate? Such a segregation seemed almost inevitable, but it would bring a danger which must not be overlooked. The public health doctor must not be cut off from clinical pediatrics. He must be well grounded in it at the start, and only in so far as he could keep abreast of its advances could he properly fulfil his function. The laboratory worker must maintain a contact with the clinic, from which he must draw his problems, and which alone could furnish him with the proper perspective as to their value. The practitioner must keep in touch on the one hand with the advances of the laboratory and on the other with the field of preventive medicine. And the American Pediatric Society, diverse as its interests had become and would continue to be, might still perform a useful function in cementing these individual groups and strengthening each by keeping it in touch with the other.

This was the last meeting of the Pediatric Society he was to attend. The society had been charged with its ideals for the future. It held the idealist in all reverence and affection. A recognized leader among them he had been for years. But a leader who can weather wrinkles and white hair and still retain the open mind of youth, the interest in new ideas, coupled with the wisdom of experience, is something more. He was indeed the grand old man of American pediatrics.

The rewards had all come, now.

XX

FAR HORIZONS

THERE was one more adventure ahead—one which was to take him to the Orient.

Western medicine had penetrated Japan, but it had made little progress in China. More than one hundred years before, some Dutch traders had established themselves on an island off the coast of Japan, and from their doctors the Japanese had acquired their first ideas of Occidental medicine. The new ideas spread, surreptitiously at first, and later openly. It was the first step in the modern development in that country which proceeded with surprising rapidity. The renaissance of Occidental medicine found the Japanese wide awake; their students and physicians studied abroad, particularly in Germany, and the Land of the Rising Sun underwent a development of medical thought, teaching and research quite comparable to that in Europe and America. But the Land of the Dragon was still somnolent. There were a few modern hospitals run by medical missionaries, but the Chinese as a whole clung to the herb doctors who practised the medicine of a thousand years ago, sublimely unconscious of what was going on in the rest of the world. Such habits could not be changed overnight, but nevertheless it seemed as if a modern medical school to educate the Chinese in China would be a step in the right direction. Ultimately it could be turned over to Chinese teachers. The project was hatched by the Rockefeller Foundation: it was one more enterprise in whose development and launching Welch had played a leading part. The Peking Union Medical College was well under way in 1920.

There were difficulties in bringing to China the best that western medicine had to give. Men with careers established or in sight in America or Europe were not anxious to abandon them, especially with the prospect of being ultimately displaced by the Chinese. The Foundation adopted the expedient of sending to China young men for terms of three or four years, and to back them up they sent over each year two or three distinguished physicians to stay for a few months only. They were to serve as a stimulus—an inspiration to the students and the younger men. It was in this capacity that Dr. Holt's aid was sought in 1923. He was invited to lecture at the college for the winter term and assist in organizing the recently formed pediatric service at the hospital. It was an intriguing prospect: the Orient, which he had never seen; a trip around the world; a worth-while task in what was practically a virgin field. There seemed to be no reason why he should not accept. The plans were made, and in August of that year he set sail with Mrs. Holt and Miss Anne Whitney of the Child Health Organization who was to assist him in making some studies of Chinese children. The story of the trip is told for the most part in his letters.

(*To his son Calvert*)

San Francisco, August 22, 1923

DEAR CALVERT:

Your night letter came this morning and we were glad to get news of you. So far everything has gone smoothly "according to schedule" as the Germans used to say regarding their war campaigns. It was hard to say good-by to you all at the Grand Central, and it is harder still to think when we go on board to-morrow and sail through the Golden Gate, that it will be so long before any news can reach us. . . .

Our San Francisco friends are as usual quite swamping us with invitations—more than we are able to accept. All the same it is nice to be welcomed. I am wondering if it will be the same in Peking.

Well, I am glad you are going to Upper Saranac. You will enjoy seeing the old place again. Please give our love to the Lyons, old and young and to Sam and family. How I would like to see it all. . . .

On Board *S. S. Pres. Wilson,* Aug. 28, '23

This is a great day for writing letters. In a few hours we will reach Honolulu and this will be our last chance to write you for some time. We like the ship, the people, the table and especially our fine cabin, fully twice the size of those on most Atlantic steamers. We cannot be too thankful that we chose the Southern route; smooth seas, beautiful blue water, bright sunny days and glorious moonlight nights. If we only had all our family with us we would have nothing to wish for. We see plenty of missionary families returning to the East—who seem to be *all* here—at least three and some with four or five small children. But what a fine time these youngsters have! It is so warm they are nearly all barefooted and scamper all over the ship in a way that seems to Mother most reckless; but their parents don't seem to mind it and so far none have fallen overboard. We are entertained by talks on China, Japan and Korea by the missionaries, moving pictures, dances and the usual ship games of shuffleboard, etc. Mother is quite an expert and quite set up by her success at this and at our game of *Auction Pitch* which we three play every evening. Our score now stands: LMH 450, LEH 345, Anne 410. We are having lots of fun keeping the record of the trip....

Off coast of Japan, Sept. 12, '23

We are at sea again after a three-day stop in Yokohama harbor which has been hot and in many respects trying, but full of interest and with some thrilling experiences, if not our own, at least those of new friends which we have made.

The 'quake was a week old when we anchored in the bay, about two miles from the ruins of the city. I did not get ashore, and very few did and the tales they brought back did not create in the rest of us any desire to see for ourselves, nor was it altogether a safe excursion for in Yokohama there has been little order preserved, and looting and even the killing of foreigners go on before the eyes of the police and sometimes by them. I do not know that any Americans or Europeans have been badly dealt with, but their anger is especially against the Chinese and Koreans, the mob having raised the cry that these people, mild and harmless, were setting fires and committing all sorts of depredations.

The stories of rescues and escapes would make your hair stand up—these we hear from the refugees, of whom we are taking on board 300 or 400 here.

One lady who was on the quay walking, to save herself from fire jumped into the water and was not rescued for five hours. It is lucky the water is warm. She kept herself afloat by pieces of wreckage. Another just leaving Cook's office just escaped, as she entered the street, the walls of two falling buildings one from each side of the way and then found herself in a deep crevasse up to her neck. One man here, it is said the only one saved from the Grand Hotel—the principal one in Yokohama—was sitting in a barber's chair when the ceiling began to come down. He rushed into the lobby where he was protected by two girders which fell across one another in such a way that he was not hit tho the man just in front was crushed to death.

So I could go on filling pages of just such stories heard from the lips of the men and women with whom we talk on deck—people *just like ourselves.* Some show the strain they have been through, hunting for days for family and friends with very little food and no change of clothing for a whole week.

I think Mother wrote of a collection that was taken up on shipboard for relief. It amounted to over $1100 and was turned over to a Committee of three appointed. I was one, the others were Dr. Morris and a Mr. Reimer. The Captain—his name is January—authorized us to form another committee to look after clothing—to collect and distribute to those most in need.

The response from the passengers has been generous and amusing in many cases. The resulting costumes are sometimes becoming and sometimes ridiculous.

Anne has served on the clothing committee and has witnessed the generosity as well as the selfishness of our shipmates. This is a time when real character shows. In the main the refugees are brave and courageous, tho some have lost everything they had in the world.

We were all glad to learn from one of our friends who went to Tokio (18 mi. up the bay) yesterday regarding the magnificent work the American Embassy was doing for all U. S. citizens and many Europeans. The British Embassy was doing next to nothing. As the Ambassador—Mr. Woods—was coming down in a destroyer to see the Admiral on his flagship the *Huron* which is anchored a short distance from the *Pres. Wilson,* the Committee decided to call upon him and ask his advice as to how the passengers' relief fund should be used.

So we three of the Committee got Capt. January to send us over to the *Huron* last night for our call. Admiral Anderson we found a cordial, quite delightful gentleman of about 60, looking very handsome in the white uniform which all the officers wear. The Ambassador was not so attractive in his pongee suit with a moist collar and negligee shirt and a rather ancient tie. Still we liked him better as we talked. They gave us what you boys would call the *inside dope* on the situation. How suspicious the Japanese had been of any offers of outside help, thinking some selfish motive was behind. They didn't want any one but themselves to send accounts of conditions here, so they "messed up" air conditions and our destroyers had to go 60 miles out before they could radio successfully. When the destroyers appeared here to give relief the populace thought they had come for an attack or to land troops at least. That they were only now after 10 days beginning to comprehend our altruistic motives in lending aid, etc. etc. "Now," said the Admiral, "I want you gentlemen to hear the account of the N. Y.

Tribune correspondent who has just come here from Peking and who has spent the day tramping thro' the ruins at Yokohama."

So the man was sent for and for half an hour told us what he had seen with his own eyes—in large sections no streets could be made out—only piles of ruins filled with dead bodies and an occasional soldier wandering about. Some looting was still going on. One Japanese coolie asked the correspondent's assistance to crack a safe which he had been vainly attacking for some time with a crowbar—only a short distance from soldiers.

How pestilence can help following in the wake of so much that is bad in a sanitary way seems incredible. The Japanese have even declined to accept water offered by the destroyers apparently thinking it was contaminated. They have in Y. completely lost their heads. The canals are filled with dead bodies which even float out in the bay as far as the ship. The horrors beggar description.

We stayed in the flagship until after eleven o'clock. While there the Admiral read us a wireless dispatch just received from Manila with the news of the sailing of a relief ship with supplies of food, tents, blankets, disinfectants and a corps of doctors and nurses. He was overjoyed. There are in the bay here seven or eight destroyers, which are picking up refugees and transferring them to nearby places where they can be cared for.

The officers and men come aboard at night and I am sure you would enjoy talking with these boys. They impress one as a fine lot. We are giving them all our books we have read and they are very glad to get them.

I hope to send this to-morrow from Kobe by a U. S. steamer.

With much love,
FATHER

(*To his son Emmett*)

Hotel Kyoto, Kyoto, Japan
Sept. 18, 1923

MY DEAR EMMETT:

You will see from the heading of this that we have changed our plans since we cabled that we were going direct to Shanghai. But the earthquake has upset all our calculations. We lay over in the harbor of Yokohama for three days, though we were not allowed to land. We saw plenty of evidence of the disaster in dead bodies floating about the Bay....

When we reached Kobe, 24 hours from Yokohama, we found things had been much exaggerated. While Kobe, which was the port to which most of the refugees were taken, was crowded, we learned that there was no trouble in getting hotel accommodations here and at Nara, the two places in Japan, next to Tokio, we wanted most to see.... This is the old capital and the place to see old Japan, Tokio being the place to see *new* Japan. We are having a glorious time shopping and doing the sights.

Since most of my medical letters were to men in Tokio, Kitasato and others, I feared I should be able to see very little of professional interest here. There is no one in Kyoto whose name I knew. I found out who the president of the Medical School was and decided the best I could do was to find him and then the head of the pediatric department. In the office I learned that the president had gone to Tokio, but the secretary, who spoke English quite well, took me through the

University. He had met Drs. Welch and Flexner when they were here some years ago, knew Noguchi also, and gave me lots of information about medical instruction in Japan. He then took me to the pediatric department, which I found was in charge of Dr. Hirai, a man with whom I had corresponded last year when I wanted to get some information regarding the diet of children in Japan. I sent him last year the last edition of my large book.

He was overjoyed to meet me, apparently; he spoke no English whatever, but we got on very nicely in German. I found in his library two earlier editions of my book—the latest one he said he kept at his house. ... On the whole I passed a most delightful and instructive morning.

The medicine here is mainly German medicine. Hirai had studied in Germany and most of their teachers had done so. Their histories were an amusing mixture of Latin and German terms with Japanese descriptions of symptoms. They all read German and many of them English, too, though few speak it fluently.

In spite of their restricted diet the Japanese children one sees in the streets are healthy-looking, comparing very favorably with what one sees in the United States. Such things as slums or crowded districts like the East Side in New York I have not seen.... The people here are quiet, kindly and rather childlike. The contrast is great to what one would have seen in Tokio, which was a hustling, bustling modern city.

We are looking forward to settling down in Peking where we shall have a home feeling and where we can look forward to some home mail. Give our best to the Howlands and write us often.

Ever so much love,
FATHER

From Kyoto the Holts were able to see something of rural Japan—shrines, small villages dependent on cormorant fishing for centuries, a night spent at a primitive Japanese inn which might have been enjoyable if there had been pillows, if the beds had been made up appropriately and if the bamboo sliding screens which separated the rooms from the curious natives gathered outside had not been transparent.

(To his daughter Evelyn)

Grand Hotel de Pekin, October 1923

DEAR EVELYN:

Mother has written you so frequently that you have been kept aware of all our doings, but this afternoon she is away, and I am going to seize the opportunity to have a little letter to you all by myself. We are so happy here after our wanderings, and to feel that for some months we shall not have to consult time tables, catch trains, fee porters and pack bags. We are still living in our hand baggage.

We had a most cordial welcome here on our arrival; Mr. Roger Greene and three of the doctors from the hospital met us at the station and we have had calls and invitations—many, almost too many—already. . . .

We have a fine large room on the southwest corner, third floor, of this large hotel. It is a combination bedroom and sitting room, with windows on two sides giving extensive views of the western hills and sunsets. In the foreground of the hills lies the Forbidden City with its golden tiled roofs. There are very few chimneys to spoil the view as there were in Japan. The P.U.M.C. (Peking Union Medical College) is only a few minutes' walk away, and the legation quarter quite as near in the opposite direction.... As this is likely to be our home for some time I am enclosing a little diagram. You see it is very spacious and sunny practically all day. The first floor lobby suggests the Waldorf somewhat, and has many shops. But above this floor it is a very quiet place and homelike. The meals are excellent, much like those you get in any French or other continental European Hotel.

The waiters wear long white gowns reaching to their feet, and over this a short, pale blue jacket, without sleeves, always starched and fresh. It gives them a very nice appearance. Most of them have shaved heads, and all seem very neat. A lady who has lived in the hotel for three years says there has been almost no change in personnel since she has been here. They take a great personal interest in our welfare, always selecting the best fruit, pointing out the choice pieces of meat or chicken on the dish. We grow very fond of them. They are simple, childlike, always good-natured, and appreciate a joke very much....

There is much variety in our days. I am now regularly at work and like my surroundings and my students. I have an office in the P.U.M.C. where on Monday and Thursday mornings I see any private patients who wish to take advantage of my presence and consult me gratis. It is pleasant to be a fulltime man and not consider the business side of medicine.

On Mondays and Fridays I give a lecture from five to six and on Saturday mornings hold a clinic. This will be my regular program for the next six weeks. So you see I will be kept pretty busy. I spend most of the morning at the P.U.M.C., get home for lunch; then we usually do some sightseeing in the afternoon until dark, now about 5:30, and take a nap until time to get ready for dinner which is 8:30 or after....

We take to rickashas like ducks to water and no longer feel as if we were being drawn in a large baby carriage....

The children here in Chinese dress are adorable, and Mother pictures little Marion in one of these quaint costumes.

We are all well and happy, finding lots of friends and making many new ones.

Much love to all,

Affectionately,
FATHER

(*To his son Emmett*)

Peking, November 4, 1923

MY DEAR EMMETT:

... I wish you and Olivia might look in and see us this Sunday night in our cozy room, and look out over this large and picturesque city on the sights we get from our window. The scenes are as varied and as fascinating as those of Egypt, and after a month we feel very much at home among them. The time flies fast, as we are so busily occupied, and our three months' stay will seem a short one, I am sure....

I am doing more teaching than I anticipated. Besides ward rounds I have a clinic every Saturday morning and now am giving a course of two lectures a week on Nutrition—eight lectures in all. All my lectures are well attended by the students, many members of the assistant staff, a few heads of other departments, a number of "faculty wives," several of whom were trained nurses, and some outside doctors. On the 16th I am to give the monthly public lecture in the auditorium, seating about 400 and usually filled. My subject will be, "What Preventive Medicine has done for

Children," illustrated by lantern slides showing New York mortality curves.

Besides my formal and informal teaching I have an office hour in the Hospital where twice a week I see private patients by appointment. Every mother, or at least every English-speaking mother, in the Far East has brought up her children on "the book," and as many seem desirous of having their offspring passed upon I am kept pretty busy. The P.U.M.C. staff are a fine bunch; we dine out with some member two or three times a week.

Tell Dr. Howland rickets is surprisingly rare both here and in Japan. I have not seen a single example of marked deformity yet. I am also making a good many observations upon teeth. The Chinese children make a much better showing than the Japanese or than our New York Children. I don't know yet what the explanation is but sweets certainly have something to do with it. The Japanese are great consumers of sweets, while these Chinese children get practically none, and in this school (an orphanage) they get no sugar, either....

Anne has made a number of addresses here and has done finely. Every one is delighted with her and much impressed with her presentations.

We think of you all every day and reckon on what you are doing at a given hour.

Much love,
FATHER

(*To* Mrs. William Brown Meloney, *editor of* The Delineator)

Grand Hotel de Pekin, Pekin
November 10, 1923

Dear Mrs. Meloney:

On several occasions I have felt prompted to write you a line and tell you what a marvelously successful trip we are having. I am prompted to do so now by the receipt of a letter from my daughter telling of your kindness to her....

I am dying for news from home relating to the A. C. H. A., Mr. Hoover, Miss Jean and others. Some one, Miss Dodge I think, wrote me the articles by doctors had none of them been printed and I am wondering what you and Mr. Page have finally decided to do.

I see the *Delineator* here regularly. The November issue was on the news stand in the Hotel shortly after the first of the month; so I can understand your reasons for printing so long in advance.

The health problem as regards children here in the Orient is a colossal one. One is confronted constantly by the low estimate the oriental places upon human life, particularly infant life. This with their superstitions and prejudices make the introduction of an American plan for promoting the health and saving the lives of children seem very remote. Still there are many who are eager for better conditions and them we are trying to help as best we may.

This is a wonderful city—Everything on a grand scale with no end of interest to the foreign visitor. You must see it some day.

Cordially yours,
L. Emmett Holt

(*To Dr. Nathaniel R. Norton*)

Peking, Dec. 13, 1923

DEAR DR. NORTON:

In our package of letters from home yesterday it was good to get one from you and to hear how things were going 12,000 miles or so away.

Yours was especially welcome since it was the first bit of Hospital news I have had since I left, now four months ago. X's resignation is a disappointment. I had hoped better things of him than throwing up his job when his service was only half over. The young men of to-day seem in so many cases to have such a small sense of obligation; it is certainly to be deplored. I am wondering if he realizes how much his future prospects may be injured by such a course.

The appointment of McIntosh meets with my cordial approval. He is a man whom we must attach strongly to the Hospital and I think the appointment made will do this. By all odds he is the most promising man for future advancement.

I am also wondering what has become of Mr. Hoyt's scheme for the Columbia alliance. The latest news I have heard as to the Columbia-Presbyterians building program was of postponement, so I suppose that nothing is likely to happen for some time yet.

Pediatric material in the Hospital is small but interesting. I have been giving two didactic and one clinical lecture a week—a little too much I found and am now having a week's entire rest, for the social engagements though most enjoyable are wearisome with the late hours which prevail.

Intestinal parasites play a large part in medicine here and besides there is a great deal of tuberculosis due to want of cleanliness and to bad economic conditions. The struggle for existence here is very keen.

The diets which the children past infancy get in China would surprise you. No milk, butter or cheese; eggs very seldom and meat usually only on special festivals. They live chiefly upon *mantou,* which is a steamed bread dough, rice and millet without sugar, butter or milk—but with vegetables in fair amount, especially cabbage, and some vegetable oils. Cabbage soup which is little else than the water in which the vegetable is cooked is a staple article in all homes. Cabbage apparently is the one food stuff which protects them against the deficiency diseases—scurvy and beri-beri are both very rare here.

The poor quality of the food of the natives is also shown in the low commercial value of their stools. The night soil here, as in all Eastern cities, is collected and used as fertilizer. That from the houses of foreigners commands the highest price; that from the houses of wealthy Chinese comes next; while that from the Chinese poor is ranked the poorest. It is removed from the houses in small tubs which are transported in large wheelbarrows to just outside the City walls where it is sun-dried and then marketed. Interesting, isn't it?

I am collecting some material upon "diet and teeth" which is most suggestive. As a rule the children here have excellent teeth. I personally examined the mouths of 100 in an orphanage—ages 7 to 14 years—and *86% had not a single cavity.* They get no sugar or sweets. A similar group in Japan had an average of *five cavities to each child and only 2% had no cavities.* The Japanese consume large amounts of sweets and their diet is chiefly carbohydrates. I have picked up a great deal of useful information and am keeping records. I hope to have some things to tell you when I return.

With kind regards to Bartlett and the rest of the staff, Cordially yours,

L. EMMETT HOLT

The weeks went by rapidly—excursions to the Ming Tombs, to the Great Wall, the Forbidden City; contacts with interesting people from all over the world; the street life of a fascinating Oriental city.

The lecture course was practically over, and he had been asked to speak before the local medical society. The paper given that evening, published after his death, was a memorable one, on a subject which had been in his mind for some years back—"Outgrowing Disease." It concerned the ultimate results of disease, not four or five years afterward, but twenty-five or thirty years afterward. There was a real lack of knowledge here. Hospital records could not provide the answer; hospital populations are shifting ones, and few patients are followed for any length of time. The answer could come only from one who had been in practice for many years, one who followed his patients long after they were grown and who kept accurate records all along the line. Into that paper went a wealth of experience of more than forty years in the practice of pediatrics, and the message gained from that experience was a hopeful one. For there were records of disease causing damage which had been regarded as irreparable—disease of the lungs, the kidney, the nervous system, but more particularly the heart—which the passage of years had obliterated to an unbelievable extent; often in their entirety. The young organism had powers of recuperation unmatched by the adult.

This was his final contribution to pediatric literature.

(A family letter)

Peking, Dec. 24

DEAR "CHEEPO":

Our hearts were made glad this morning by the receipt of two cablegrams from New York. One said "Merry Christmas," and was signed "Sawyers." The other, with the same message, was signed by the cryptic word, "Cheepo." Mother got out her "Mission Code Book," and was seeking vainly through the C. H. E.'s for the word's meaning when Anne exclaimed, "Why, it's the children's initials!" and so it proved....

We have finally, after much discussion and protracted thought, decided to give up our trip through India and Suez, and return home via the Pacific. The chief reason for this change is the fact that my heart has not been behaving as well as it should for a few weeks past. I have had a little too much of everything to do, I guess, with the teaching and other lectures, sightseeing, shopping, and perhaps most of all the social engagements, which have been interesting and enjoyable, but too many.

Since my teaching was finished nearly two weeks ago I have been taking a modified rest cure. We go out in the "rickashas" shopping, usually for two or three hours in the morning, and I spend the greater part of the early afternoon lying down, in the later afternoon usually receiving visits from some of the doctors of the P.U.M.C., who come in to gossip about their cases and their teaching....

We are somewhat disappointed in many ways, but there is much still to see in China; and now that our work is done we shall enjoy playing around here a while longer. Just where we shall be the rest of the time we are not sure. We are so comfortable here in our big sunny rooms that we are likely to remain in Peking for some weeks at least....

There is nothing in the world so nice as friends, and especially when your relatives are also your dear friends; but most of all your children. We do appreciate you all more and more the longer we are away, and the greater the distance which separates us. Separation and absence seem to be necessary to place these things in their true value in life....

. . . .

This was Dr. Holt's last letter home. On the morning of the twenty-fourth he spent some pleasant hours shopping for furniture with Mrs. Holt. In the afternoon he worked with Miss Whitney on some height-and-weight tables of Chinese school children which he was preparing. But next morning, after a bad night, it was apparent that his overtaxed heart would require absolute rest and the best of care if he were to return safely to America. For a few days he seemed to grow better. On the thirteenth of January, though still strong enough to work occasionally at his health tables, he went to the hospital. On the afternoon of the fourteenth came an attack from which he did not rally. He died five hours later, peacefully and with little pain.

So ended a singularly well directed life. The trip to the Orient was, almost to the last, a serene and happy adventure. The final task had been well done. If its purpose had been to inspire that group by contact with a strong personality, the imprint of that personality could not have been thrown into sharper relief than by his laying down his life at the close of the effort. Nowhere was the shock of his death more profound than in that little circle of workers at the far end of the earth. But New York had not forgotten him. There was a vacant seat left in many an enterprise that could not well be filled, an example that many would cherish. "I thought I would work a little harder that day," wrote one of his colleagues in New York.

The race had been well run. He had been true to his ancestry. In him there had burned the spirit of those pioneers who had hewed trails through the forest, who had seen the vision of orchards and green fields in the midst of the wilderness and had made it a reality, who had not hesitated to part with the past —comfortable homes in Massachusetts or Connecticut —when the future called. It was the same force that had driven the country's pioneers of industry by methods not always too scrupulous, but this time it was tempered by an idealism nurtured from the cradle, a faith in a human and rational purpose in the universe. That, too, had been his mother's religion imparted in the tranquil boyhood years on the farm in Webster.

INDEX

Aboilard, M., 151
Adams, Dr., 94, 99, 131
Allgemeine Krankenhaus, 79
Ambulance service, first, at Bellevue, 50
American Child Health Association, 229-230
American Child Hygiene Association, 229
American Journal of Diseases of Children, 204-205
American Medical Association, 93
American Pediatric Society, 94-97, 99, 101, 264
American Red Cross, 229, 232
American Relief Association, 229
Anderson, Admiral, 272-273
Anderson, Martin B., 24, 25-27, 42
Antitoxin, diphtheria, 99-101
Appendicitis, treatment of, 50
Archives of Pediatrics, 93
Ashby, Dr., 154
Association for the Prevention of Infant Mortality, 172, 228-229
Autopsy, 50

Babies' Hospital, 107-114, 115, 118, 136, 164, 173, 181, 203, 210, 262
Baginsky, Dr., 147-148
Baker, S. Josephine, 229
Baldwin, Edward R., 233, 237
Barlow, Sir Thomas, 97, 154
Barthez, Dr., 82
Bartlett, Dr., 136
Behring, 99
Belais, Mrs. Diana, 140
Bellevue Hospital, 49-53, 150, 202
Beri-beri, 207-208
Bernstorff, 241
Biggs, Hermann, 138, 139, 218, 233, 236, 237, 238, 250, 251
Binet, Dr., 149
Bismarck, 83
Blackader, Dr., 94, 127, 265
Bloch, 208
Blood transfusion, 161
Body-snatching, 44
Bokay, J., 157
Bolling, Richard, 211
Bologna, 77-78
Bourbon, Princesse de, 250

288 INDEX

Bourré, 151-153
British Museum, 74
British Pediatric Society, 155
Brown, Dr., 131
Buffalo, University of, 39-41
Bulkley, Benjamin, 29
Burghcleve, Lady, 251
Burr, Mr., 243

Calmette, 164
Calvary Baptist Church, N. Y., 55-57
Calvert, John B., 26, 43, 54, 55, 66, 67, 84, 91, 192, 261
Care and Feeding of Children, The, 116-118, 173, 262
Carlisle, Secretary, 132
Carnegie Foundation, 192, 259
Carrel, Alexis, 142, 161
Cauldwell, Charles M., 54, 55, 57, 59, 120
Caxton, Commissioner, 216
Chapin, Mrs. Robert, 115
Chapin, Henry Dwight, 63, 93, 94, 171, 215n
Cheeseman, Eliza Holt, 20, 21-22, 32, 57-58, 90, 122-123, 146
Cheeseman, Eugene, 20, 122-123
Chemistry, in pediatrics, 200-210
Child health, interest in, 214-231
Child Health Organization, 218-229, 259

Children's Clinical Club, London, 154-155
China, medicine in, 267-268
Cohnheim, 51
Coit, Henry L., 169
College of Physicians and Surgeons, 43-44, 51, 136, 263
Commonwealth Foundation, 259
Connecticut Agricultural Experiment Station, 205
Cook, Dr., 79
Cornell Medical College, 99
Courtney, Dr., 203
Coutts, Dr., 154
Crothers, Samuel McChord, 158
Currier, Andrew F., 93
Curtice, Ebenezer, 10
Curtice, Henry, 9-10
Curtice, Mary, 10
Curtice, Sabrah. *See* Holt, Sabrah Curtice.
Curtice, Ziba, 10
Cutter, Mr., 243
Cyclopedia of Diseases of Children, ed. by Keating, 96, 118

D'Andrea, Novella, 77-78
Daniels, Secretary Josephus, 235, 236
Dart, Sally, 8
Dart, Sibyl, 8
Davison, Henry P., 232, 239, 242-243, 244, 248, 249, 252

INDEX

De Gassicourt, Cadet, 82
Delafield, Francis, 50
Dennett, Roger H., 215n, 217
Department of Labor, Children's Bureau of, 231
Deutsche Gesellschaft für Kinderheilkunde, 82, 153
Dewey, John, 218
Diarrhea, infantile, treatment of, 166-171
Diarrheal diseases, article on, 96
Diet, child, in China, 282
Diphtheria, fatality of, 97; progress in control of, 97-101
Diphtheria antitoxin, 95
Diseases of Infancy and Childhood, 118-121, 173, 201
Donkin, Dr., 154
Downes, William A., 211
Dresden, 84

Ebert, 241, 242
Egypt, 192-199
Ehrlich, Dr., 161
Eijkman, 208
Eliot, Charles W., 218
Erysipelas, 49
Escherich, 153
Experiments, animal, 205-206, 207

Fales, Dr., 203
Farrand, Livingston, 234
Faunce, Mr., 128, 130

Feer, Emil, 153, 174-175
Fifth Avenue Baptist Church, 138
Finkelstein, Dr., 112
Finley, John, 218
Flexner, Abraham, 264
Flexner, Simon, 139, 142, 144, 156, 218, 275
Florence, 77
Food, Health and Growth, 210
Forschheimer, Dr., 94
Fox, George, 61
Fredet-Rammstedt operation, 211
Frölich, 208

Gates, Frederick T., 138n
Gerhardt, Carl, 82
Germany, conditions in, 1919, 240-242, 247
Gibney, Virgil P., 44-45, 59, 106, 121, 124, 127
Gilmore, Joseph H., 28-30, 38
Gladstone, Mr., 74
Goodhart, Dr., 154
Gorgas, General, 222
Gorner Grat, 84-85
Greene, Roger, 276

Haas, S. V., 215n
Halsted, William Stewart, 51
Hamill, Samuel McC., 233, 236, 237, 238, 244
Hartley, Robert, 166-167

INDEX

Harvey, 221
Haynes, Royal S., 215n, 217, 259
Heiser, Victor, 218
Henoch, Professor, 96, 112, 171
Henry Street Settlement, 171, 172, 263
Herter, Christian A., 112-113, 120n, 138, 139, 159, 168, 203
Hindenburg, 241
Hirai, Dr., 275
Holmes, Oliver Wendell, 49
Holst, 208
Holt, Abiel, 7
Holt, Calvert, letters to, 181-185, 189-191, 257-260, 261, 269-274
Holt, Constant, 7-9
Holt, Curtice, 20, 30, 31, 59, 129
Holt, Eliza. *See* Cheeseman, Eliza Holt.
Holt, Emmett, Jr., letters to, 186-189, 260-261, 262, 274-275, 278-279
Holt, Evelyn, letter to, 276-278
Holt, Henry, 261
Holt, Horace, father of Emmett, 10-12, 16, 146
Holt, Kenneth, death of, 181
Holt, Linda Mairs, 67, 89-91; letters to, 119-135, 234-252
Holt, Luther Emmett, an educator, 3-4, 173; chemical work, 203-213; childhood, 20-24; college, 24-35; death in China, 285; European trips, 69-86, 146-157, 192-199, 234-252; family life, 157-160, 179-181; hospital work, 104-105, 107-114, 203-213; letters, 23, 28, 44-48, 56-59, 64, 67, 69-90, 119-135, 181-191, 234-252, 257-262, 269-285; marriage, 87-91; medical training, 39-53; practising physician, 54-61, 102-104; president of Pediatric Society, 121, 264-266; publications, 63, 116-121, 173, 201, 210, 262, 283; Puritan background, 4-19; Red Cross committee, 233-256; Rockefeller Institute, 138-145; specialization in pediatrics, 61-68; teaching, 36-38, 61, 64-65, 106, 136, 263; trip to China, 268ff.
Holt, Nathan, 7
Holt, Nicholas, 7
Holt, Sabrah Curtice, mother of Emmett, 10-12, 16-19, 31-32, 42, 52, 56, 59-60, 64, 65-67, 86-87, 91, 146
Holt, William, 8
Hoover, Herbert, 229, 240
Hospital for the Ruptured and Crippled, 42-48, 61, 129-130
Hospital for Sick Children, London, 155

INDEX

House, Colonel, 240
Howland, John, 136, 200-202, 204, 262

Infant mortality, fight against 161-178; rate of, 1, 3, 176-177
Intubation, 97-98
Isaacs, Marion, 69

Jacobi, Abraham, 94-95, 97, 106, 136, 264
Jacobs, Dr., 150
James, Walter B., 156, 191, 192, 264
January, Captain, 271, 272
Japan, Western medicine in, 267, 275
Jean, Sally Lucas, 219
Jenner, 221
Johns Hopkins Medical School, 51, 144, 202
Junior Red Cross, 254

Kaiser Wilhelm II, 241, 247, 251
Kaiser Wilhelm Institute, 137
Kane, Mr., 74
Keating, John M., 94, 95, 118
Keller, Dr., 153
Kerley, Charles G., 62
Klebs, 99
Knight, James, 43, 47-48
Kobe, 274
Koch, Robert, 3, 92, 164

Koplik, Dr., 94
Kyoto, 274-276

La Fetra, Dr., 136
Lane, Franklin K., 216, 225
Lattimore, Samuel, 24, 27-28
League of Nations, Health Organization of, 254, 255-256
League of Red Cross Societies, 233, 253-254
Lee, Ivy, 252
Lees, Dr., 154
Leslie, Frank, 167
Levene, P. A., 142, 203
Lindsay, Samuel McC., 218
Lister, Joseph, 3, 49, 221
Lister Institute, 137
Liverpool, 73
Loeb, Jacques, 142, 172
Loeffler, 99
London, 73-75
Louvre, 75
Lovejoy, Owen, 218
Lucas, Dr., 233
Ludendorf, 241
Lumbar puncture, 163
Lusk, Graham, 202
Luxembourg, 76

Magnin, Dr., 150
Mairs, Linda. See Holt, Linda Mairs.
Malaria, 63
Malthus, 1
Marchiafava, Dr., 246

292 INDEX

Mason, Dr., 136
McAneny, Leonard, 245
McCollum, E. V., 208
McNutt, Julia G., 108
McNutt, Sarah J., 108
Medicine, teaching of in 1876, 39-42
Meigs, Dr., 94
Meloney, Mrs. William Brown, 280
Meltzer, Samuel, 142
Mendel, Lafayette B., 205-206, 208, 209
Meningitis, cerebrospinal, epidemic of, 162-164
Merchant, Jessie, 69
Meyer, Dr., 112
Microscope, first use of, 50
Milk, boiled, 168; certified, 169; contaminated, 166-168
Milk commissions, 169
Mitchell, Mrs. John A., 140
Morgenthau, Henry, 234, 235, 237, 239, 247, 248, 250, 255

National Gallery, 74
Newsholme, Sir Arthur, 251
New York Academy of Medicine, 100, 191, 264
New York Foundling Asylum, 104, 118
New York Infant Asylum, 61-63, 96, 118
New York Medical Record, 63

New York Nursery and Child's Hospital, 63, 104, 118
New York Polyclinic Hospital, 106, 118
Ninth International Medical Congress, 93
Noguchi, Hideyo, 275
Northcote, Sir Stafford, 74
Northrup, Dr., 94, 99, 131
Northwestern Dispensary, 61, 63
Norton, Nathaniel R., 281
Nurse, visiting, 171
Nurses, training of at Babies' Hospital, 115-116
Nurses' training school, first, at Bellevue, 50
Nutrition, science of, 205

O'Dwyer, Joseph, 94, 97-98, 99
Olds, Mr., 243
Osborne, Thomas B., 205-206, 208, 209
Osler, Sir William, 6, 94, 121, 127, 150, 192, 204

Paris, 75-76
Paris Academy of Medicine, 49
Park, Edwards A., 208
Parker, Joseph, 75
Pasteur, Louis, 3, 49, 92, 164, 221
Pasteur Institute, 137, 246

INDEX

Pasteur-Liebig controversy, 41
Pasteurization, compulsory, 170
Peace Conference, Versailles, 240
Pediatrics, 1-2; chemical advance in, 200-213; German lead in, 82; growth of American, 92-101
Peking Union Medical College, 268, 276-277
Peterson, Mrs. Frederick, 219
Phelps, Captain, 238
Pinard, Dr., 250
Pirquet, 153, 164
Pompeii, 76-77
Protein milk, 112
Prudden, T. Mitchell, 138, 139
Public Health Service, Child Hygiene Division of, 230
Puerperal fever, 49
Puritanism, 4-6
Pyemia, 49
Pyloric stenosis, 210-213

Quincke, 163

Reed, Walter, 221
Research, medical, 136-145
Rhees, Rush, 263
Rhine, 86
Rickets, 208; in China, 279
Rilliet, Dr., 82
Rist, Dr., 246

Riverside Academy, Wellsville, N. Y., 36-38
Rochester University, 24-35, 263-264
Rockefeller, John D., Jr., 138
Rockefeller, Mrs. John D., 129-130
Rockefeller Institute, 138-145, 154, 161, 172, 192, 203, 246, 264, 268
Rome, 76
Roosevelt, Theodore, 218
Rotch, Thomas Morgan, 107, 120, 121, 131, 156, 206, 264
Roussy de Sales, Comtesse, 247
Roux, Dr., 99, 246
Royal Society of Medicine, Section on Children's Diseases, 155
Russell, Dr., 245

St. Bartholomew's Hospital, London, 74
Salon Carré, 75
Salpetriere, 150
Salt solution, injection of, 96, 171
Salvarsan, 161
Schaudinn, 161
Schloss, Oscar, 101
Schlossmann, Dr., 148-149
Schools, public health in, 215-216
Scurvy, 95, 207-208; infantile, 97

INDEX

Semmelweiss, 49
Shipley, 208
Sibley, Polly, 8-9
Simmonds, 208
Simplon, 84
Sims, Marion, 106
Sistine Chapel, 76
Smith, C. E., 215n
Smith, Eustace, 154
Smith, J. Lewis, 94, 127
Smith, Theobald, 138, 139
Smith, Thomas, 74
Soxhlet, 168
Spargo, John, 218
Speedwell Society, 172
Spurgeon, 73
Squires, James Duane, 54, 55-56, 66, 67, 84, 91
Starr, Louis, 94, 127
Still, George, 154, 155
Stoddard, Dr., 41
Strasbourg, 86
Strauss, Nathan, 169-170, 174-175
Streptococcus, 49
Strong, Richard P., 233, 245
Surgery, in 1880, 49
Syphilis, treatment of, 161-162

Talbot, Dr., 233, 237
Teachers College, 226
Teeth, condition of, in Orient, 282
Thomson, John, 154, 156, 211
Trudeau, E. L., 51, 156

Tuberculin test, 164-165
Tuberculosis, test for, 164-165

Vanderbilt Clinic, 136
Van Ingen, Dr. Philip, 229
Van Slyke, Dr., 203
Van Vorst, John, Jr., 93
Vendôme, Duchesse de, 250
Venice, 78
Verne, Jules, 77
Vienna, 78-82, 83-84
Virchow, 50
Visp, 68, 84, 85
Vivisection, campaign against, 140
Von Recklinghausen, 51
Voorhees, Senator, 132

Wald, Lillian D., 171
Walker-Gordon Company, 168-169
Wangenheim, 235
Warburg, Felix, 218
Wassermann test, 161, 165
Waterlow, Lady, 250
Watson, William Perry, 93
Webster, N. Y., 7, 8; life in, 12-16
Webster Academy, 23
Welch, William H., 51-52, 112, 137, 138, 139, 218, 227-228, 233, 236, 237, 238, 240, 246, 248, 251, 268, 275
Welles, 151

INDEX

Wentworth, A. H., 163
Whipple, George, 264
Whitbeck, J. W., 42
White, Henry, 240
Whitney, Anne, 268*ff.*
Wiesbaden, 86
Wilbur, Ray Lyman, 218
Wilcox, Herbert B., 136, 215*n*, 217
Williams, Linsley, 247
Willington, Conn., 7, 8
Wilson, Woodrow, 240, 241
Winters, Joseph E., 99-101
Wirt, William, 218
Wollstein, Dr., 120

Wood, Thomas D., 218
Woods, Ambassador, 272
World War, 214*ff.*
Wyeth, John A., 106

Xerophthalmia, 208

Yersin, 99
Yokohama, earthquake in 270-274

Zermatt, 84-85

CHILDREN AND YOUTH
Social Problems and Social Policy

An Arno Press Collection

Abt, Henry Edward. **The Care, Cure and Education of the Crippled Child.** 1924

Addams, Jane. **My Friend, Julia Lathrop.** 1935

American Academy of Pediatrics. **Child Health Services and Pediatric Education:** Report of the Committee for the Study of Child Health Services. 1949

American Association for the Study and Prevention of Infant Mortality. **Transactions of the First Annual Meeting of the American Association for the Study and Prevention of Infant Mortality.** 1910

Baker, S. Josephine. **Fighting For Life.** 1939

Bell, Howard M. **Youth Tell Their Story:** A Study of the Conditions and Attitudes of Young People in Maryland Between the Ages of 16 and 24. 1938

Bossard, James H. S. and Eleanor S. Boll, editors. **Adolescents in Wartime.** 1944

Bossard, James H. S., editor. **Children in a Depression Decade.** 1940

Brunner, Edmund DeS. **Working With Rural Youth.** 1942

Care of Dependent Children in the Late Nineteenth and Early Twentieth Centuries. Introduction by Robert H. Bremner. 1974

Care of Handicapped Children. Introduction by Robert H. Bremner. 1974

[Chenery, William L. and Ella A. Merritt, editors]. **Standards of Child Welfare:** A Report of the Children's Bureau Conferences, May and June, 1919. 1919

The Child Labor Bulletin, 1912, 1913. 1974

Children In Confinement. Introduction by Robert M. Mennel. 1974

Children's Bureau Studies. Introduction by William M. Schmidt. 1974

Clopper, Edward N. **Child Labor in City Streets.** 1912

David, Paul T. **Barriers To Youth Employment.** 1942

Deutsch, Albert. **Our Rejected Children.** 1950

Drucker, Saul and Maurice Beck Hexter. **Children Astray.** 1923

Duffus, R[obert] L[uther] and L. Emmett Holt, Jr. **L. Emmett Holt: Pioneer of a Children's Century.** 1940

Fuller, Raymond G. **Child Labor and the Constitution.** 1923

Holland, Kenneth and Frank Ernest Hill. **Youth in the CCC.** 1942

Jacoby, George Paul. **Catholic Child Care in Nineteenth Century New York:** With a Correlated Summary of Public and Protestant Child Welfare. 1941

Johnson, Palmer O. and Oswald L. Harvey. **The National Youth Administration.** 1938

The Juvenile Court. Introduction by Robert M. Mennel. 1974

Klein, Earl E. **Work Accidents to Minors in Illinois.** 1938

Lane, Francis E. **American Charities and the Child of the Immigrant:** A Study of Typical Child Caring Institutions in New York and Massachusetts Between the Years 1845 and 1880. 1932

The Legal Rights of Children. Introduction by Sanford N. Katz. 1974

Letchworth, William P[ryor]. **Homes of Homeless Children:** A Report on Orphan Asylums and Other Institutions for the Care of Children. [1903]

Lorwin, Lewis. **Youth Work Programs:** Problems and Policies. 1941

Lundberg, Emma O[ctavia] and Katharine F. Lenroot. **Illegitimacy As A Child-Welfare Problem, Parts 1 and 2.** 1920/1921

New York State Commission on Relief for Widowed Mothers. **Report of the New York State Commission on Relief for Widowed Mothers.** 1914

Otey, Elizabeth Lewis. **The Beginnings of Child Labor Legislation in Certain States;** A Comparative Study. 1910

Phillips, Wilbur C. **Adventuring For Democracy.** 1940

Polier, Justine Wise. **Everyone's Children, Nobody's Child:** A Judge Looks At Underprivileged Children in the United States. 1941

Proceedings of the Annual Meeting of the National Child Labor Committee, 1905, 1906. 1974

Rainey, Homer P. **How Fare American Youth?** 1940

Reeder, Rudolph R. **How Two Hundred Children Live and Learn.** 1910

Security and Services For Children. 1974

Sinai, Nathan and Odin W. Anderson. **EMIC (Emergency Maternity and Infant Care):** A Study of Administrative Experience. 1948

Slingerland, W. H. **Child-Placing in Families:** A Manual For Students and Social Workers. 1919

[Solenberger], Edith Reeves. **Care and Education of Crippled Children in the United States.** 1914

Spencer, Anna Garlin and Charles Wesley Birtwell, editors. **The Care of Dependent, Neglected and Wayward Children:** Being a Report of the Second Section of the International Congress of Charities, Correction and Philanthropy, Chicago, June, 1893. 1894

Theis, Sophie Van Senden. **How Foster Children Turn Out.** 1924

Thurston, Henry W. **The Dependent Child:** A Story of Changing Aims and Methods in the Care of Dependent Children. 1930

U.S. Advisory Committee on Education. **Report of the Committee, February, 1938.** 1938

The United States Children's Bureau, 1912-1972. 1974

White House Conference on Child Health and Protection. **Dependent and Neglected Children:** Report of the Committee on Socially Handicapped — Dependency and Neglect. 1933

White House Conference on Child Health and Protection. **Organization for the Care of Handicapped Children, National, State, Local.** 1932

White House Conference on Children in a Democracy. **Final Report of the White House Conference on Children in A Democracy.** [1942]

Wilson, Otto. **Fifty Years' Work With Girls, 1883-1933:** A Story of the Florence Crittenton Homes. 1933

Wrenn, C. Gilbert and D. L. Harley. **Time On Their Hands:** A Report on Leisure, Recreation, and Young People. 1941